D0927454

Multicultural America

Volume VI
The European Americans

Multicultural America

Volume VI

The European Americans

Rodney P. Carlisle
GENERAL EDITOR

An imprint of Infobase Publishing

Multicultural America: Volume VI: The European Americans
Copyright © 2011 by Infobase Publishing

Facts On File, Inc.
An Imprint of Infobase Publishing
132 West 31st Street
New York NY 10001

Library of Congress Cataloging-in-Publication Data
Multicultural America / Rodney P. Carlisle, general editor.
    v. cm.
    Includes bibliographical references and index.
    Contents: v. 1. The Hispanic Americans — v. 2. The Arab Americans —
v. 3. The African Americans — v. 4. The Asian Americans — v. 5. The
Jewish Americans — v. 6. The European Americans — v. 7. The Native
Americans.
    ISBN 978-0-8160-7811-0 (v. 1 : hardcover : alk. paper) — ISBN
978-0-8160-7812-7 (v. 2 : hardcover : alk. paper) — ISBN
978-0-8160-7813-4 (v. 3 : hardcover : alk. paper) — ISBN
978-0-8160-7814-1 (v. 4 : hardcover : alk. paper) — ISBN
978-0-8160-7815-8 (v. 5 : hardcover : alk. paper) — ISBN
978-0-8160-7816-5 (v. 6 : hardcover : alk. paper) — ISBN
978-0-8160-7817-2 (v. 7 : hardcover : alk. paper) 1.
Minorities—United States—History—Juvenile literature. 2.
Ethnology—United States—History—Juvenile literature. 3. Cultural
pluralism—United States—History—Juvenile literature. 4. United
States—Ethnic relations—Juvenile literature. I. Carlisle, Rodney P.
    E184.A1M814 2011
    305.800973—dc22   2010012694

Facts On File books are available at special discounts when purchased in bulk quantities for businesses, associations, institutions, or sales promotions. Please call our Special Sales Department at (212) 967-8800 or (800) 322-8755.

You can find Facts On File on the World Wide Web at http://www.factsonfile.com

Text design and composition by Golson Media
Cover printed by Art Print, Taylor, PA
Book printed and bound by Maple Press, York, PA
Date Printed: March 2011
Printed in the United States of America

11 10 9 8 7 6 5 4 3 2 1

CONTENTS

Volume VI

The European Americans

AMERICANS HAVE HAD a sense that they were a unique people, even before the American Revolution. In the 18th century, the settlers in the 13 colonies that became the United States of America began to call themselves Americans, recognizing that they were not simply British colonists living in North America. In addition to the English, other cultures and peoples had already begun to contribute to the rich tapestry that would become the American people.

Swedes and Finns in the Delaware River valley, Dutch in New York, Scots-Irish, and Welsh had all brought their different ways of life, dress, diet, housing, and religions, adding them to the mix of Puritan and Anglican Englishmen. Lower Rhine German groups of dissenting Amish and Mennonites, attracted by the religious toleration of Pennsylvania, settled in Germantown, Pennsylvania, as early as 1685. Located on the western edge of Philadelphia, the settlers and later German immigrants moved to the counties just further west in what would become Pennsylvania Dutch country.

The policies of other colonies tended to favor and encourage such group settlement to varying extents. In some cases, as in New Jersey, the fact that each community could decide what church would be supported by local taxes tended to attract coreligionists to specific communities. Thus in the colonial period, the counties of southern New Jersey (known in colonial times as West Jersey) tended to be dominated by Quakers. Townships in New Jersey closer to New York City were dominated by Lutheran, Dutch Reformed, and Anglican churches and settlers.

Ethnicity and religion divided the peoples of America, yet the official tolerance of religious diversity spawned a degree of mutual acceptance by one ethnic group of another. While crossreligious marriages were frowned upon, they were not prohibited, with individual families deciding which parents' church should be attended, if any. Modern descendants tracing their ancestry are sometimes astounded at the various strands of culture and religion that they find woven together.

To the south, Florida already had a rich Hispanic heritage, some of it filtered through Cuba. Smaller groups of immigrants from France and other countries in Europe were supplemented during the American Revolution by enthusiastic supporters of the idea of a republican experiment in the New World.

All of the 13 colonies had the institution of African slavery, and people of African ancestry, both slave and free, constituted as much as 40 percent of the population of colonies like Georgia and South Carolina. In a wave of acts of emancipation, slaves living in the New England colonies were freed in the years right after the Revolution, soon joined by those in Pennsylvania, New York, and New Jersey. Although some African Americans in the south were free by birth or manumission, emancipation for 90 percent of those living south of Pennsylvania would have to wait until the years of the Civil War, 1861–65. Forcibly captured and transported under terrible conditions overland and across the ocean, Africans came from dozens of different linguistic stocks. Despite the disruptions of the middle passage, African Americans retained elements of their separate cultures, including some language and language patterns, and aspects of diet, religion, family, and music.

Native Americans, like African Americans, found themselves excluded from most of the rights of citizenship in the new Republic. In the Ohio and Mississippi Valley, many Native Americans resisted the advance of the European-descended settlers. In Florida, Creeks and Seminoles provided haven to escaped slaves, and together, they fought the encroachment of settlers. Some of the African Americans living with the Seminoles and other tribes moved west with them on the Trail of Tears to Indian Territory in what later became the state of Oklahoma. Other groups, like the Lumbees of North Carolina, stayed put, gradually adjusting to the new society around them. Throughout scattered rural communities, clusters of biracial and triracial descendents could trace their roots to Native-American and African ancestors, as well as to the English and Scotch-Irish.

The Louisiana Purchase brought the vast Mississippi Valley into the United States, along with the cosmopolitan city of New Orleans, where French exiles from Canada had already established a strong Creole culture. With the annexation of Texas, and following the Mexican-American War (1846–48), the United States incorporated as citizens hundreds of thousands of people of Hispanic ancestry. Individuals and communities in Texas and New Mexico preserve not only their religion, but also their language, cuisine, customs, and architecture.

As the United States expanded to the west, with vast opportunities for settlement, waves of European immigrants contributed to the growth of the country, with liberal naturalization laws allowing immigrants to establish themselves as citizens. Following the revolutions of 1848 in Europe, and famines in Ireland, new floods of immigrants from Central Europe, Ireland, and Scandinavia all settled in pockets.

As waves of immigrants continued to flow into the United States from the 1880s to World War I, the issue of immigration became even more politicized. On the one hand, older well-established ethnic communities sometimes resented the growing influence and political power of the new immigrants. Political machines in the larger cities made it a practice to incorporate the new settlers, providing them with some access to the politics and employment of city hall and at the same time expecting their votes and loyalty during election. The intricate interplay of ethnicity and politics through the late 19th century has been a rich field of historical research.

In the 1890s, the United States suddenly acquired overseas territories, including Hawaii, Puerto Rico, and Guam. People from the new territories became American citizens, and although the great majority of them did not leave their islands, those who came to the continental United States became part of the increasingly diverse population. The tapestry of American culture and ancestry acquired new threads of Polynesian, Asian, Hispanic, and African-Hispanic people.

During the Progressive Era, American-born citizens of a liberal or progressive political inclination often had mixed feelings about immigrants. Some, with a more elitist set of values, believed that crime, alcoholism, and a variety of vices running from drug abuse through prostitution, gambling, and underground sports such as cockfighting, all could be traced to the new immigrants. The solution, they believed, would be immigration reform: setting quotas that would restrict immigrants from all but Great Britain and northern Europe.

Other reformers took the position that the problems faced by new immigrants could be best dealt with through education, assistance, and social work. Still others approached the questions of poverty and adjustment of immigrants as part of the labor struggle, and believed that organizing through labor unions could bring pressure for better wages and working conditions. Meanwhile, immigrants continued to work through their churches, community organizations, and the complexities of American politics for recognition and rights.

Ultimately, two approaches emerged regarding how different ethnic groups would be viewed and how they would view themselves in America. For some, the idea of a melting pot had always held attraction. Under this way of thinking, all Americans would merge, with ethnic distinctions diminishing and the various cultures blending together to create a new American culture. Such a process of assimilation or integration appealed to many, both among American-born and immigrant groups. Others argued strongly that ethnic or racial identity should be preserved, with a sense of pride in heritage, so that America would continue to reflect its diversity, and so that particular groups would not forget their origins, traditions, and culture.

In 1882 the Chinese Exclusion Act prohibited further immigration of Chinese, and it was extended and made more restrictive in several amendments through 1902. Under the law, Chinese were prohibited from obtaining U.S. citizenship. In 1924 immigration legislation was enacted establishing quotas, based upon earlier census figures, so that the quotas favored those from northern Europe. Under that law, Chinese were excluded, although between 1910 and 1940, more than 50,000 Chinese entered under claims they were returning or joining families already in the United States. The racial nature of the Chinese Exclusion and Immigration Acts tended to prevent the assimilation of Chinese into American society, with many cities, particularly in the west, developing defined Chinatowns or Chinese districts.

Whether an individual ethnic group should become homogenized, integrated, and assimilated into the total culture, or whether it should strive to maintain its own separate cultural identity, was often hotly debated. For some, like the Chinese, Native Americans, and African Americans, armed power of the state, law, and social discrimination tended to create and enforce separate communities and locales. For others, self-segregation and discrimination by other ethnic groups, and the natural process of settling near relatives and coreligionists led to definable ethnic regions and neighborhoods. Among such diverse groups as African Americans, Asians, Hispanics, Italians, Arab Americans, and Native Americans, leaders and spokesmen have debated the degree to which cultural identity should be sacrificed in the name of assimilation. In the 21st century, the debates have continued, sometimes with great controversy, at other times, the dialogues went on almost unnoticed by the rest of the country.

Armed conflict, race-wars, reservation policy, segregation, exclusion, and detention camps in time of war have shown the harsh and ugly side of enforced separation. Even though the multiethnic and multicultural heritage of the United States has been fraught with crisis and controversy, it has also been a source of strength. With roots in so many cultures and with the many struggles to establish and maintain social justice, America has also represented some of the best aspirations of humanity to live in peace with one another. The search for social equity has been difficult, but the fact that the effort has continued for more than two centuries is in itself an achievement.

In this series on Multicultural America, each volume is dedicated to the history of one ethnocultural group, tracing through time the struggles against discrimination and for fair play, as well as the effort to preserve and cherish an independent cultural heritage.

THE EUROPEAN AMERICANS

The other volumes in this series treat the social and cultural experiences of a wide variety of ethnic groups in America, groups that in the early 21st century, still have minority status, that is, they make up varying percentages of the total American population. As will be seen in looking at those volumes, those minorities range from a few percentage points of the total population to more than 10 percent of the population, in the case of African Americans. The American people of European ancestry have represented the "majority" since the colonial period.

However, the story of European-Americans is far more complex than implied in that simple assertion of "majority" status. For one thing, in the early 21st century, the combined birth rate and immigration rate of people of European ancestry is smaller than those of African Americans or people of Latin American ancestry, leading demographers to conclude that the "majority" will become a "minority" by sometime in the mid-21st century. And looking backward, as well as forward in time, the history of the European majority is itself extremely complicated.

During the colonial period, the various colonies that became the independent United States were first settled by peoples from different countries or regions of Europe. The Delaware River saw settlements by Swedes and Finns; New Amsterdam, that became New York, saw settlement from the Netherlands. New England was first settled by English dissidents, seeking to establish their own states dominated by their own Puritan version (and sects within that version) of the Protestant Christian religion. William Penn established a colony in Pennsylvania that offered religious freedom, attracting not only members of the Society of Friends (Quakers, mostly British), but later, members of dissident sects (especially the Amish and Mennonites) from regions of what would later became Germany. New Jersey set up a colonial charter in which each community could determine what its own established church would be, leading to great diversity in that state that soon attracted not only Quakers, but also Dutch Reformed settlers, and people of mostly British ancestry but belonging to different Protestant sects.

As spelled out in this volume, the complex quilt of settlers from Europe continued to grow more complicated, with Irish, Scotch-Irish, and others. With the uprising of slaves in Haiti against the French colonial regime in the 1790s, French families moved to various locations in the south, especially Louisiana, where French-Canadian refugees had settled earlier after evacuating what became Canada. Later in the 19th century, European immigration received boosts from a famine in Ireland, from a wave of revolutions in central and eastern Europe in the 1840s, and then later waves of immigrants from Scandinavia who sought to escape harsh economic conditions.

By the early 20th century, two conflicting patterns had emerged. One was the "melting pot" in which many people of diverse European ancestry intermarried, with their children and grandchildren losing a strong sense of identity with a particular European country—whether it be England, Germany, Holland, France, or another nation or region. At the same time, groups of more recent European immigrants gave a characteristic flavor to whole regions, with Scandinavians in the upper Midwest; Germans in Missouri; and Italians and Irish in cities like New York, Boston, Philadelphia, San Francisco, and New Orleans. Immigration restriction legislation passed in the 1920s represented an attempt to establish quotas that would limit the numbers of immigrants from southern European countries and favoring immigration from northern European countries. Some of the ethnic and cultural neighborhoods, pockets or regions survived and thrived; others appeared to "melt away." The story of those communities, their varying length of survival, and the reasons for their integration into, or isolation from, the "mainstream" majority ethnic culture makes the subject of this volume particularly intricate.

RODNEY CARLISLE
GENERAL EDITOR

CHAPTER 1

The Colonial Era: Beginnings to 1776

DURING THE 15TH century, the rise of wealthy Italian city-states helped set in motion a race for dominance that eventually led to European exploration and settlement of North America. These city-states were the richest, most powerful political units in Europe. In large part, they gained these riches and the power wealth brought because the strategic geographic location of the Italian peninsula allowed them to control the lucrative trade routes between Europe and the Middle East, the gateway to the spices, precious gems, silk, fruit, and other merchandise of Asia that was in great demand in Europe. By controlling the trade routes, the Italian merchants were able to act as retailers of Asian and Middle Eastern commodities to the rest of Europe, building fortunes for themselves in the process. With riches came political power.

When it became apparent that trade led to riches and political power, other European countries sought to emulate the Italian example, but were not sufficiently powerful to directly challenge the Italians for control of the Mediterranean trade routes. Thus, the newcomers sought other routes to the riches of the Orient. One of the first nations to succeed in finding an alternate route to Asia was Portugal. To avoid direct confrontation with the Italians, the Portuguese sailed south along the coast of Africa, rounded the Horn of Africa, then sailed east across the ocean to India and China. Though the route was considerably longer than the direct course through the Middle East, the Portuguese never-

1

theless gained enough riches to control the western Mediterranean, much as the Italians controlled the eastern portion of that sea.

The Spanish were also interested in tapping into the Asian market, but were not strong enough to directly contest either the Italians or the Portuguese. Seeking another alternate route, they were receptive to Christopher Columbus's proposal to lead an expedition west across the great ocean to reach the Orient. Hoping to unlock the riches of Asia for themselves, the Spanish monarchs agreed to finance a voyage of discovery. Although Columbus never did find a new route to Asia, he did, discover America. Within a very few years, riches from the Western Hemisphere poured into the Spanish treasury, propelling Spain to a position of hegemony as the only superpower of the day.

Out of this sequence of events came a new theory of political economics— mercantilism. Those nations that enjoyed profitable trade grew rich, and with riches came national political power. Royal courts throughout Europe began to believe in this new mercantilist theory—the strength of a nation was determined by its wealth. Soon, others joined the Portuguese and the Spanish in seeking lucrative new trade routes and eventually establishing overseas colonies, because colonies could produce raw materials for the nation that owned them; colonies also offered markets for the finished products of the imperial homeland. Since the initial impetus to European overseas exploration was economic, a primary factor stimulating early European migration to America was economic. After the Portuguese came the Dutch, French, Swedes, English, and others, all seeking gold, silver, and the elusive Northwest Passage through the New World to the riches of Asia. Although they found little in the way of precious metals and there proved to be no water route through North America to Asia; early explorers, traders, and colonists established a lucrative trade in furs with the indigenous peoples; found abundant fishing off the North American coasts; shipped lumber, tobacco, and other agricultural products back to Europe; and found rich farmlands more plentiful than any available in Europe. All of these lured Europeans to the New World.

EARLY EXPLORATIONS

Scandinavians, often referred to as the Norse or the Vikings, explored west across the northern Atlantic Ocean before 1000 c.e. They landed in Iceland and established a colony in Greenland as early as the 980s under their leader, Erik the Red. The population eventually grew to as many as 5,000 people, but declined in the 14th century, and was largely defunct by the end of the following century. In the same decade the Greenland colony was established, Norse seafarers sighted the eastern coast of what is today Canada. In 1001, Leif Eriksson spent the winter somewhere along the coast of Newfoundland, and three years later his brother Thorvald also wintered at the same location, but was killed in a skirmish with the natives. Similar voyages of exploration, some including brief residence in the new land, may have reached the Maine

These sod-covered dwellings are part of a recreation of the short-lived Viking settlement at L'Anse aux Meadows in Newfoundland, which was established around 1000 C.E. These reconstructions are based on archeological digs at the site that uncovered the remains of eight buildings.

coast, or perhaps even farther south. Yet, their presence was transitory. They established no permanent colonies.

The Portuguese explorer João Vaz Corte-Real is believed to have reached modern Newfoundland in 1474, nearly two decades before Columbus's first voyage, and named the area Terra do Bacalhau (Land of Cod). In the decade following Columbus's voyage to the New World, other Portuguese mariners explored the coastal areas of North America. In 1501, Corte-Real's sons Gaspar and Miguel sailed along the coast of contemporary Newfoundland and Labrador where they captured around 60 natives they later sold into slavery. The brothers set sail for their return voyage separately, and only Miguel survived. The following year he sailed to North America in search of his missing brother, but was never seen again. João Álvares Fagundes established a settlement in Newfoundland or Nova Scotia, but it lasted only five years.

NUEVA ESPAÑA—NEW SPAIN

Sailing for Spain, the Italian Christopher Columbus arrived in the New World while he was attempting to find a trade route to Asia. For the better part of the next two centuries the Spanish, and other Europeans who arrived later, explored the continent in vain attempts to find a passage to Asia. Among the first to explore lands that would later become the United States were Ponce de León who investigated Florida, followed by a number of Spanish expeditions into Florida and the adjoining lands. Juan Ponce de León was the first known

Financial support from the Spanish, who were in competition with the Italians and Portuguese, allowed Christopher Columbus to make his expedition. This print depicts Columbus returning to the Spanish court in 1493 displaying trade goods and six captured Native Americans.

explorer of the region in 1513. In 1526, Lucas Vázquez de Ayllón attempted to establish the colony of San Miguel de Guadalupe somewhere along the coastline of Georgia or South Carolina, and two years later, Pánfilo de Narváez led a disastrous expedition of between 300 and 600 Spaniards into the peninsula, but after hostilities with the indigenous peoples, lack of food, and storms that wrecked their ships, most of the men died, including their leader. Only four are known to have traveled overland to Mexico and survived. In 1539, Hernando de Soto explored northward through Florida into modern Georgia in search of gold. From Georgia he moved west, discovering the Mississippi River somewhere near Memphis, Tennessee, but he died shortly after the discovery. De Soto's initial expedition was followed by Pedro Menéndez de Avilés, who established the first permanent European colony in North America at St. Augustine (San Agustín) in Florida in 1565.

Florida continued under Spanish rule until 1763, when it was ceded to Great Britain under the Treaty of Paris ending the French and Indian Wars. By the beginning of the American Revolution, there were an estimated 3,000 Spanish residents in Florida, most of whom supported the Revolution. At the end of the Revolutionary War, the Treaty of Paris of 1783 returned Florida to

Spain, which had been an ally of the colonials against Britain, and it remained Spanish territory until purchased by the United States in 1819.

Among the first Spanish explorers to penetrate into what would become the American southwest was Francisco Vásquez de Coronado, who journeyed through Arizona, New Mexico, Colorado, and some surrounding areas in 1540, claiming all of the lands for Spain. The first permanent settlement in the area appears to have been San Juan de los Caballeros, founded by Don Juan de Oñate in New Mexico in 1598. In 1609, Santa Fe came into existence, serving as a point for further exploration and colonization. Among the early creations were the prototypes of the typical western cattle ranches in Texas. Juan Bautista de Anza, who was born in Mexico in 1736, blazed a trail through California, leading to the founding of what would become the cities of Los Angeles, San Jose, and San Francisco.

Beginning in 1769, the Franciscan missionary Junípero Serra established the *misión* (mission) of San Diego de Alcalá, the first of 21 similar settlements that formed the famous California mission system. Founded to spread Christianity to the indigenous population, the missions established Spanish culture throughout California. Many remain today with the original place names, reflecting the Spanish heritage that continues to shape America, including the popular Mission Revival style of architecture. Among the other Spanish contributions to American culture was the name *dollar*, which the Continental Congress later adopted for its coinage, the famous French Quarter in New Orleans that was actually constructed by the Spanish, and a host of words adopted into English in the early colonial period, terms such as *padre* (father), *hacienda* (manor house), *plaza* (a central public town square), *villa* (country house), *patio* (an open courtyard in a home), *siesta* (a nap), *loco* (crazy), *bandido* in its anglicized form of "bandit," *rancho* (the English "ranch," and *fiesta* (festival).

NOUVELLE-FRANCE—NEW FRANCE

The French had a fishing presence in the fertile marine banks off Newfoundland and Nova Scotia before the celebrated voyage of Columbus in 1492. In 1524, Italian Giovanni da Verrazano, sailing for King Francis I of France, explored the North American coast from Florida north through Newfoundland, giving his name permanently to the narrows leading into what would be New York Harbor. Beginning with Jacques Cartier 10 years later, the French started to explore the coast on a regular basis and attempted to found small trading and fishing colonies. Between 1541 and 1604, several efforts were made to establish settlements in what would become Canada, Maine, South Carolina, and Florida, but none proved successful because of harsh weather, illness, and Spanish offensives.

With the Spanish success in developing their economy and political might from their overseas trade with the New World, the French determined to press

This print shows Indians assisting French explorer Samuel de Champlain during his travels in Canada.

on in search of gold or other riches and the hoped-for water passage to Asia. In 1608, Samuel de Champlain established what would become the city of Quebec with 28 men. The stark winters and disease killed many settlers prematurely, resulting in very slow development—only about 355 Europeans were reported in the settlement by 1640. What the French found were natives willing to trade valuable furs for European goods, furs that were in great vogue in Europe, where they could return a small fortune to a perceptive investor. The French viewed the Indians as necessary economic partners. After their early failures, they were successful in settling along the St. Lawrence River and the adjoining coastal areas. French policy was to form economic and strategic alliances with the Indians to capture the lucrative trading routes. Early French traders tended to live with the Indians, to intermarry, and even to adopt some elements of Indian culture. As more French began to arrive, they established their own settlements and priests began missions to convert the natives to Catholicism, but they continued to regard the Indians as trading partners and political allies.

Beginning in 1627, France took a much greater economic interest in its North American claims. In that year, Cardinal Richelieu formed the Company of One Hundred Associates as an economic venture. In addition to the fur trade, Richelieu began a semi-feudal system of land grants designed to encourage permanent settlement and the development of the region's agricultural potential. In 1658, Pierre d'Esprit, Sieur de Radisson, and Médard Chouart, Sieur de Grosseilleurs, began a two-year exploration of Lake Michigan and Lake Superior, traveling through the areas of modern-day Wisconsin, Minnesota, and the upper Mississippi Valley. In 1669–70, René-Robert Cavelier, Sieur de la Salle, pushed French claims into the Ohio Valley.

In 1673, Louis Jolliet, accompanied by Jesuit priest Jacques Marquette, traveled by canoe along the trading routes through the Great Lakes to the area around modern Green Bay, Wisconsin, then up the Fox River and down the Wisconsin River to the Mississippi. They went as far south as the Arkansas River, then returned north along the Illinois River, the Chicago River, and back along Lake Michigan. Nine years later, the Sieur de la Salle again explored the waters from Lake Ontario through Lake Michigan, as well as the Ohio and lower Mississippi Valleys, claiming the land as far south as the Gulf of Mexico for France and naming it Louisiana in honor of King Louis XIV. French traders who had adopted many of the ways of the natives, known as *coureurs des bois* (runners of the woods), were exceptionally valuable in pushing French influence into the Great Lakes area and the Ohio and Mississippi Valleys, even though they acted without legal authority from the government of New France.

By 1712, the territory claimed by New France included everything from Newfoundland to Lake Superior, down the Mississippi River to the Gulf of Mexico, and as far east as the Ohio Valley, western Pennsylvania, and western New York. In addition to locations in Canada, it included settlements at Detroit (1701), Green Bay, St. Louis, New Orleans (1718), Biloxi, Mobile, and Baton Rouge. Between 1719 and 1729, Jesuit Pierre François-Xavier de Charlevoix journeyed from the St. Lawrence River west along the Great Lakes to modern Chicago, then south through Illinois and the Mississippi Valley to New Orleans, leaving some of the earliest written accounts of this area.

In 1755, the British forced the removal of French-speaking settlers from Nova Scotia, known to the French as L'Acadie (Acadia), with most settling in Louisiana, where they became known as the Cajuns, a distortion of the name *Acadian.* The distinctive Cajun culture makes Louisiana unique among the American states with its Creole and Cajun-influenced music, Cajun Creole dialect, and French nomenclature and legal precedents. In time, Louisiana's cultural heritage would be the source of *Dixie*, a term applied to the entire American south, but originating from "*dix*," the French word for "10," appearing on the local Louisiana currency that was printed in French even after the American Revolution.

The expedition of René-Robert Cavelier, Sieur de la Salle, unloading supplies in North America in an engraving published in 1698.

Peter Faneuil, who funded the original construction of Boston's Faneuil Hall (shown above in the late 1980s) was the son of early French immigrants to New York.

Peter Faneuil

The son of Huguenot parents who fled religious persecution in France, Faneuil was born in New Rochelle, New York, in 1700. He moved to Boston at around age 18, where he secured a job in his uncle's successful commercial business trading with England and with Spanish possessions. Upon his uncle's death, Faneuil inherited his business, a fashionable Beacon Hill mansion, and a sizeable fortune in cash and stock.

One of the richest men in America, Faneuil was also noted for his philanthropy, especially toward the downtrodden. He donated Faneuil Hall to the city of Boston in 1742. Although heavily damaged by a fire in 1761, it was rebuilt and became the meeting site for patriots leading up to the American Revolution. For that reason, it has sometimes been referred to as the Cradle of Liberty.

To assert its claims over the lands it explored, France began constructing a series of fortifications including Fort Duquesne on the site of modern Pittsburgh to guard the Ohio Valley from English incursions. This rivalry for control of the Ohio Valley ignited the French and Indian War when a force of Virginia militia under Major George Washington were driven from the area by a French and Indian force under Claude Pierre Pécaudy, Sieur de Contrecoeur, in 1754. Known as the Seven Years War in Europe, the conflict raged until 1763 when the Treaty of Paris required that France cede its territory in North America to England.

Although New France came to an end, elements of the early French culture survived in the United States. French architecture, arts, and cuisine (itself a French word) are ubiquitous in American society. It has also been estimated that some 15,000 French words or phrases form the basis for expressions used today such as *à la carte* (on the menu), *à la mode* (in the fashion; in the United States it means "with ice cream"), *apéritif* (cocktail), *art déco* (decorative art), *au jus* (in the juice), *avant-garde* (experimental), *café au lait* (coffee with milk), *chic* (stylish), *déjà vu* (already seen), *de jour* (of the day), *fiancé* (betrothed person), *petite* (small, short), RSVP (*Répondez, s'il vous plaît*; respond please), *sauté* (fry over high heat), and *souvenir* (keepsake).

NIEUW-NEDERLANDT—NEW NETHERLAND

The Dutch first settled in and around present-day New York City—then New Amsterdam—in New Jersey, and up the Hudson River Valley to Albany, but the Dutch East India Company explored the area from the Delaware River north to the Connecticut River, with occasional forays beyond those landmarks. The Dutch were primarily traders, establishing a permanent colony at a point where there was an excellent harbor with wide river access to the interior. Through their early negotiations with the Indians, they developed a thriving barter economy, trading goods—pots, pans, knives, and other finished products—for furs, food, and other articles supplied by the Indians. The fur trade routes, in particular, reached deep into the interior of the continent. In later years, Dutch trading goods would be found among Indian tribes in the Midwest and as far west as the Rocky Mountains.

Serious Dutch efforts to explore, and later colonize, North America began in 1602 with the chartering of the Dutch East India Company, often known by its Dutch initials VOC (Vereenigde Oostindische Compagnie), with the mission of exploring for a passage to Asia. Seven years later, the VOC contracted with Englishman Henry Hudson to continue its search for the elusive passage. Hudson, acting largely in violation of his original contract, entered what came to be known later as New York Harbor and explored up the river that would bear his name as far north as modern Albany. Hudson was followed by Adriaen Block who, five years later, continued exploration of the area around Manhattan Island and gave his own name to Block Island. A map originating with Block's voyage was the first to label the region of exploration as New Netherland.

In 1615, the Dutch established their first trading post, Fort Nassau, on Castle Island in the Hudson River near modern Albany, later to be replaced by Fort Orange on the site of New York's capital city. Permanent settlers arrived after the reorganization of Dutch overseas trading with the granting of a monopoly to the Dutch West India Company (WIC, Westindische Compagnie) in 1621. When the settlers began to arrive two years later, several additional

NIEUW AMSTERDAM ofte NUE NIEUW JORX oft TEYLANT MAN

This Dutch painting shows the harbor of New Amsterdam in 1664, the year the Dutch lost their colony in what would become New York to the English.

trading posts were added. Thirty families arrived in May 1624 to establish a settlement on today's Governor's Island off lower Manhattan, and in the following year, 45 more colonists arrived, most of whom were Walloons, French Huguenots, and Africans, the latter being slaves. They also brought with them various livestock including horses, cows, pigs, and sheep.

Pieter Minuit arrived in 1626 as director of New Netherland. Under his leadership, land was obtained, ostensibly by purchase, from the indigenous tribes on the southern tip of Manhattan Island where Minuit established a fort he named New Amsterdam—the future New York City. From its very beginning, the new settlement was populated by diverse peoples. Minuit was a Walloon born in Germany. New Netherland's early colonial population included other Germans, as well as Dutch, French Huguenots, Scandinavians, English Protestants, Poles, Portuguese, Spanish, Africans, South Americans, and many others, including various indigenous peoples. By 1643, at least 18 different languages could be heard in New Amsterdam. While most of these settlers were members of Protestant groups, the Union of Utrecht that established the Dutch Republic in 1579 guaranteed freedom of religious belief, so the colony also included Catholics, Quakers, Anabaptists, and both Ashkenazi and Sephardic Jews. The Dutch colony was the first in North America to offer an unconditional guarantee of religious freedom.

The Dutch quickly expanded their trading routes into the Iroquois Confederacy in central New York, and New Amsterdam became a major port for a lucrative trade in furs, lumber, and tobacco. At the same time, they also began serious efforts to populate the Hudson Valley and neighboring areas of today's Long Island, New Jersey, and Connecticut. In 1629, the West India Company began offering vast tracts of land to people who would agree to settle at least 50 families on the land to make it productive. Called "patroons," these landowners were endowed with quasi-feudal rights to create courts, appoint local officials, and otherwise exercise control over their domains. Settlers worked the land as tenant farmers. These patroons and their descendants would exercise significant political power in New York State even into the 20th century.

The most influential governor of New Amsterdam was Pieter Stuyvesant, who arrived in 1647 with a directive from the WIC to maximize profits. Although his stern methods did not endear him to the colonists, New Netherland experienced rapid growth under his leadership. He defeated the colony of New Sweden and incorporated its lands into New Netherland, trade prospered, and the Dutch tradition of individual freedom of religious conscience was maintained. Yet, it was also during Stuyvesant's time in office that, on August 27, 1664, four English warships arrived in the harbor off New Amsterdam and demanded its surrender. Unprepared for a war, since England and

An artist's conception of Pieter Stuyvesant's surrender of the inadequately defended colony of New Amsterdam on August 27, 1664, as English ships loom in the harbor at right.

the Netherlands were at peace, Stuyvesant had little choice but to capitulate, and New Netherland became New York.

Although the Dutch colonial era was at an end in North America, their considerable influence remained. Uniquely Dutch architecture, characterized by brick structures with high gabled ends, can be seen even today in Albany, New York, and the intervening towns. The blue, white, and orange colors of the Dutch flag from the colonial era are today represented in the flags of the cities of Albany and New York, and in the uniforms of the New York Mets baseball team, the New York Knicks basketball franchise, and the New York Islanders hockey club. Dutch place names abound, such as: Amsterdam, Schuylkill (*Schuylkil*), Fishkill (*Viskil*), Catskill (*Kaatskil*), Kinderhook (*Kinderhoek*), Bronx (named for the Bronck family who settled there), Staten Island (*Staaten Eylandt*), Harlem (*Haarlem*), Brooklyn (*Breukelen*), Coney Island (*Conyne Eylandt*), and Gravesend Bay (*Grave Sant*).

American culture has been enriched by traditions such as Santa Claus (*Sinterklaas*), which originated with the festival of Saint Nicholas celebrated by settlers in New Netherland. Dutch folklore from the Hudson Valley prompted stories such as "Rip Van Winkle" and "The Legend of Sleepy Hollow" written by Washington Irving, and formed the basis for other American literature. And the American lexicon was enriched by Dutch words in common use in America, such as: Yankee (*Janke*), yacht (*jaght*), buoy (*boei*), cookie (*koekje*), booze (*busen*), coleslaw (*koolsla*), dike (*dijk*), patron (*patroon*), and boss (*baas*), to name just a few.

NYA SVERIGE—NEW SWEDEN

In the 17th century, Sweden was a major player in European politics, encompassing not only the Sweden of today, but also Finland, Estonia, and portions of northern Germany, Latvia, Poland, and Russia. Anxious to profit from the growing fur trade with the New World, investors formed the New Sweden Company and outfitted an expedition of two ships that left Gothenburg under the command of Pieter Minuit in late 1637. They arrived in Delaware Bay in March 1638 and established Fort Christina, named in honor of Queen Christina. In time, this small settlement, the first permanent European settlement in the Delaware Valley, would become the modern city of Wilmington, Delaware.

The area along Delaware Bay had earlier been claimed by the Dutch, a fact that Minuit knew since he had previously been director of the Dutch West India Company. Nevertheless, the governor of New Sweden ignored this inconvenience and convinced the local *sachems* (leaders) of the Delaware and Susquehannock tribes to sell the Swedes land on the western side of the Delaware River. Eventually, the Swedes would claim lands in what is today Delaware, southeastern Pennsylvania including the city of Philadelphia, northeastern Maryland, and western New Jersey.

When Minuit died on a return voyage to Sweden, he was replaced as governor by Johan Björnsson Printz, who served from 1643 to 1653. The colony grew to about 600 settlers who were mostly Swedes and Finns, but also included a few Germans and Dutch. Historians have estimated that between one-third and one-half of the settlers were probably Finns. A large majority made a living by farming, and a few lived in the scattered small towns as merchants or craftsmen. Though relatively small in number, New Sweden prospered and enjoyed generally good relations with the local indigenous population. Some historians credit the Swedes with bringing to America the basic design for what would become known as the American log cabin, which closely resembled similar structures in Sweden during that period.

In 1654, Johan Rysingh replaced Printz as governor after complaints about Printz's autocratic rule. Unfortunately for the future of New Sweden, Rysingh promptly determined to remove Dutch settlers from an area claimed by the Swedish colony. In May of that year, the Swedes captured Fort Casimir from its Dutch garrison. In response, Pieter Stuyvesant, the Dutch governor of New Amsterdam, dispatched an army into the Delaware Valley in the summer of 1655. The Dutch forces recaptured the fort and then moved on to force the surrender of Fort Christina as well. The Swedish colony ceased to exist when it was formally incorporated into New Netherland on September 15, but Stuyvesant allowed it some degree of local control and permitted the settlers to maintain their religion, culture, traditions, and even a local militia.

Despite modern additions, this 1643–53 Delaware County, Pennsylvania, house, which was built by a Swedish settler, still shows evidence of Swedish log cabin construction methods.

Despite its conquest by the Dutch, Swedish and Finnish settlers continued to move into what had been New Sweden. The settlements they founded included a log blockhouse where the city of Philadelphia now stands. It was located on the site where they later constructed the Gloria Dei Church in about 1700. Swedish remained a viable language in the former colony until into the 18th century, but the lands the colonists occupied changed hands once again when the British took New Amsterdam from the Dutch in 1664. John Morton, a descendant of Martti Marttinen, one of the original Finnish colonists in New Sweden, voted in favor of the Declaration of Independence in the Continental Congress.

THE SCOTS-IRISH

In 1683, King Charles II granted 24 proprietors title to East Jersey, half of them Scots. One of the latter, Robert Barclay, a Quaker, became the first governor of the colony. Some 700 Scots settled on these lands, about half of them initially indentured servants, who were a mixture of Quakers, Episcopalians, and Presbyterians. Every governor of the colony was a Scot until 1697. In 1702, East Jersey and West Jersey were combined into what is today New Jersey, with the Scottish population retaining political and economic influence in the colony for some time thereafter. Another Scottish colony was established in Darien, Georgia, in 1736; it was among the first settlements to issue an official protest against slavery in America.

While these colonies were established by people from Scotland, most of those of Scottish descent who came to America in the colonial period were the Scots-Irish. During the first decade of the 17th century, King James I of England attempted to consolidate his control over the northern portion of Ireland by redistributing land ownership to Protestants from England and Scotland. Many of the latter, who were Calvinist Presbyterians, settled on what was called the Plantation of Ulster, where they were joined by members of other dissenting groups including French Huguenots, German Palatines, and English Baptists throughout the balance of the century. By the beginning of the 18th century, high rents and religious discrimination convinced many, known in Great Britain as the Ulster Scots, to move to North America. There they became known as the Scotch-Irish, or Scots-Irish, despite the fact that many had no direct Scottish or Irish ancestry.

Researchers estimate that between 1717 and 1770, some 250,000 Scots-Irish migrated to the English colonies that would become the United States. About 70 percent of the arrivals were Presbyterians, and most came as indentured servants who worked off their indentures before moving farther inland. The first large group arrived in Boston in 1718, and many moved inland to New Hampshire and Maine. They brought the potato with them, which quickly became a staple crop in the areas where they settled. This became a familiar pattern with Scots-Irish immigrants. Arriving after much of the better coastal lands were already occupied, and wishing also to settle away

John Dunlap

A Scots-Irish immigrant, John Dunlap was born in Ireland in 1747 and moved to Philadelphia at age 10. After learning the printing trade in his uncle's business, Dunlap later purchased it. In 1771, he began publishing the weekly newspaper *Pennsylvania Packet, or General Advertiser*, but when the American Revolution began, he enlisted as an officer in a Philadelphia mounted unit and fought at Trenton and Princeton. Being a Philadelphia printer and a patriot, Dunlap was retained as the official printer for the Continental Congress, and it was in this capacity that John Hancock asked Dunlap to print the first copies of the Declaration of Independence on the evening of July 4, 1776. The following year he began publishing the *Journals of the Continental Congress*. He died in 1812.

from the control of other religious groups, a high proportion of Scots-Irish immigrants moved to what were then frontier areas, especially in Pennsylvania; from there they gradually moved down the Shenandoah Valley into the western portions of Virginia, North Carolina, and South Carolina. Most migrated in family groups, so their communities usually consisted of large extended families. By the time of the American Revolution, there were Scots-Irish in every colony, and after the Revolutionary War, some of those living on the frontier were among the first to settle across the Allegheny Mountains in Kentucky and Tennessee.

Because their communities were located mostly on the frontier, the Scots-Irish were heavily involved in warfare with the indigenous tribes as they moved west, pushing the original inhabitants before them. Because of this they were disproportionately represented in the militias of the colonies with western frontiers and acquired a reputation as skilled fighters. They were also responsible for the massacre of peaceful Conestoga Indians in Lancaster County, Pennsylvania, and other depredations committed by the infamous Paxton Boys.

In America, the Scots-Irish dislike for the British government was compounded by their residence on the frontier or backcountry areas that were remotely located from the centers of political and economic power in the lowland areas. Residents of the backcountry often felt a sense of neglect, with a frequent complaint being that the only time they saw any evidence of government concern was when the tax collector arrived. For these reasons, the majority of Scots-Irish appear to have supported the American Revolution. Historian James G. Leyburn noted in his *The Scotch-Irish: A Social History* that the largely Scots-Irish community of Mecklenburg, North Carolina, declared its independence a year before the Declaration of Independence when it adopted the Mecklenburg Declaration in 1775. The heavily Scots-Irish Virginia and North Carolina militia won the critical Battle of Kings Mountain that caused the British to abandon their Southern Campaign. Leyburn quoted a British major general as stating that "half the rebel Continental Army were from Ireland." He quotes a Hessian officer serving with the British forces in a similar vein: "Call this war by whatever name you may, only call it not an American rebellion; it is nothing more or less than a Scotch Irish Presbyterian rebellion." These were likely exaggerations, but the testimony nonetheless acknowledged the significant support of the Scots-Irish for the revolutionary cause.

DIE DEUTSCHEN IM AMERIKA—THE GERMANS IN AMERICA

Although there were some Germans present in the Dutch and Swedish colonies in North America and four or five German woodcrafters in the early Jamestown colony, the first substantial arrivals began in the early 1680s. In 1682, a group of Quakers arrived and in the following year, 13 Mennonite families led by Franz Pastorius arrived in Pennsylvania where they purchased 43,000 acres of land and established the settlement of Germantown some six miles to the north and west of Philadelphia. William Rittenhouse, one of this group, constructed the first paper mill in America. The Pastorius group also issued the first document protesting African slavery in America. Because of this early settlement, Pennsylvania became a destination for many of the early German immigrants to America. It has been estimated that some 200,000 Germans migrated to America during colonial times.

Chief among those who followed were the Pennsylvania Dutch. Originating in the German states and the Low Countries, these people were not really Dutch, but Germans whose name for themselves—the German word *Deutsch* (German)—was corrupted by English speakers into "Dutch." A large number began arriving from the Palatinate after Queen Anne granted refuge to some 2,100 in 1709. In 1710, another 3,200 arrived in New York, where most settled on Robert Livingston's manor along the Hudson River to work until they had paid off the costs of their passage. Many then moved on to the New York frontier where, beginning in 1723, they were the first Europeans allowed to purchase farmlands in the Mohawk Valley west of Little Falls. By 1750, more than 500 German families were spread out along some 12 miles of the Mohawk River, with the largest community named German Flats (modern Herkimer).

The most famous of these Germans arriving in New York is thought to be John Peter Zenger, who came from the Palatinate as an indentured servant. In 1733, he established *The New-York Weekly Journal* and became a leader in the movement for freedom of the press. Johann Peter Rockefeller arrived in New Jersey to work on a farm in 1733. One of his descendants would be oil magnate John D. Rockefeller. Among those who came to Pennsylvania were the Studebaker brothers, who arrived in 1736. They established a successful business making wagons—the famous Conestoga wagon—and their descendants later produced artillery for the Union army during the Civil War, and still later operated the prominent Studebaker Motor Company.

The Germans contributed to America's emerging religious diversity. Most adhered to either the Evangelical Lutheran or German Reformed Churches, but they also included Amish, Hutterites, Swiss Mennonites, Seventh-Day Baptists, Moravians, Anabaptists, Schwenkfelders, and Waldensians. Once in America, many became early converts to Methodism. Culturally, the Germans contributed to America's musical traditions through the distinct hymns of the various religious denominations. Chief among these was the influential *Die Turteltaube*, a hymnal based on the unique harmonic system of Johann Conrad Beissel of the Ephrata Cloister in Ephrata, Pennsylvania.

Music societies and choral groups formed in any community large enough to support them, and Germans crafted organs, pianos, and other popular musical instruments. Skilled German artisans were also responsible for much of the early colonial furniture industry; their tables, chairs, cabinets, and desks were especially noted for their intricate carved designs and decorations of painted flowers and birds. Germans also created much of the popular pottery of the colonial era, turning out an assortment of stylish and traditional plates, bowls, and containers of various kinds.

Another contribution preserved in American society today is the wide variety of German cuisine that first appeared with the early colonial German settlements. Today's hot dogs are the descendants of the *frankfurter* brought from Frankfurt-am-Main and the *wiener* originating in Vienna. Various varieties of German sausages—*bratwurst, blutwurst, knackwurst, leberwurst, weisswurst—sauerkraut, schnitzel,* and *hamburger* appear in grocery stores throughout America, while bakeries sell the popular *strudel* and the *pretzel,* also German inventions. And the German-dominated production of beer in the United States had its origins

A prayer room at the Ephrata Cloister, which was founded by German Americans in Pennsylvania.

John Peter Zenger

John Peter Zenger, born in 1697, was a German who became the owner and editor of *The New-York Weekly Journal*, the second newspaper published in New York City, in 1733. The following year he printed an article written by James Alexander that attacked New York governor William Cosby. Angered by the critical article, Cosby had Zenger arrested on charges of "seditious libel." At the urging of Benjamin Franklin, Philadelphia attorney Andrew Hamilton agreed to defend Zenger after his first two lawyers had been dismissed from the case by the court.

Although Zenger's action in printing the critical article probably violated the established law at the time, Hamilton was successful in convincing the jury that publishing the article was not libelous because the statements it contained were based on fact. Zenger's case is considered a landmark in the establishment of liberty because it set the precedent that truth was a valid defense against charges of libel. It also led to the coining of a popular phrase, "Philadelphia lawyer," that originally referred to someone of great ability.

in these communities. In fact, lager beer, the most commonly sold type of beer in the United States, was initially brought to America by these German immigrants during the colonial period.

POLACY W AMERYCE—THE POLES IN AMERICA

Although Poland was not among the European nations supporting early exploration and colonization of North America, its natives were among the first New World settlers. The first documented Poles in America arrived in the Jamestown colony in 1608, only a year after its founding and 12 years before the arrival of the Pilgrims at Plymouth, Massachusetts.

Initially only three or four in number, they were skilled artisans that the Virginia Company of London contracted to produce export goods in the new colony. Although there is debate among historians as to the exact function of the Poles and other artisans described in the records as "Dutchmen," the most recent scholarship suggests that the Poles were skilled in the manufacture of tar, pitch, and glass, all important trade products, and that the "Dutchmen," whom some believe to have actually been Germans, were skilled woodworkers.

There is also an intriguing report in the court books of the Virginia Company for July 21, 1619, that reads: "Upon some dispute of the Polonians resident in Virginia, it was now agreed (notw[th]standing any former order to the contrary) that they shalbe enfranchised, and made as free as any inhabitant

Old World Ethnic and Racial Groups in the British Mainland Colonies, 1700 and 1775

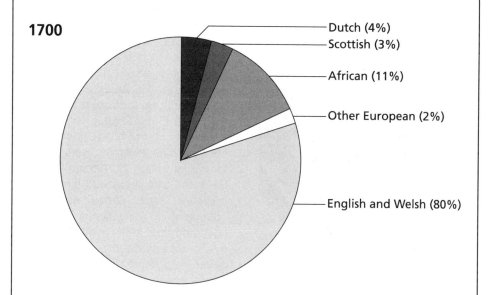

1700

- Dutch (4%)
- Scottish (3%)
- African (11%)
- Other European (2%)
- English and Welsh (80%)

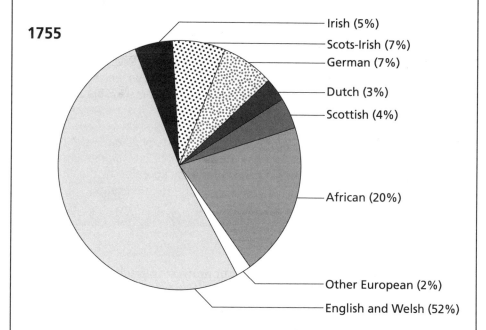

1755

- Irish (5%)
- Scots-Irish (7%)
- German (7%)
- Dutch (3%)
- Scottish (4%)
- African (20%)
- Other European (2%)
- English and Welsh (52%)

Source: Thomas L. Purvis. "The European Ancestry of the United States Population," *William & Mary Quarterly* 61 (1984): 85–101.

© Infobase Publishing

Tadeusz Kosciuszko

This print from the 1830s celebrates the military service of Polish-American hero Tadeusz Kosciuszko.

Born in the Polish-Lithuanian Commonwealth in 1746, Tadeusz Kosciuszko was educated in Warsaw and Paris. In 1776, he arrived in Philadelphia, where he offered his services to the American Revolution, which was in great need of military engineers. After working on the defenses of Philadelphia along the Delaware River, his work came to the attention of General Horatio Gates who appointed him chief engineer when Gates assumed command of the colonial army in northern New York. In that capacity, he was credited by Gates with being instrumental to the pivotal patriot victory at the Battle of Saratoga that led to the crucial French alliance. From there, Kosciuszko went on to a position as chief engineer for the construction of West Point, where the U.S. Military Academy is now located. After the American Revolution, he led an unsuccessful Polish revolt against Russian rule. Before leaving for Europe, however, he wrote a will, naming his friend Thomas Jefferson as executor, in which he left his American estate, the result of payments and land grants for his service in the Revolution, to be used to purchase the freedom of slaves and to educate them to become self-sufficient citizens. Kosciuszko was one of only two foreign officers elected to membership in the prestigious Society of the Cincinnati and was promoted by brevet to the rank of brigadier general. The building in which he lived in Philadelphia is today operated by the National Park Service as the smallest national park in the United States.

there whatsoever: And because their skill in making pitch & tarr and sopeashees shall not dye wth them, it is agreed that some young men, shalbe put unto them to learne their skill & knowledge therein for the benefitt of the Country hereafter." What this appears to describe is a "dispute" over enfranchisement, and possibly freedom, the latter most likely in the sense of civil liberties rather than literal freedom. As a result of this, it was agreed that the Poles would be enfranchised and be "made as free as any inhabitant there whatsoever." Apparently in return, the Poles would teach their skills to some young men for the greater benefit of the colony. Thus, it would appear that the Poles protested disenfranchisement and were successful in gaining equal civil and political rights with the English citizens.

Aside from the Jamestown episode, there were a number of Poles resident in the Dutch colony of New Netherland including Daniel Litscho, who was an officer in Pieter Stuyvesant's military forces, and Albert Zaborowski (or Zabriskie), who was a trader, Indian interpreter, justice of the peace, and owner of large tracts of land in what is today Bergen County, New Jersey. Other Poles were landowners in colonial Pennsylvania and New York, including Anthony Sadowski, who settled near Philadelphia and whose sons became pioneers beyond the Alleghenies in what today is Kentucky, Tennessee, and Ohio. Of course, these were isolated individuals and families, with no recognizable Polish communities forming until well into the 19th century when immigration from Europe increased.

PROMINENT POLISH AMERICANS

The most important Pole to arrive in America is considered to be Tadeusz Kosciuszko, who arrived in 1776 to offer his services to the revolutionary cause. An engineer by trade, his skills were particularly important to the colonial military forces that lacked officers with these skills. After an initial assignment building defenses along the Delaware River to protect Philadelphia, he was taken north by General Horatio Gates to oppose the British drive into New York from Montreal under General John Burgoyne. Kosciuszko's skill as an engineer was instrumental in the critical American victory at the Battle of Saratoga, after which the Pole was assigned as the chief engineer for the construction of West Point, where the U.S. Military Academy stands today.

Another Pole who arrived shortly after Kosciuszko was Kazimierz Pułaski, who was appointed by General George Washington as the first commander of mounted troops, earning for him the title "Father of the American Cavalry." Pułaski was later killed leading an assault on the British fortifications at Savannah, Georgia. Both Kosciuszko and Pułaski were accorded the rare distinction of honorary U.S. citizenship, both have prominent statues in Washington, D.C., and Pulaski Day is celebrated as a holiday in many states today, especially those with large Polish-American populations.

THE ENGLISH COLONIES

As early as 1497, only five years after Columbus's first voyage to the Americas, John Cabot, who was actually the Italian Giovanni Caboto, explored the North Atlantic coast, seeking a Northwest Passage to Asia and in the process claiming the lands he sailed along for King Henry VII of England. Although Henry Hudson sailed for the Dutch as noted above, there is little doubt that he shared the knowledge he gained from exploring the North Atlantic coast of America, and in particular the river that now bears his name, with his countrymen in England. Sir Humphrey Gilbert explored for a Northwest Passage to Asia in 1583, landing in Newfoundland and Nova Scotia. The real stimulus to British settlement in North America, however, was Sir Walter Raleigh, who explored the coastal areas of North Carolina and Virginia in 1584 and 1587. In 1587, he established the unsuccessful colony on Roanoke Island that subsequently disappeared. His explorations and efforts on behalf of England in North America eventually led to formation of a joint stock company for the purpose of further exploring and colonizing English claims in North America.

In 1606, the Virginia Company of London began planning to establish a colony in Virginia, an effort that led to the founding of Jamestown in the following year. Although most of the colonists perished during the first winter, it eventually prospered, with 11 plantations in operation by 1619, the same year that slaves were introduced into the colony. The following year, the *Mayflower* arrived off Cape Cod in modern Massachusetts, with 101 colonists who landed at Plymouth to establish another settlement, this one of small farmers. Although these were "English" colonies, they were far from homogenous.

RELIGIOUS AND ETHNIC DIVERSITY

From their very beginnings, the English colonies contained much religious diversity. The Plymouth colony was founded by dissenters from the Church of England, the official religion of that nation, because it retained too much pomp and pageantry. They sought a place where they could establish their own more austere lifestyle. In 1634, Cecil Calvert, the second Lord Baltimore, obtained the permission of King Charles I to establish the colony of Maryland as a refuge for Catholics. The colony adopted a strict law against religious discrimination with the Maryland Toleration Act in 1649. In 1636, Roger Williams established Providence and Rhode Island as a haven for religious dissenters unhappy with life in Puritan Massachusetts. In 1681, Pennsylvania was founded by Quaker William Penn, who invited people seeking religious freedom to settle on his lands. In addition to Quakers, those attracted to Pennsylvania included people from Lutheran, Reformed, and other denominations. The first Jewish synagogue in America appeared in New York City in 1728. To the south, French Huguenots began arriving in South Carolina in 1562 and also established communities in Philadelphia, Massachusetts, New York, Virginia, and Rhode Island. A study of religious organization in 1775 identified 668 Congregational churches, 558 Presbyterian, 495 Anglican, 494 Baptist, 310 Quaker, 159 German Reformed, 150 Lutheran, 120 Dutch Reformed, 65 Methodist, 56 Catholic, and six Jewish congregations.

Religion was not the only aspect of diversity in the English colonies. New England included Scots-Irish, especially along the early frontier areas, and Dutch settlers in western Connecticut. New York had large Dutch and German populations, as well as a myriad of people in New York City. New Jersey contained an influential Scots-Irish population, along with both Catholic and Presbyterian Irish. Pennsylvania included a French community in Philadelphia and heavily German districts outside the city. Scots-Irish farmers predominated in many of the backcountry areas of the south. In Virginia, until they were supplanted by slaves, Irish and English indentured servants provided the primary labor force on the colony's plantations. In the Carolinas, many of the English settlers arrived from Barbados, bringing African slaves with them, while Charleston contained a large French community. In 1699, about 90 percent of the population of the English colonies was of English descent. By the time of the first U.S. census in 1790, the approximately 2.8 million people included 1.3 million of English descent, 180,000 Scots and Scots-Irish, 156,000 Germans, 54,000 Dutch, 44,000 Irish, and 13,000 French, with a scattering of other groups.

This Congregationalist church in Farmington, Connecticut, was built in 1771. By 1775, there were 668 Congregational churches in the colonies.

While the early English colonies contained the religious and ethnic diversity that would become hallmarks of the United States, they also provided the template for how the United States would deal with the indigenous population. Unlike the French—who often lived among the Indians, learned their languages, and treated them as trading partners and allies against the Dutch and later the English—the English policy was to purchase or conquer land and then remove the Indian inhabitants. It was this model that was later pursued by the English colonies once they gained their independence as the United States of America.

GENDER ROLES, THE LAW, AND LITERACY

The status of women in early America was largely a reflection of colonial English traditions. In the German-speaking areas of the colonies, women often worked in the fields alongside men, and in both the German and Dutch areas, wives enjoyed ownership of their personal property and could bequeath it in wills. This was not true among the English colonists. Among New England Puritans, women seldom worked in the fields and, once married, they lost any right to ownership of property. Anything they brought to the marriage became the husband's legal property at marriage, to do with as he pleased. A woman could not make a will, could not testify in court against her husband, could not file a legal action, could not inherit property in her own name, and had no role in politics. It was these English traditions that shaped American law after the Revolution, and it would not be until the 1850s that individual states, beginning with New York, began to enact married women's property laws giving women the right to hold property in their own name if married.

The legal system of the United States is derived from English common law, and its political system is also largely an adaptation of English traditions that were established in colonial times. When the North American colonies were established, England was governed by a monarch along with a parliament consisting of a House of Commons and a House of Lords. To a certain extent, this general framework was mirrored in America, where each colony had a governor who corresponded to the role of the king in local colonial matters. The governor had a council of advisers, that might equate to the House of Lords, and a colonial assembly that roughly corresponded to the House of Commons. The same general structure can be seen in the modern president, Senate, and House of Representatives.

Much of modern America's educational tradition also derives from the early English colonists, especially those in New England. The Puritans who first settled the area believed that every person ought to be able to read in order to properly study the Bible. Because of this, they established mandatory primary schools in each town. It has been estimated that by 1750 almost all adult males in New England could read, and about 90 percent of the women, ratios far in excess of other areas in the English colonies. The need to train ministers led to the founding of Harvard College (1636) and Yale College (1701), while Baptists founded Rhode Island College (modern Brown University, 1764), and Congregationalists established Dartmouth College (1769). In the south, only the College of William and Mary (1693) approached these early New England institutions. The New England tradition spread quickly to the Middle Atlantic colonies, and eventually, after the Civil War, to the south as well. Perhaps because of its early tradition of education, New England also led the development of an American literary tradition, producing more literary works than all of the other regions combined.

CONCLUSION: BEGINNINGS OF THE AMERICAN REVOLUTION

There were nearly 3 million people in the English colonies at the outbreak of the American Revolution. Although there is no definitive way of knowing, some historians believe that about one-third of these people sided with the revolutionaries, one-third remained loyal to Great Britain, and the remaining one-third were mostly ambivalent. At the same time, about 85 percent of the white colonial population hailed from the British Isles—English, Irish, Welsh, and Scottish, 8.8 percent were of German ancestry, and 3.5 percent were of Dutch descent. Some of these groups were much more prone to support the Revolution than others.

Historical experiences help account for why some groups were more inclined to support the Revolution. Unlike the other English colonies, Maryland had been founded by Cecil Calvert, the second Lord Baltimore, as a refuge for Catholics. Sir George Calvert, the first Lord Baltimore, had been stripped of his possessions by England's Protestant rulers when he declared himself Catholic. Although generations passed between the founding of the colony and the beginning of the Revolution, many of Maryland's Catholics nevertheless supported the revolutionary cause against an English monarchy that was permanently associated with rule by and taxation to support the Church of England.

Similarly, the Scots-Irish, whose ancestors moved from Scotland to Northern Ireland, then on to North America, were mostly Presbyterians who settled in Pennsylvania and along the frontier edges of the southern colonies. They resented having to pay taxes to support the established Church of England, but in America they also resented the Navigation Acts and other impediments to manufacturing, and, because so many resided in the frontier areas, they tended to support the Revolution as a means of freeing themselves from colonial governments they believed were neglecting the interests of those who lived in areas remote from the coastal seats of political influence. Many of the Scots-Irish supported the Revolution as a means of shedding not only English rule, but rule of their frontier areas by the propertied classes of the seacoast area.

In New York, the German and Dutch farmers in the Hudson, Mohawk, and Schoharie Valleys were under the political control of English landlords, or in the case of the Hudson Valley, the descendants of the Dutch patroons who had formed a political alliance with the British to maintain their economic and political position. The Germans and most of the Dutch tended to support the revolutionary cause as a means to eliminate the political and economic control of the English landlords. This was seen in the Mohawk and Schoharie Valleys, where the American Revolution quickly turned into a local civil war. The German and Dutch population, together with some English small farmers, forced the leading English families to flee

Charles Thomson, a Scots-Irish immigrant who served in the Continental Congress and designed the Great Seal of the United States.

to Canada, from where the Loyalists staged raids and at least one major invasion of central New York in attempts to regain their lands.

William Penn, the proprietary owner of Pennsylvania, had invited German colonists to settle on his lands. They responded, many prompted by the religious wars raging in Europe. By 1766, fully one-third of all the residents in Pennsylvania were of German birth or ancestry. They brought with them a fierce loyalty to their language and heritage that led them to resist English cultural influences. Regarded as "inferior" by the English, the Germans in Pennsylvania proved to be strong allies of the Revolution.

JAMES S. PULA
PURDUE UNIVERSITY

Further Reading

Brading, David A. *The First America: The Spanish Monarchy, Creole Patriots, and the Liberal State, 1492–1867.* Cambridge: Cambridge University Press, 1993.

Glasgow, Maude. *The Scotch-Irish in Northern Ireland and in the American Colonies.* Bowie, MD: Heritage Books, 1998.

Haiman, Miecislaus. *Polish Past in America 1608–1865.* Chicago, IL: Polish Museum of America, 1974.

Holbrook, Sabra. *The French Founders of North America and Their Heritage.* New York: Atheneum, 1976.

Jacobs, Jaap. *New Netherland: A Dutch Colony in Seventeenth-Century America.* Leiden, Netherlands: Brill, 2005.

Johnson, Amandus. *The Swedish Settlements on the Delaware, 1638–1664,* 2 vols. Philadelphia, PA: International Printing Co., 1911–1927.

Leyburn, James G., *The Scotch-Irish: A Social History.* Chapel Hill, NC: University of North Carolina Press, 1962.

Miller, Kerby. *Emigrants and Exiles: Ireland and the Irish Exodus to North America.* New York and Oxford: Oxford University Press, 1988.

Nelson, Helge. *The Swedes and the Swedish Settlements in North America,* 2 vols. New York: Arno Press, 1979.

Roeber, A. G. *Palatines, Liberty, and Property: German Lutherans in Colonial British America.* Baltimore, MD: Johns Hopkins University Press, 1998.

Voorhees, David William. *Dutch New York: The Roots of Hudson Valley Culture.* Yonkers, NY: Fordham University Press, 2009.

Weslager, C.A. *New Sweden on the Delaware 1638–1655.* Wilmington, DE: Middle Atlantic Press, 1988.

Wytrwal, Joseph A. *America's Polish Heritage.* Detroit, MI: Endurance Press, 1961.

CHAPTER 2

The American Revolution: 1775 to 1783

AT THE OUTSET of the Revolutionary Era, American culture was predominantly English, but with significant ethnic and regional variations. Whereas 90 percent of American colonists in 1690 were of English descent, a substantial influx of German, Scots-Irish, Welsh, and French settlers over the course of the 18th century—together with a thriving Atlantic slave trade that brought Africans to North America against their will—had altered the ethnic composition of the American colonies. By the late 18th century, European Americans of English descent comprised less than 50 percent of the nearly 2.5 million colonists, and the American landscape included a variety of languages, dialects, and ethnicities. The steady flow of immigrants temporarily abated with the outbreak of the Revolutionary War in 1775, but by that point recent immigrants or the children of recent immigrants comprised nearly half the population of the 13 colonies.

New England was the most populous and the most culturally homogeneous region; its 400,000 European Americans were predominantly dissenting Protestants of English background. Almost as populous as New England, Virginia included English Anglicans and African slaves in a ratio of roughly two to one, with substantial pockets of Germans and Scots-Irish as well. The more sparsely populated Deep South was also biracial, where African Americans outnumbered European Americans nearly two to one. Pennsylvania was the

27

Landung einer Französischen Hülfs-Armee in America, zu Rhode Island, am 11ten Julius 1780.

This print shows French troops who participated in the American Revolution disembarking at Newport, Rhode Island, in 1780.

third most populous region, and the area with the greatest cultural and ethnic diversity. Roughly 100,000 Germans had immigrated to the colonies in the half-century preceding the Revolutionary Era, and most of them had spread across Maryland and Pennsylvania. The Middle Colonies included (among other religious groups) large communities of Lutherans, Quakers, Anglicans, and Dutch Reformed, along with relatively smaller groups of Dutch Mennonites, German Baptists, French Huguenots, and Portuguese Jews. The nearly 250,000 Scots-Irish who had come to America throughout the colonial period clustered in distinctive settlements throughout the Cumberland and Shenandoah Valleys and into the backcountry of the Carolinas.

Philadelphia, with a population of 20,000, was the largest city in North America and was second only to London as the most populous city in the British Empire. New York was the second largest and the most culturally diverse American city. Besides a few densely populated areas such as Philadelphia, New York, and Boston, however, the country was overwhelmingly rural. The vast majority of colonial Americans were small farmers, and most never traveled more than 30 miles from their place of birth. Despite considerable variations in ethnic background and social class, European Americans during the Revolutionary Era endured a number of hardships, as well as opportunities, which over time contributed to the formation of a new, distinctly American, national identity.

The nation that emerged from the struggle, however, would include a mosaic of ethnicities, many of European descent. These groups would embrace Americanization at different rates, but would also continue to preserve aspects of their unique ethnic cultures.

British soldiers (at left) drop their weapons before a contingent of Scottish Highlanders in Boston in this British cartoon from 1775. The Scottish were influential both in the colonies and among British forces, and were feared by both sides during the Revolution.

Ethnic Loyalties

Like many of his Scots-Irish compatriots, James Caldwell emigrated from Ulster to Philadelphia shortly before the outbreak of the American Revolution. Once there, he joined kinsmen who were already established merchants, and who would later aid Philadelphia's protest against Britain's colonial policies. The following excerpt is from a letter Caldwell wrote to his brother in Ireland in December 1774 shortly before the outbreak of hostilities. Caldwell discusses the loyalties of various ethnic groups within Philadelphia:

. . . The English are divided, some espousing our quarrel (as it is called) from real hatred to Tyranny, and others from attachment to the descendants of their Pilgrim relatives and Countrymen, and to the religion which they professed; but the greater part, at all hazard, determined to support the claims of the British Government be they right or wrong, to unconditional submission— The Scotch with very few exceptions are advocates for and friendly to those principles for which so many of them fought in 1715 & 1745 and of course opposed to the measures pursued by the Colonists; indeed they seem anxious to wipe away the stigma & remembrance of their resistance and disafection to the house of Hanover, by the most unbounded loyalty to George the third & his measures, so true is it, that new converts are apt to become the most violent and jealous partizans; but among the Irish, nine tenths espouse the American Cause, and our Countrymen of the North add the sagacity and calmness of the calculating Scotch Lowlander, to the enthusiastic chivalry of the native of the Emerald Isle in supporting the rights of the People.

FAMILY LIFE AND CHILDHOOD

For most European-American females during the Revolutionary Era, there was little alternative to matrimony. Girls were trained in the domestic arts by their mothers, and 16 was considered an appropriate age for marriage. The small percentage of women who did not marry typically lived in the homes of relatives and helped out with housework and child care in exchange for room and board. By the late 18th century, arranged marriages were becoming less common than they had been earlier in the century. The Revolution accelerated the trend toward self-determination in courtship and marriage, as democratic ideals contributed to a decline in patriarchal authority. Among the upper classes especially, however, parents continued to have considerable influence over the selection of a marriage partner. Women were legally subordinated to their husbands and divorce, though legal in some states, was rare. With the exception of widows and the relatively few women who never married, adult females in the second half of the 18th century seldom worked outside of the home. Even in urban areas, less than 10 percent of the female population was employed, although that figure would rise temporarily during the war years when circumstances necessitated women taking over their husbands' roles.

Information about controlling reproduction was not widely disseminated until long after the Revolutionary War, so women could expect to be pregnant numerous times during their childbearing years. Most married women in the late 18th century were pregnant every other year. Birthrates were somewhat lower during the Revolutionary Era, due in part to the physical separation of spouses during wartime. Even so, many European-American women typically bore five to six children. Although it was customary among the wealthier urban classes for a woman to avoid strenuous activity for a month after giving birth, farmers' wives or women without domestic servants could not afford the luxury of "lying in." Child mortality rates were high—half the children born in the late 18th century never reached their fifth birthdays—and it was not unusual for parents to name a child after a deceased sibling.

Children constituted over half the population of British North America at the outset of the Revolutionary period. Although notions of childhood were beginning to change—a trend that would continue in the decades following the Revolutionary War—parents in the late 18th century still tended to treat their children as small adults. Mothers trained their daughters in the domestic arts, which included cooking, sewing, and embroidery. Young children sometimes attended dame schools, private elementary schools typically taught by women in their homes. Some poor children attended religiously affiliated charity schools, while others went without formal education. Extended schooling was uncommon for girls, although many daughters in the middle and upper classes were expected to learn to read and write and to play a musi-

European-American girls were typically trained in domestic chores and managing a household. This whimsical print from just after the Revolution shows a young girl who has dropped a pie in Lombard Street, Philadelphia, being helped by laughing chimney sweeps.

cal instrument. Most girls spent their days helping with a seemingly endless routine of household chores that might include cooking, mending, spinning thread, churning butter, grinding wheat, and caring for younger siblings. On southern plantations or in upper-class urban homes, the daughters of wealthy European Americans (most typically those of English descent) were trained to manage a household staff of servants.

Most European Americans during the Revolutionary Era made their livings as subsistence farmers. Farmers' sons were expected to help their fathers with such tasks as clearing the land, planting crops, plowing fields, and butchering hogs. Younger boys might help their mothers with household tasks, but by the age of 10 or 12, sons in farming families were expected to work alongside their fathers. In rural villages, it was common for European-American boys to learn a trade by serving an apprenticeship with a local craftsman. In maritime towns and villages, boys were commonly apprenticed to seamen at a young age. Elsewhere, vocational choices were often limited according to which local artisans had openings for apprentices. Boys in urban settings were likely to receive more formal schooling than their rural counterparts, although urban sons might also be apprenticed to learn a practical trade. Education tended to consist largely of rote memorization and to emphasize spelling, penmanship, and arithmetic. The national average for length of formal schooling was only three years.

RELIGION AND MATERIAL CULTURE

Although church membership and attendance reached record lows during the Revolutionary Era, religion continued to occupy a central place in the lives of most European Americans. The Bible was by far the most widely available book, and biblical references were reflected in everything from children's names to public speeches to everyday conversations. Among men who served in the military, religious services were a very important part of army camp life. The overall decline in church attendance was largely due to disruptions caused by the war. Many Anglicans who supported the Loyalist cause fled to the safety of Canada or England once fighting broke out. Pastors from various other denominations served as chaplains or even soldiers, and the absence of so many laymen from the congregations meant more empty seats in the pews. Although they seldom were given a public role, European-American women played a crucial part in sustaining organized religion during the turbulent Revolutionary Era.

The Revolution also affected material culture, from architecture and furniture to fashion. For both pragmatic and ideological reasons, styles became

The Claus Rittenhouse House in Philadelphia was built by German immigrants around 1707, and remained in use throughout the 18th and 19th centuries. Generations of Rittenhouses farmed and ran several early paper mills near the site.

Religion and the Revolution

Near the end of 1775, as hostilities between the Crown and the colonists showed no sign of abating, a group of German Mennonites defended before the Pennsylvania Assembly their position as conscientious objectors:

The Advice to those who do not find Freedom of Conscience to take up Arms, that they ought to be helpful to those who are in Need and distressed Circumstances, we receive with Chearfulness towards all Men of what Station they may be—it begin our Principle to feed the Hungry and give the Thirsty Drink;—was have dedicated ourselves to serve all Men in every Thing that can be helpful to the Preservation of Men's Lives, but we find no Freedom in giving, or doing, or assisting in any Thing by which Men's Lives are destroyed or hurt—We beg the Patience of all those who believe we err in this Point.

Another traditionally pacifist group, the Society of Friends, underwent a schism over the question of taking up arms against the British. When a group calling themselves Free Quakers espoused the conviction that they could, in good conscience, join the fight against the Crown forces, they were disowned by the more numerous traditional Quakers and subsequently established their own Meeting House in Philadelphia.

Anglicans, who were primarily of English descent, found themselves in a particularly difficult position with the outbreak of hostilities. Since the British monarch was the head of the Anglican Church, many Anglicans feared that allegiance to him and prayers for "victory over all his enemies" might reasonably be construed as treasonous during wartime. Many Anglican preachers remained loyal to the British cause and fled to Canada for protection. Some Anglican churches, however, responded to the crisis by issuing Revised Books of Common Prayer, which either omitted prayers for the royal family entirely, or replaced them with prayers for the Continental Congress.

simpler during the Revolutionary Era. Neoclassical styles of architecture and furniture became popular, reflecting the Republican opposition to ornamentation and ostentatious displays of wealth. At the same time, consumer boycotts, non-importation agreements, and a naval blockade made ornate textiles and other luxury items from Britain difficult to obtain. Popular fashions during the Revolutionary Era lent themselves to homespun fabrics and allowed for greater freedom of movement; men began to wear loose trousers and jackets, while women donned looser dresses with high waists. Changes in fashion extended to children as well. Throughout most of the 18th century, it had been the common practice among European Americans to dress their young children in layers of petticoats and stiff bodices. Around the time of the Revolution, however, boys began to exchange their petticoats for trousers at the age of three or four. Among the radical patriots, hairstyle and fashion became expressions of political sentiment: Benjamin Franklin, most famously, dressed plainly and eschewed the use of powdered wigs or other elaborate hairstyles associated with the English aristocracy.

FOOD AND MEDICINE

The diet of European Americans during the Revolutionary period varied from one region to the next according to the ethnic composition of a region and the availability of food items. In general, salted meats, root vegetables, and seafood were common staples in the European-American diet. Settlers in the Pennsylvania and southern backcountry, the majority of Scots-Irish descent, depended on hunting and fishing for their primary food supply and prepared their food using techniques learned from Native Americans. Rural farmsteads in New England and the Middle Colonies were typically self-sufficient where foodstuffs were concerned. Game from hunting supplemented meat raised for consumption, and whatever meat was not consumed immediately was usually preserved by drying, smoking, or salting. Fruits and vegetables were canned to last throughout the winter and early spring.

The menu in the Middle Colonies, where German and Dutch settlers had introduced a number of foods, was typically more varied than that in either New England or the south. Milk and fresh meat were comparatively rare in the south due to the challenges posed by the warm climate. Root cellars and, less commonly, ice caves might be used to slow the rate at which food spoiled, but refrigeration in the modern sense was not available. Given the likelihood of impurities in the drinking water, cider or beer accompanied most meals.

At the time of the Revolution, slightly over 10 percent of American medical practitioners (400 out of an estimated 3,500) had received formal training, and Philadelphia was home to one of only a very few hospitals. Many of the doctors who had trained professionally had done so in Edinburgh. Once ties with Britain were broken, several American medical schools were established, including those at Dartmouth College, Harvard University, and the College of William and Mary. Medical associations also sprang up during the Revolutionary Era in an effort to professionalize medicine. Even so, trained doctors were available only to the wealthiest Americans. Most people had to depend on care from relatives or neighbors, even in cases of serious injury or life-threatening illness. Doctors were seldom involved in childbirth, leaving midwives to assist in sometimes extremely risky deliveries. It was only near the end of the Revolutionary Era that male doctors began to study fetal development and practice obstetrics, though in rural areas midwives continued to deliver babies.

Little was known about the causes of infection or disease in the late 18th century. Epidemic diseases such as smallpox, diphtheria, and yellow fever periodically swept through regions of the country, wiping out large segments of the population. A shortage of medical supplies and lack of proper sanitation made disease, not gunfire, the primary cause of soldiers' deaths during the Revolutionary War. Exsanguination, or bloodletting, was an approved treatment for a variety of afflictions. Based on the medieval belief that the body's four "humors" had to be kept in proper balance to maintain good health, bloodletting was prescribed for everything from diphtheria to mental illness. Either by lancing the flesh or by applying live leeches, medical practitioners (or barbers) might extract up to a pint or more of a patient's blood per day. Surgery, including the amputation of wounded soldiers' limbs, was performed without anesthesia or antiseptics until well into the 19th century.

RECREATION AND ENTERTAINMENT

During the Revolutionary Era, the Continental Congress encouraged states to ban such "frivolous" activities as horse racing, gambling, and even attending the theater. Religious and political leaders considered such activities morally questionable and antithetical to the Republican ideology. Despite local bans on gambling, European-American men continued to bet on everything from dice and cards to cockfights. The upper classes, particularly in urban areas controlled by the British, continued to host formal balls and other social events—though not on the same scale as before the war—or passed time playing chess, checkers, backgammon, whist, or cribbage. Reading, particularly on religious, philosophical, or practical topics, was a popular pastime among the literate. Often urban ladies or girls would gather to listen to someone read while they worked on their sewing or mending.

Social gatherings in rural communities often combined work and pleasure. Barn raisings, harvest gatherings, and husking bees, for example, gave farming families an opportunity to assist one another and to socialize at the same time. When the work was done, the gatherings provided an excuse to drink, dance, and enjoy the company of neighbors. Many young men and women in rural villages also attended singing schools taught by itinerant musicians. Classes typically met two or three times a week for several months before culminating in a public concert of religious psalms. The singing schools not only kept young people interested in church, but they also improved the quality of musical performance and inspired a taste for music as a form of social recreation and entertainment. A new composition style introduced secular and national themes to psalms sung outside church, wherever young people gathered. Then, as now, various ethnic groups contributed to the development of American music. The Scots-Irish frontiersmen strongly influenced what would come to be called "bluegrass" music, while the Moravians began the tradition of American chamber music.

DUTCH AND GERMAN AMERICANS

Although the English had long since taken over control of the former Dutch colony of New Netherland, a Dutch presence was still evident in the mid-Atlantic region by the late 18th century, particularly in the river valleys of New York and New Jersey. A century and a half after the first Dutch settlers had arrived on Manhattan Island, elements of Dutch culture persisted in the place-names, and architecture of the region. While the descendants of Dutch settlers in and near urban areas had been largely Anglicized by the Revolutionary Era, enclaves of Dutch Americans in certain rural areas were still easily identifiable by their distinctive clothing, religious practices, and language. Scholars have attributed such cultural retention among the rural Dutch to a number of factors, including settlement patterns that established tight-knit communities in which Dutch settlers and their descendants interacted continually with members of the same ethnic background and religious faith. Family farms provided homes for multiple generations, and families connected through ties of kinship, marriage, friendship, and religion lived in close proximity to one another. A vibrant religious and social life that centered on the Reformed Dutch Church afforded additional opportunities for cultural preservation; well into the 18th century, the Reformed Dutch preached and sang in the Dutch language and read from a Dutch translation of the Bible. By

A VIEW of the late *PROTESTANT DUTCH CHURCH* in the CITY of ALBANY.
This Venerable Edifice was situated at the junction of State, Market & Court Streets. It was erected AD 1715, and pulled down AD 1806. It included within its Walls the site of a Church the corner stone whereof was laid by Roger Jacobsen AD 1656.

This Protestant Dutch church stood for most of the 18th century in Albany, New York, a city with a strong Dutch influence in its culture and architecture.

The Plight of a Redemptioner

During the colonial period, more than 70,000 German immigrants arrived at the port of Philadelphia, a great many of them traveling as "redemptioners" whose services were sold to the highest bidder upon arrival in America. With a legal status hardly better than that of a slave, the redemptioner was beholden to his new master for a period sufficient to pay off the debt incurred on the voyage. Typically it took several years as a house servant or manual laborer for a redemptioner to earn his freedom, and then many more years before he could save enough money to buy tools and, eventually, land. By 1775, hundreds of destitute redemptioners were crowded into dockside boardinghouses in Philadelphia, waiting for someone to purchase their services. The following excerpt is from the memoir of a German redemptioner who arrived in America during the Revolutionary Era.

I happened to be under Deck when they arrived but by receiving Tidings that Masters were come I went up on Deck in order to look at them for little I expected. And they soon were inclosed by a ring of Men who offered their Service. Some said they could plow and sow and others again could reap and mow, some could drive [a] Team [of horses or oxen] and others were Tradesmen. I for my part thought it not worthwhile to enter the ring or to encroach upon them which made [me] keep off a small distance but it was my good fortune to be eyed by the said Mordecai Lee who beckoned to me to come near him, which I did joyfully. he then, like the rest of [the] Masters, first enquired after my Debt and having acquainted him with it, he replied it was very high and [asked] how long I purposed to serve for it, to which [I] replied I thought six Years were sufficient . . . [He] then replied that . . . if I would give in six Months more he would redeem me at a venture, to which I replied that it seemed a long Time to serve, especially if I should have the ill fortune to get an ill natured Master or Mistress. to which he said he could assure me if I was a good Boy I should have no reason to complaint but if I proved to the contrary I might also expect the same from my Master. Upon this . . . I agreed to serve the aforesaid Time.

the late 18th century, younger generations of Dutch Americans were speaking English and calling for the use of English in church services. Change came about only gradually, however, particularly in some of the rural parishes where the use of Dutch continued into the 19th century.

Much larger than the Dutch population in revolutionary America was the population of German-speaking immigrants and their descendants. Beginning with the settling of Germantown, Pennsylvania, by a group of German Mennonites in 1683, entire communities of immigrants from various German principalities had come to America in search of religious toleration or improved economic opportunities. Although small enclaves of Germans could be found throughout the colonies, their greatest presence could be felt in the mid-Atlantic region. Pennsylvania's founder William Penn not only welcomed the new arrivals, but also actively recruited these diverse religious groups and helped to establish transportation networks through his connections with Rotterdam merchants. Small German-speaking religious groups including the Swiss Mennonites, German Baptists (Dunkers), Schwenkfelders, Amish, Waldensians, and Moravians settled in Pennsylvania, as did much larger numbers of German-speaking immigrants belonging to the main Lutheran and Reformed churches. An estimated 27 percent of white immigrants who arrived in the colonies between 1717 and 1775 were German-speakers, and more than 80 percent of these arrived by way of Philadelphia. Most settled in southeastern Pennsylvania, western Maryland, and the backcountry of Virginia and Maryland.

It is worth noting that Germany did not exist as a unified nation at this time, but rather as a group of distinct principalities and regions. It was upon arrival in the New World that German-speaking immigrants from the Palatinate, Hesse, Wurtemberg, Alsace, Switzerland, and elsewhere received the appellation "Pennsylvania German" or "Pennsylvania Dutch." (The latter term derives from the German word *deutsch*, meaning German, and was applied to the spoken language—a fusion of German dialects and some English—different from "high," or "pure," German). The lumping together of these groups under a common label tends to obscure important differences. The Mennonites, for example, deliberately set themselves apart from the affairs of the world and confined education to a few years' worth of basic instruction, whereas the Moravians—who established the settlement of Bethlehem, Pennsylvania, in 1742—strongly emphasized both missionary work and education. Nevertheless, in the American context, differences among German-speakers paled in comparison to the distinctions separating them from their non-German neighbors. The German-speakers thus came to be regarded and to self-identify as a distinct ethnic group. Already by the Revolutionary Era, well-to-do German Americans in port cities such as Philadelphia and New York had formed charitable organizations to assist other German-speaking immigrants. Singing societies, theater clubs, and other ethnic associations soon followed.

THE SCOTS-IRISH

The majority of Irish immigrants to the American colonies were Presbyterians from the north of Ireland, commonly called "Scots-Irish" (or "Scotch-Irish") to differentiate them from the Irish Catholics who came to dominate Irish immigration to America in the 19th century. The Scots-Irish left Ulster to come to the New World partly in response to the religious intolerance they faced in Ireland. As Protestant dissenters (non-members of the Church of Ireland), Presbyterians were barred, along with Catholics, from holding civil or military offices. The Irish government attempted to suppress Presbyterianism by closing churches and schools, and Presbyterians, like Catholics, were forced to pay heavy taxes in support of the established church to which they did not belong. Despite such religious oppression, economic hardship was likely an even greater catalyst for leaving Ireland; the largest waves of Irish immigration in the 18th century correspond to crop failures, rent increases, and the decline of the linen industry.

Loyalists

Too often, the Revolutionary War is depicted as a monolithic struggle between the colonists on one side and the British Crown on the other. In reality, nearly every European-American ethnic group was divided over its support for the Revolution. From the outset of hostilities, Loyalists—Americans who remained loyal to the British Crown—were driven from their homes and either imprisoned or run out of town. In many instances, radical patriots tarred and feathered or otherwise humiliated suspected Loyalists and torched their household belongings. State governments passed laws to deprive Loyalists of their property, voting rights, and personal liberties. The following excerpt was written by the wife of a Loyalist merchant, Henry Barnes, who was forced to flee his home to avoid capture. The letter speaks to the plight not only of Loyalists, but also of women on both sides of the conflict, many of whom feared for their personal safety in the absence of their husbands.

. . . The greatest terror I was ever thrown into was on Sunday last. A man came up to the gate and loaded his musket, and before I could determine which way to run he entered the house and demanded a dinner. I sent him the best I had upon the table. He was not contented, but insisted upon bringing in his gun and dining with me; this terrified the young folks, and they ran out of the house. I went in and endeavored to pacify him by every method in my power, but I found it was to no purpose. He still continued to abuse me, and said when he had eaten his dinner he should want a horse and if I did not let him have one he would blow my brains out. . . . His language was so dreadful and his looks so frightful that I could not remain in the house, but fled to the store and locked myself in. He followed me and declared he would break the door open. Some people very luckily passing to meeting prevented him doing any mischief and staid by me until he was out of sight, but I did not recover from my fright for several days. The sound of drums or the sight of a gun put me into such a tremor that I could not command myself.

Although Presbyterians from the north dominated Irish immigration, a number of Catholics (roughly 20–25 percent of Irish immigrants) also left Ireland to come to the American colonies. Unlike the Scots-Irish, whom the colonists actively recruited to settle the land, Irish Catholics were discouraged from coming by means of anti-Catholic legislation. Those Catholic immigrants who did come were typically single men, often traveling as indentured servants. Most Scots-Irish, by contrast, traveled as families (particularly in the early decades of the 18th century) and settled among others who shared their ethnic background and religious faith. A small minority of Scots-Irish settled in New England. Most found the Puritan climate of Massachusetts unwelcoming, but had much better success settling the town of Londonderry, New Hampshire. There was also a sizable presence of Scots-Irish, many of them cotton-spinners and weavers, in New York by the start of the Revolutionary Era.

In the decades immediately preceding the American Revolution, the majority of Irish immigrants arrived via Philadelphia. Many became successful merchants, artisans, or professionals and played an active role in revolutionary politics (14 of the 56 signers of the Declaration of Independence were Scots-Irish). The Philadelphia Irish also formed such ethnic associations as the Irish Club, founded in the mid-1760s, and the Society of the Friendly Sons of Saint Patrick, founded in 1771. Philadelphia also had its share of destitute Irishmen, whom Benjamin Franklin described as "extremely poor, living in the most sordid wretchedness, in dirty hovels of mud and straw, and clothed only in rags." Far more typical than the Scots-Irish who remained in Philadelphia, however, were those who joined the ranks of pioneers settling the frontier. By the late 18th century, Scots-Irish comprised 50 percent of the white population in the Appalachian region, which stretched from Pennsylvania to Georgia and west to Kentucky and Tennessee.

THE ACADIANS

In the decades preceding the American Revolution, pockets of another ethnic group of European origin—the Acadians— could be found throughout several of the British colonies. Largely of French descent, the Acadian community had been built by 17th-century migrants from Europe to present-day Nova Scotia and southern New Brunswick. After the French surrender of the Acadian colony to the British in the Treaty of Utrecht (1713), the Acadians eventually agreed to swear an oath of loyalty to the British Crown in exchange for neutrality during wartime. By the time the compromise was reached in 1730, the Acadian community was thriving both economically and culturally. As the British consolidated their hold on Nova Scotia and populated the area with loyal English-speaking settlers, British authorities came to regard the Acadians as not only expendable, but also potentially dangerous given their presumed French sympathies.

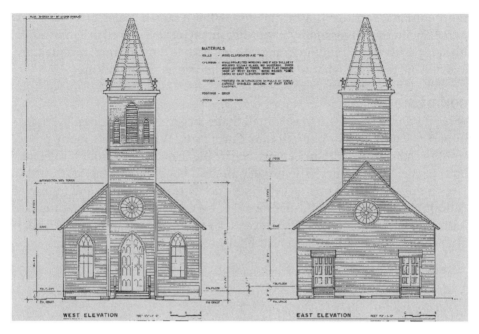

MATERIALS

Acadian exiles from Nova Scotia created the original timber framing of the St. Gabriel Catholic Church in Iberville Parish, Louisiana, around 1769. By 1803, over 3,000 Acadians had resettled in the Mississippi Valley.

Fearing the rapidly expanding Acadian population—particularly with the outbreak of the French and Indian War in 1754—and coveting the community's rich farmlands, Major Charles Lawrence, lieutenant-governor of Nova Scotia, decided in 1755 to expel the Acadians from the region and scatter them instead in small groups throughout the British colonies. Under orders from Lawrence, British soldiers detained the Acadians, torched their homes and looted their property, placing more than 6,000 of them on British ships to be relocated. By scattering the Acadians, British authorities hoped that the community of French-speaking Catholics would be swallowed up by the dominant English-speaking culture in the British colonies.

By 1763, approximately 1,000 recently transplanted Acadians lived in Massachusetts, with roughly another 800 in Maryland, 600 in Connecticut, and several hundred each in New York, Pennsylvania, Georgia, and South Carolina. Still others had returned to France or relocated to the French colony of Saint-Domingue (present-day Haiti) after their expulsion from Nova Scotia. When the Peace of Paris concluded the Seven Years' War in that same year, many Acadian refugees relocated again (this time voluntarily) to Spanish-controlled Louisiana, where they established settlements on both sides of the Mississippi River. Acadian immigration to Louisiana continued for the next several decades. Between 1764 and 1803 (when the United States acquired the Louisiana Territory), an estimated 3,000 Acadian exiles created a new homeland in the Mississippi Valley. Migrants typically arrived as family units, bringing with them (and adapting) Acadian styles of clothing, architecture, and cuisine to create what would become known as Cajun culture.

CONCLUSION

After the Revolution, the new United States began to expand rapidly, thanks in part to continued immigration by Europeans. While life for many people would remain rural, urban centers began the growth that would accelerate later in the 19th century. The population also began migrating westward in large numbers, helped by a growing network of transportation and improved communications. These advances would also contribute to building the new nation's identity, something that became a growing concern for many leaders after the war for independence was finally over.

KATHLEEN RUPPERT
INDEPENDENT SCHOLAR

Further Reading

Allison, Robert J., ed. *American Eras: The Revolutionary Era, 1754–1783*. Detroit, MI: Gale Research, 1998.

Berkin, Carol. *First Generations: Women in Colonial America*. New York: Hill and Wang, 1996.

———. *Revolutionary Mothers: Women in the Struggle for America's Independence*. New York: Vintage, 2006.

Burg, David F. *American Revolution: An Eyewitness History*. New York: Facts on File, 2001.

Cogliano, Francis D. *Revolutionary America, 1763–1815: A Political History*, 2nd ed. London and New York, Routledge, 2000.

Dolan, Jay P. *The Irish Americans: A History*. New York: Bloomsbury Press, 2008.

Faragher, John M., ed. *Encyclopedia of Colonial and Revolutionary America*. New York: Facts on File, 1990.

Finkelman, Paul, ed. *Encyclopedia of the New American Nation: The Emergence of the United States, 1754–1829*. Detroit, MI: Charles Scribner's Sons, Thomson Gale, 2006.

Grunwald, Lisa and Stephen J. Adler. *Women's Letters: America from the Revolutionary War to the Present*. New York: Dial Press, 2005.

Gunderson, Joan R. *To Be Useful to the World: Women in Revolutionary America, 1740–1790*. Chapel Hill, NC: University of North Carolina Press, 2006.

Huff, Randall. *The Revolutionary War Era*. Westport, CT: Greenwood Press, 2004.

Kierner, Cynthia A. *Southern Women in Revolution, 1776–1800: Personal and Political Narratives*. Columbia, SC: University of South Carolina Press, 1998.

Klepp, Susan E. et al., eds. *Souls for Sale: Two German Redemptioners Come to Revolutionary America*. University Park, PA: Pennsylvania State University Press, 2006.

Library of Congress. "Religion and the American Revolution." Available online, URL: http://www.loc.gov/exhibits/religion/rel03.html. Accessed February 2010.

Marten, James, ed. *Children in Colonial America*. New York: New York University Press, 2007.

Martin, James Kirby, ed. *Ordinary Courage: The Revolutionary War Adventures of Joseph Plumb Martin*. New York: Brandywine Press, 1993.

Metz, Elizabeth R. *I Was a Teenager in the American Revolution: 21 Young Patriots and Two Tories Tell Their Stories*. Jefferson, NC: McFarland & Co., 2006.

Middlekauff, Robert. *The Glorious Cause: The American Revolution, 1763–1789*. Oxford and New York: Oxford University Press, 2005.

Miller, Kerby A. et al. *Irish Immigrants in the Land of Canaan: Letters and Memoirs from Colonial and Revolutionary America, 1675–1815*. New York: Oxford University Press, 2003.

Mintz, Steven. *Huck's Raft: A History of American Childhood*. Cambridge, MA: Harvard University Press, 2004.

Neimeyer, Charles P. *The Revolutionary War*. Westport, CT: Greenwood Press, 2007.

Norton, Mary Beth. *Liberty's Daughters: The Revolutionary Experience of American Women, 1750–1800*. Ithaca, NY: Cornell University Press, 1996.

Panetta, Roger, ed. *Dutch New York: The Roots of Hudson Valley Culture*. New York: Fordham University Press, 2009.

Skidmore, Max J. "Ideas and the Arts: Germanic Music in Early Pennsylvania." *Journal of Popular Culture,* v.31/3 (Winter 1997).

Society of Mennonites. "A short and sincere declaration . . . to whose sight this may come be they English or Germans." [Philadelphia: Printed by Henry Miller, November 7, 1775]. Available online, URL: http://hdl.loc.gov/loc.rbc/rbpe.14401300. Accessed February 2010.

Volo, Dorothy Denneen and James M. Volo. *Daily Life during the American Revolution*. Westport, CT: Greenwood Press, 2003.

Werner, Emmy E. *In Pursuit of Liberty: Coming of Age in the American Revolution*. Westport, CT: Preager, 2006.

Wokeck, Marianne S. "German and Irish Immigration to Colonial Philadelphia." *Proceedings of the American Philosophical Society.* v.133/2 (June 1989).

CHAPTER 3

The Early National Period and Expansion: 1783 to 1859

THE UNITED STATES remained a predominantly rural nation throughout the early national period. The population in 1790 was approximately 4 million people, 95 percent of whom lived east of the Appalachian Mountains. Philadelphia and New York were the largest cities, with populations of roughly 42,000 and 33,000, respectively. Over 90 percent of the nation's population lived in rural villages or towns of fewer than 2,000 inhabitants. Nevertheless, urban populations throughout the period increased at a rapid and, many people felt, an alarming rate due to both the influx of European immigrants and the migration of young people from the outlying rural areas seeking employment in the cities. The combination of urbanization and western expansion caused massive population shifts throughout the period and, together with industrial development, greatly affected the organization of social and economic life.

The opening decades of the 19th century witnessed a revolution in communications and transportation that helped to bring European Americans in different parts of the nation into closer contact. The Post Office Act of 1792 gave the federal government an expanded role in communications and encouraged the circulation of national newspapers. Partly for that reason, the early national period witnessed a remarkable proliferation in the availability of newspapers and other periodicals. Whereas in 1780, there were only 39

American newspapers in publication; by 1820, the number had increased to 42 daily newspapers and over 400 weeklies. In addition to improving roads, state governments and private investors also financed the construction of over 3,000 miles of canals between 1815 and 1840. By 1850, America boasted 30,000 miles of railroad—more than the rest of the world combined. While distinct regional and ethnic sub-cultures persisted, the improved communication and transportation networks helped to forge the beginnings of a more unified national culture.

Federal census returns for 1790 and 1820 show a remarkable expansion in both population and land area during the first decades of the nation's existence. According to the first federal census, taken in 1790, the population of the United States was 3,929,214 and the land area was only 867,980 square miles. By 1820, a high birthrate and European immigration had caused the population to grow to 9,638,453, and westward expansion had increased the young nation's land area to 1,753,588 square miles. In the decades following the War of 1812 especially, continued population growth, westward expansion, and improved transportation networks all contributed to an ever-expanding market for consumer goods. The growth of a market-based economy had

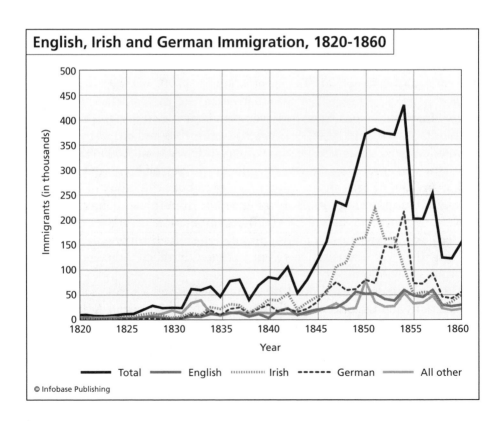

English, Irish and German Immigration, 1820-1860

© Infobase Publishing

significant repercussions for the daily lives of most European Americans, as did the beginnings of a shift toward an industrialized society. As production increasingly moved out of the household, American society found itself reevaluating everything from gender roles and conceptions of childhood to education and patriarchal authority.

DEFINING THE NATION

The ethnic and linguistic diversity among European Americans, to say nothing of distinct racial groups, is often obscured in traditional accounts of the early national period. Yet "white" America at the time of the nation's founding included not only the culturally dominant Anglo-Americans, but also significant populations of Americans of Irish, Scotch, Welsh, German, Dutch, Swiss, French, and Swedish ancestry. The forging of a national identity, therefore, posed a rather unique challenge in the United States, given the nation's multiethnic demography.

One of the key issues that emerged in the early decades of the republic had to do with the naturalization of foreign-born residents. Initially, the residency requirement for citizenship was set at two years. In an atmosphere of Francophobia caused by the French Reign of Terror, Congress increased the residency requirement to five years in 1795. Three years later, the Federalist-supported Alien and Sedition Acts included a Naturalization Act that further lengthened the residency requirement to 14 years and mandated that all foreigners living in the United States must register. The legislation was allowed to lapse once Democratic-Republican Thomas Jefferson took office, but antiforeign sentiment remained prevalent and would peak again in response to increased immigration in the middle decades of the 19th century.

Closely related to the question of citizenship was the matter of a national language. Not only was the adoption of an official national language not legislated in the early national period, but the nation's founding documents were issued in German, French, Dutch, and Swedish for the benefit of those Americans who did not understand English. Nevertheless, many Anglo-Americans, including Benjamin Franklin, encouraged the use of English as a means of promoting national unity. In many cases, it was pressure from within an ethnic community, rather than purely external forces, that helped to promote Anglicization.

Cognizant of the antiforeign animus provoked by adherence to a non-English native tongue, some established German Americans advised newer arrivals that by continuing to speak German they would perpetuate their image as strangers and arouse the suspicion of fellow Americans, including potential employers. Despite such warnings, a number of German-American enclaves chose to take on the appearance of a "nation within a nation" by retaining not only their own language and customs, but also their own schools, churches, and newspapers.

The domed ceiling of Saint Patrick's Roman Catholic Church of New Orleans. The church was built in 1838 to cater to the large increase in Irish immigration in the 1830s.

THE CHANGING FACE OF IRISH IMMIGRATION

In 1790, approximately 44,000 people of Irish birth (14–17 percent of the white U.S. population) called the United States home. The vast majority were Protestants, primarily Ulster Presbyterians. A few prominent Irish Catholics had been remarkably successful, including Charles Carroll, a Maryland State and U.S. senator and the only Roman Catholic to sign the Declaration of Independence. Most of the Irish Catholics who had immigrated to the United States prior to the Revolution, however, had done so as convicts or indentured servants and so had not established a particularly strong ethnic community. Prior to 1820, most Catholics who left Ireland in search of work chose England or Catholic Europe as their destination. But beginning in the 1820s, a number of factors, including the eviction of many Irish tenant farmers, an economic recession in the United Kingdom, and the demand for unskilled labor to build the U.S. transportation infrastructure coincided with lowered shipping fares to encourage an upswing in Irish Catholic immigration.

The welcome these early waves of Irish Catholics received was far from warm, given the prevalent anti-Catholic sentiment of the time. Although the scale of Irish Catholic immigration in the 1820s and 1830s was not great enough to provoke quite the same level of nativist hostility that ensued in the following decades, early anti-Irish hostility did exist. This was particularly the case during economic downturns, when competition for jobs was at its highest. Competition with African Americans for unskilled job opportunities helped to foster racial tension between the two groups. During the depression of 1837–44, Irish Catholics competed with other whites as well as with blacks for increasingly scarce jobs, and the resultant hostility included both ethnic and religious overtones.

With the onset of the Great Famine in Ireland, mass immigration brought more and more Irish, most of them lacking education and skills, and all of them impoverished, to North American cities. Irish females, many of whom emigrated alone rather than in a family unit, were often fortunate to find work as domestic servants, while most of the males sought whatever day labor they could find—working on the docks, for instance, or helping to build roads and canals. Their urban dwellings were overcrowded and unsanitary, and the Irish poor in particular were the object of much stereotyping and scorn in the press and the popular culture.

Despite the obstacles, Irish Americans managed to build a vibrant ethnic culture that centered on the parish church, but also included mutual aid societies and fraternal organizations. As Irish Catholics increasingly became the

As Irish immigration increased, anti-Catholic fears were expressed in the media by cartoons such as this one from 1855. The perceived threat of growing influence from the Catholic Church in the United States is represented here by an image of the Pope stepping ashore in America.

The state militia, called in to quell the violent anti-Catholic riots in Philadelphia in 1844, are shown engaged in street battles in this July 1844 print.

The Know-Nothings

By the 1840s, nativist prejudices were widespread and were most often directed against working-class Irish Catholics. At times tensions erupted into violent outbreaks, as was the case during the Philadelphia Riots in May and July of 1844 when Catholic homes, churches, and nearby buildings were destroyed and dozens of people were wounded and killed. The violence was condemned by middle-class reformers, but nativist sentiment continued to grow across class lines. In the early 1850s, a nativist political party, the American or Know-Nothing Party, campaigned successfully on an anti-immigrant platform. The Know-Nothings maintained that only Protestantism was compatible with American values and political liberties, and that Catholics and non-natives should not be allowed any political power in America:

DESCENDANTS OF THE PILGRIMS! . . . are you slumbering at your posts in the assurance that "all is well?" The danger is all around you. It has not come upon you unawares; but the storm has been brooding for a quarter of a century. The West—the mighty West—is a swift witness against you. From the shores of the Atlantic to the Pacific; along the banks of the Ohio to the populous cities upon our Lake shores, is one vast bee-hive of foreign population. With this tide of immigration, rolls on in rapid succession, battalions of Romish Priests, to first plant upon our soil, its accursed institution. . . . Fellow citizens, there is NO SECURITY in the hour of danger. Our danger is not so much to be dreaded from outward foes as those from within. An outward foe can be met upon his own battlements in a fair and open fight; but an enemy at home, is one much to be dreaded.

targets of nativist prejudice and hostility, Ulster-Presbyterian immigrants and their offspring came to embrace the designation "Scots-Irish" in order to differentiate themselves from their Catholic compatriots. In the process, Irish America became intimately identified with Catholicism in the post-Famine consciousness.

HOME AND FAMILY

Young people in the early national period were given more freedom than before to select their own marriage partners, and increasingly, the choice was guided by the ideals of romantic love. The expectations of married life also underwent a transformation, as most people came to believe that marriage should bring happiness and fulfillment to both partners. Couples began calling each other by their first names and openly expressing their mutual affection. With a greater say in whom to marry and when, European-American couples tended to marry later in life than had been the case in the colonial period—the average bride in the post-Revolutionary Era was between her late teens and early 20s, while most grooms were in their mid-20s. Marriage ceremonies, which typically took place at the bride's family home, tended to be simple and unpretentious affairs.

Due to delayed marriages, economic changes, and the increased availability of contraceptive methods (however primitive), the birth rate declined significantly between 1790 and 1820. The average family size in the early national period—two parents and four children—was smaller than in the colonial period, but still larger than the average western European family at that time. The decline in family size was particularly marked among the middle and upper classes, suggesting that many European-American couples consciously chose to limit the number of children they had. Even women who used some form of contraception typically bore two or three children, however, and families on the frontier tended to be considerably larger than that. Most rural women were still assisted in childbirth by midwives, though obstetricians were becoming more common in urban areas. Women who survived the rigors of childbirth still had to worry about the health of their children—infant mortality rates in the 19th century ran as high as 25 to 30 percent.

With a decline in the birth rate, the introduction of labor-saving devices, and the commercial availability of household goods formerly produced from scratch, middle-class mothers had more time to devote to raising their children. As fathers increasingly sought employment away from the home, mothers assumed almost sole responsibility for the raising of children. A new genre of advice literature emerged to address topics about children and childrearing, such as education, clothing, diet, discipline, and religious training. A new conception of childhood developed in which children ceased to be regarded as miniature adults. The proliferation of children's toys and books at the time reflected the emerging view of childhood as a time to be cherished in its own right and essential to proper development. At the same time, children's toys reflected an increasingly rigid ideology of gender roles. Girls' toys, such as needle books and dolls, were intended to encourage femininity and a nurturing personality. Boys were far more likely to play with toy guns or swords. While girls were encouraged to be quiet and demure, boys were given horns to play and drums to bang.

As transformations in the traditional household economy diminished the economic role of children, increased emphasis was placed on the importance of play as part of a healthy and wholesome childhood. The assumption of adult responsibilities, at least according to the advice literature, was to be deferred as long as possible. The middle class "cult of childhood," however, had little relevance for working families who relied on their children's labor to help put food on the table or required older children to supervise their younger siblings so that the mother could seek paid employment. Similarly, families in the less-settled frontier regions required the labor of every able-bodied family member to keep the household running smoothly; most frontier children performed essential chores by age 5. Orphans or children from destitute families were often "bound out" to perform farm labor or domestic service for more prosperous households. Ethnic background also influenced conceptions of

This farmstead in St. Clair County, Illinois, was one of the first in the area to become home to a German immigrant family, the Merkels, in the 1830s. The buildings are typical of German immigrant farm families at the time and housed the Merkel family's wine-making operations.

childhood. German and Russian immigrants, for example, emphasized strict discipline and hard work from an early age.

While some extended families continued to live together in the early republic, the nuclear family was becoming the typical household unit. Although it was rare for two or more married couples to live under the same roof, many households included unwed or widowed kinfolk as well as paid lodgers or apprentices. The more prosperous households also included hired farm laborers or domestic servants. The average dwelling was somewhat larger than most colonial homes, but—except among the most prosperous families—seldom included more than two or three rooms. Houses were typically furnished and decorated quite simply, and only the well-to-do landscaped their yards or painted their houses.

PROTO-INDUSTRIALIZATION AND THE GROWTH OF CITIES

In the late-18th and early-19th centuries, the majority of American families (as many as 80 percent in 1800) still engaged in some form of agriculture. The percentage of farming families began to decline with the expansion of commerce and manufacturing, but even as late as 1840, only one in nine Americans lived in cities or towns of more than 2,500. Agriculture remained the largest sector of the economy throughout the early national period, and the seasonal rhythms of farm work shaped the daily lives of most European Americans. Although the United States was still predominantly agricultural, the shift to an industrial economy began to occur during the early national period. With proto-industrialization came urban growth; the population of U.S. cities increased by 700 percent between 1830 and 1860 due to both European immigration and the migration of young people from the surrounding areas seeking paid work in the cities.

The growth of a market economy and the early stages of a factory system disrupted traditional family structures. In antebellum New England, for example, young women left home in numbers equivalent to young men and sought paid employment in the nearby cities or burgeoning mill towns. The physical separation of more and more young people from their families and tight-knit communities, together with republican notions of equality, led to a decline in patriarchal authority.

Parents, preachers, and social reformers were left to worry that the nation's young men in particular would fall prey to the temptations of city life. Such concerns were exacerbated by the decline of the craft-guild system, as young men became paid laborers, rather than apprentices under the watchful eye of a master craftsman. Young working-class children were made to suffer as production moved out of households and into mills and factories. In 1820, children under 10 years of age comprised 50 percent of the nation's industrial labor force. Without any of the safeguards that would come later, the factory system was free to exploit working-class children.

This 1808 cartoon "dedicated to all the butchers in the United States" was published in response to the election of Simon Snyder, Pennsylvania's first governor from the state's German-American farming class.

Germans in America

In this excerpt from the 1837 book *The Americans in Their Moral, Social and Political Relations*, Austrian-born social commentator Francis J. Grund offers his view of the German community in America:

Thousands of Germans are annually emigrating to the United States; and thousands of them purchase real estates, or acquire them by persevering industry. They do not disperse and become mixed with the Americans, but increase the settlements, which are already established by their countrymen, or settle in their immediate neighbourhood. They are, therefore, in the very outset less dependent on the Americans than on their own brethren, from whom they derive the principal means of support. Their own countrymen undertake their instruction in the rules and regulations of the country; and, being for the most part, sturdy democrats, teach them to refrain from all measures not in strict accordance with that doctrine. . . . As cultivators of the soil they have the finest prospect before them; for no other country offers the same resources, or will so richly reward their industry. As farmers, the German emigrants have a decided advantage over all other settlers; for they find friends, relatives, and a home in three or four of the largest and most fertile states of the Union. There the German language is no obstacle to their progress; because thousands around them speak no other. They will find German papers, German churches, and German schools. Their officers of justice will be Germans; their physicians, and—if they should be so unfortunate as to need them—their lawyers. It will appear to them as if a portion of the land of their fathers had, by some magic, been transplanted to the New World.

EDUCATION

In the aftermath of the Revolution, republican ideology emphasized the need for education to promote civic virtue. Without an educated populace, theorists predicted, public virtue would disappear and the republican experiment would fail. Education in this broad sense was understood not strictly as intellectual training, but also as a means of inculcating self-control and respect for authority. Educational opportunities proliferated in the new republic, particularly in the northeast. Various evangelical denominations founded Sunday schools with a primarily religious curriculum in content—the Bible was frequently the only text—but one that also imparted basic literacy and writing skills to working-class children and many adults who might not otherwise receive such training.

Several state constitutions also called for the formation or expansion of public school systems. Pennsylvania's 1790 constitution, for example, required towns to establish free schools for the poor. Free public schools were slow to materialize, however, and where they did exist, they were considered unsuitable for middle- and upper-class children, who continued to attend private academies or study with private tutors. Some ambivalence accompanied the desire to create a well-educated citizenry; opposing voices warned that universal schooling might create an overly ambitious lower class. Nevertheless, more and more people came to accept the view that society had an obligation to educate its citizenry for the good of the nation.

It was not only—nor even primarily—the schools that were expected to inculcate the values of civic virtue, however. As society sought to reconcile patriarchal gender relations with the new republican political culture, women's traditional responsibilities as transmitters of culture and values came to be imbued with political significance. Magazine articles, pamphlets, lectures, and sermons hailed the contribution that Republican Mothers made in safeguarding the republic. By promoting virtue and defending the republic from corruption, women as mothers helped to ensure the success of the republican experiment. One upshot of the emphasis on Republican Motherhood was improved educational opportunities for girls. In order to prepare females for their roles as Republican Mothers, a number of academies for young women were founded in the wake of the Revolution. Particularly among European-American females in urban areas, literacy rates improved significantly in the early decades of the 19th century.

Efforts to educate the nation's citizenry were not aimed solely at children. Popularized during the Revolution, partly in response to local bans on theatrical performances, public lectures became increasingly prevalent during the 1830s. Cities and towns often used public funds to establish lecture halls at which lyceum associations—organizations devoted to promoting generalized adult education—sponsored lectures on a broad range of scientific, literary, and religious topics. Mechanics' associations and young men's associations in

A membership certificate from the 1820s or 1830s for the Charleston, South Carolina, Hibernian Society, an Irish fraternal organization founded in the city in 1801.

many cities likewise hosted lectures and similar events in an effort to improve the minds and morals of the working classes and to protect young working men from the perceived dangers and temptations of city life.

Institutes of higher learning also expanded rapidly in the post-Revolutionary era. American colleges had suffered reduced enrollments during the war years and the custom of sending sons to Europe to study had been greatly curtailed. Once the fighting ended, though, American colleges proliferated and became increasingly nonsectarian. Whereas eight out of the nine American colleges established before the Revolution had been affiliated with particular religious sects, 10 out of 14 founded between 1776 and 1796 were nonsectarian.

RELIGION

For the vast majority of European Americans in the early national period, religion was synonymous with Protestant Christianity. Under the umbrella of Protestantism, however, was an ever-expanding diversity of denominations and sects. Whereas church membership had declined significantly during the Revolutionary Era, membership rates rose steadily throughout the early national period. Growth was especially marked for the newer denominations, such as the Baptists and Methodists, who made use of large revivalist camp meetings to evangelize frontiersmen and their families west of the Appalachian Mountains. Circuit riders traveled throughout the frontier regions preaching against such vices as drinking, gambling, and dancing. American Methodism, begun in 1784, had increased its membership to over half a million adherents by 1850. The increase in membership among both the Methodist and Baptist denominations outpaced population increases.

National independence brought institutional changes to the Anglican, Reformed, and Lutheran religious denominations, which could now operate without European oversight. This new-found autonomy, coupled with evangelical revivalism, contributed to the proliferation of diverse religious traditions within the early republic. While common Christianity appeared to offer hope as a basis for national solidarity (or, at least, that was the hope among many conservative evangelicals), religious institutions in many cases served to reinforce, rather than efface, ethnic identities.

The only significant concentration of Roman Catholics in the early national period was in Maryland. The relatively few Catholics outside Maryland were predominantly immigrants, widely scattered and divided by ethnic tensions. In an era that emphasized republican ideals and civic equality, many Americans were hostile to the European Catholic tradition of papal authority. John Carroll, the first Roman Catholic bishop in the United States, faced considerable obstacles in attempting to recruit new members to the Catholic faith and to establish Catholicism on a sound institutional footing. Due in large part to the establishment of parochial schools and the charitable work of religious orders, membership in the Catholic Church in the United States increased from roughly 25,000 in 1783 to 195,000 by 1820. Subsequent waves of Irish and German immigration, along with the continued splintering of Protestant denominations, would make Roman Catholicism the largest denomination in America by 1865.

Women were at the heart of the religious revival that came to be known as the Second Great Awakening. Although female ordination was rare in most denominations, women played an important part in the evangelical drive to win converts to Christianity. Some women challenged contemporary notions of public and private spheres by becoming itinerant preachers and addressing revival meetings; by mid-century, a few women were

This 1848 illustration depicts St. Nicholas German Roman Catholic Church in New York City.

This 1817 Quaker meetinghouse in Wilmington, Delaware, which was predominantly Quaker at the time, is a good example of houses of worship built by the Quakers in the early 19th century.

even founding religious movements and denominations, including Seventh-Day Adventism and Christian Science. More common were the women who joined religious congregations and devoted their energies to charitable societies and social reform movements, activities that likewise carried women into the public sphere. Particularly on the frontier where meetinghouses were not readily available, many women also held prayer meetings in their homes and helped to support missionary work. An evangelical movement that emphasized conversion experience and emotional piety came to regard women as specially suited to safeguard the nation's moral and religious future.

ARTS AND ENTERTAINMENT

Though many Americans in the early years of the republic considered art for its own sake frivolous, early national leaders did patronize art in an attempt to promote republican virtues and national pride among the citizenry. After the War of 1812, several artists' associations and fine arts academies were founded to help cultivate a distinctly American artistic culture. Artists of the early republic such as John Trumbull, Charles Willson Peale, and John Singleton Copley were commissioned to paint historical battle scenes, famous landscapes, and portraits of patriotic leaders. Lithographic techniques made it possible to reproduce and distribute visual art to the populace on a level unknown in earlier eras. Photography, particularly photographic portraiture, also became a popular art form with the introduction of daguerreotype technology to New York in 1839.

Once the Revolutionary War ended, interest in the theatrical arts revived and the growth of urban areas made large theaters economically viable. Theater audiences were typically seated according to social class, and shows often included audience participation. A common theme among early American playwrights was the contrast between supposed European corruption and American virtue. Stock characters such as the Yankee or the Backwoodsman emerged to represent distinctly American characteristics. Like other noted playwrights of the era, Mercy Otis Warren wrote plays promoting the social and moral values deemed essential to the future of the new republic. European plays continued to be performed on American stages as well; William Shakespeare's works were among the best known and most commonly performed. Beginning in the 1820s and 1830s, theatrical performances often included short minstrel shows between acts. By the 1840s, minstrel shows—performed by white actors in blackface—had developed into full-length productions and were considered a uniquely American form of entertainment.

The lifting of formal bans after the Revolution ushered in a renewed interest in horse racing, boxing, and other sports and games. However, such pursuits frequently aroused opposition from some segments of society. Republican leaders cautioned against imitating the idle dissoluteness of European aristocrats and insisted that any form of leisure that failed to improve one's character had no place in a virtuous republic. Many religious leaders also criticized amusement for its own sake as decadent and self-indulgent. Dancing was especially controversial; although dance instruction flourished, many Baptist and Methodist ministers regarded dancing as sinful and threatened to excommunicate members who attended balls or dancing schools. Although the Second Great Awakening carried the spirit of reform and moral crusade throughout the country, southerners typically encountered fewer religious proscriptions on their leisure activities than did their compatriots in Puritan New England.

WESTWARD EXPANSION

Hundreds of thousands of European Americans migrated west in the early 19th century, particularly in the decades that followed the War of 1812. Although the land area of the United States had doubled with the Louisiana Purchase in 1803, only one in 14 Americans lived west of the Appalachians by 1812. However, major population shifts occurred after a second U.S. victory over the British in 1812 removed barriers to European-American settlement of the west. By 1840, the population of European Americans west of the Alleghenies had increased tenfold. By that time, much of the land east of the Mississippi had been settled, and families (many of them the same families who a decade earlier had settled in the frontier regions of Kentucky, Tennessee, and Ohio) pushed even farther west to seek fresh land and new opportunities in the Pacific northwest.

Letter to an Irishman

Exiled to the United States for his alleged role in the United Irishmen's 1798 Rebellion, John Caldwell soon became an active member of New York's Irish-American society. The following is an excerpt from a letter that Caldwell wrote to his fellow United Irishman and former cellmate, Robert Simms.

[I]n general, every Stranger coming here, is inclined to encrease his wealth by some means or other, the misfortune is that many of us mistake the way—the Scotch farmer or Labourer on his arrival in a transatlantic Town, calls on his Country men, advises with them, goes back to the Country & becomes a farmer & of course a respectable member of Society—the Dutch & Germans frequently with two & three Hundred Pounds Sterling of property, will bind themselves to the Pensylvania Farmer & while the Husband attends his employer through his avocations, the wife will be learning the more dome-stick business of the farm, as suited to her sex—when the engagement of the People expire—they again emigrate to an uncleared Piece of Land & sett an example of Industry by blessing the Country with the fruits of their Labour. I wish I could say so much for our Country men—the Labourer, the farmer, the weaver, on coming here, all incline to live in large Towns, this may arise from the known character of the Irish—we are to use a trite saying, so warm hearted, we wish to live together & to be in the way of hearing often from our friends, but this disposition is often attended with ruin to Individuals and dishonour to our National character—I have often seen the Man, who with his family might have made a figure a 100 Miles from Town & there been respectable as a Citizen & a man—lose his little property in the dram shop he kept—lose his time by attending to Political controversy & matters that as an Alien did not concern him or at all events which his interference could not better, & lose the respectability of himself & his family by the consequences which must generally arise from such a line of conduct.

John Caldwell

It was not merely a restless sense of adventure that prompted such a dramatic upheaval and relocation of American families, although in some cases, that played a role. Periodic economic depressions, such as occurred in 1819 and again in 1837, prompted many families to pick up their roots and seek new opportunities farther west. Other families left to escape the cholera epidemics that were beginning to plague the eastern cities. Still others had struggled to grow crops in the worn-out soil of the Midwest and sought the more fertile soil of the Pacific territory. Travel narratives and guidebooks offered some help to European Americans as they prepared for the overland trip.

In this engraving depicting a migrant family camping on the plains in the west in the 1840s, a woman cooks over an open fire while men bring game birds and deer.

During the weeks and months on the trail, pioneers mastered the new skills they would need in order to adapt to life on the frontier. For the many men and women who lacked previous trail experience (many of them from middle-class homes and accustomed to domestic servants), the adjustment to trail life could be a challenge. Chores on the trail were roughly divided along gender lines, though roles were not rigid and everyone was expected to lend a hand. Men typically drove the wagons, made necessary repairs, orchestrated countless river crossings, and took turns standing guard at night. Women prepared the meals—no small task over an open fire in the wind and rain—aired out the provisions following a rainstorm or river crossing, did the family's laundry on layover days, and supervised young children.

CONCLUSION

While immigrants in the early national period were diverse, the country would become even more so in the next few decades. Even as westward movement increased, new European immigrants would continue to pour into the growing cities on the east coast. Immigration was rapidly becoming a dominant theme as the 19th century progressed. But first, many different groups of immigrants would soon become participants in the national trauma of the Civil War.

KATHLEEN RUPPERT
INDEPENDENT SCHOLAR

Further Reading

Allison, Robert J., ed. *American Eras: Development of a Nation, 1783–1815.* Detroit, MI: Gale Research, 1997.

Bergquist, James M. *Daily Life in Immigrant America, 1820–1870.* Westport, CT: Greenwood Press, 2008.

Boylan, Anne M. *Sunday School: The Formation of an American Institution, 1790–1880.* New Haven, CT: Yale University Press, 1988.

Chambers-Schiller, Lee Virginia. *Liberty, a Better Husband: Single Women in America, the Generations of 1780–1840.* New Haven, CT: Yale University Press, 1984.

Cogliano, Francis D. *Revolutionary America, 1763–1815: A Political History,* 2nd ed. London and New York: Routledge, 2000.

Dolan, Jay P. *The Irish Americans: A History.* New York: Bloomsbury Press, 2008.

Gaustad, Edwin S. *Neither King nor Prelate: Religion and the New Nation, 1776–1826.* Grand Rapids, MI: Wm. B. Eerdmans Publishing, 1993.

———. *A Religious History of America,* rev. ed. San Francisco: Harper & Row, 1990.

Granger, L.W. *Wide Awake! Romanism: Its Aims and Tendencies. The Sentiments of a Know-nothing.* Detroit: n.p., 1854.

Grund, Francis J. *Americans in their Moral, Social, and Political Relations* (1837); in "American Notes: Travels in America, 1750–1920." Available online, URL: http://memory.loc.gov. Accessed May 2010.

Hansen, Karen V. *A Very Social Time: Crafting Community in Antebellum New England.* Berkeley, CA: University of California Press, 1996.

Holmes, Kenneth L., ed. *Covered Wagon Women: Diaries and Letters from the Western Trails, 1840–1849.* Lincoln: University of Nebraska Press, 1995.

Kenslea, Timothy. *The Sedgwicks in Love: Courtship, Engagement, and Marriage in the Early Republic.* Lebanon, NH: Northeastern University Press, 2006.

Kirby A. Miller et al. *Irish Immigrants in the Land of Canaan: Letters and Memoirs from Colonial and Revolutionary America, 1675–1815.* Oxford: Oxford University Press, 2003.

Prokopowicz, Gerald J., ed. *American Eras: The Reform Era and Eastern U.S. Development, 1815–1850.* Detroit: Gale Research, 1998.

Riordan, Liam. *Many Identities, One Nation: The Revolution and Its Legacy in the Mid-Atlantic.* Philadelphia, PA: University of Pennsylvania Press, 2007.

Schlissel, Lillian. *Women's Diaries of the Westward Journey.* New York: Schocken Books, 2004.

Volo, James M. and Dorothy Denneen Volo. *The Antebellum Period.* Westport, CT: Greenwood Press, 2004.

CHAPTER 4

The Civil War and the Gilded Age: 1859 to 1900

THE STORY OF late-19th-century America is largely the story of immigrants and their interaction with one another, with the host society, and with immigrants who had preceded them to the New World. Between the Civil War and the 1880s, roughly 10 million immigrants—primarily from Britain and Ireland, Germany, and Scandinavia—joined the 5 million immigrants from those same regions of northern and western Europe who had migrated to the United States in the decades following the Napoleonic Wars. Toward the end of the 19th century, patterns of immigration began to shift, with the "new immigrants" arriving predominantly from southern and eastern Europe. These various groups of immigrants played important roles in settling the west and building the infrastructure of the United States. They became involved in municipal, state, and federal politics to varying degrees, and fought bravely alongside native-born Americans in the Civil War. Along the way, they negotiated the day-to-day tasks of earning a living, maintaining their homes, and feeding and clothing their families. Like other immigrant groups, European Americans formed religious, ethnic, and communal organizations that helped them to maintain their cultures while adjusting to life in their new homeland.

French immigrants had been arriving in small but steady streams for over a century prior to the outbreak of the American Civil War. Most of the early settlers were well educated, skilled, and quite prosperous as arti-

English emigrants leaving for America in a wood engraving published in Harper's Weekly *in January 1870.*

sans and merchants. In the years immediately after the Civil War, unskilled workers comprised an increasingly large percentage of French immigrants. Rather than joining earlier communities of French settlers (who tended to be widely scattered, with the only appreciable concentration in Louisiana), the French who arrived in the second half of the 19th century chose to settle wherever economic opportunities presented themselves. As a result, French immigrants were geographically widespread and, with the exception of the Cajun French in southern Louisiana, quick to assimilate into the mainstream culture and society.

Also quick to assimilate were the hundreds of thousands of English migrants who entered the United States during the second half of the 19th century. The largest wave of English immigration occurred in the 1880s, when roughly 80,000 English immigrants arrived each year. Like the French, English immigrants typically eschewed separate ethnic neighborhoods or communities and instead blended in easily with the host culture. Given a shared language and familiar institutions, as well as a sense of belonging to the same ethnic stock as most native-born whites, English Americans did not establish strong group cohesiveness; whatever ethnic institutions they did establish seldom lasted beyond the second generation.

Unlike their French and English counterparts, Dutch immigrants tended to settle in ethnic enclaves and to maintain a strong group identity. The majority of 19th-century Dutch immigrants entered the United States via New York and continued west to the Great Lakes region. Most became farmers, establishing agricultural communities and small towns where for many decades Dutch immigrants and their offspring comprised at least 90 percent of the population. Group cohesiveness was relatively easy to maintain in these rural settings. However, in metropolitan areas the Dutch managed to preserve ethnic and religious ties by settling in fairly self-contained neighborhoods where they established churches, day schools, and a network of ethnic associations.

Chain Migration

Chain migration (the process by which immigrants followed relatives or acquaintances from the homeland into a community in the United States) often played a role in determining the settlement patterns of ethnic groups. In many cases, personal letters such as the following, written by an immigrant named Gjert Gregoriussen Hovland to friends back home in Norway, praised the opportunities available in America and encouraged further migration.

I must take this opportunity to let you know that we are in the best of health, and that we—both my wife and I—find ourselves exceedingly satisfied. Our son attends the English school and talks English as well as the native born. Nothing has made me more happy and contented than the fact that we left Norway and journeyed to this country. We have gained more since our arrival here than I did during all the time that I lived in Norway, and I have every prospect of earning a livelihood here for myself and my family—even if my family were larger—so long as God gives me good health.

[. . .] It would heartily please me if I could learn that every one of you who are in need and have little chance of gaining support for yourselves and your families would make up your mind to leave Norway and come to America, for, even if many more were to come, there would still be room here for all. For all those who are willing to work there is no lack of employment and business here. It is possible for all to live in comfort and without suffering want. I do not believe that any of those who suffer under the oppression of others and who must rear their children under straitened circumstances could do better than to help the latter to come to America. But alas, many persons, even though they want to come, lack the necessary means and many others are so stupid as to believe that it is best to live in the country where they have been brought up even if they have nothing but hard bread to satisfy their hunger. It is as if they should say that those who move to a better land, where there is plenty, commit a wrong. But I can find no place where our Creator has forbidden one to seek one's food in an honorable manner. I should like to talk to many persons in Norway for a little while, but we do not wish to live in Norway. We lived there altogether too long. Nor have I talked with any immigrant in this country who wished to return.

Germans were concentrated in the cities of the northeast from New York to Baltimore, and especially in both the rural and urban Midwest. Wisconsin consistently boasted the largest percentage of Germans during this period; in 1900, German immigrants and their offspring comprised over one-third of the state's population. Across the "German belt," which stretched from Ohio to Nebraska, the German population outstripped the national average both as

The illustrator of this June 1882 cartoon titled "Uncle Sam's Lodging House" used a stereotypical Irish figure causing more trouble for Uncle Sam than other immigrants to highlight tensions over Irish immigration and political involvement.

a percentage of total population and as a percentage of all first- and second-generation immigrants. Chain migration brought a continual influx of Germans throughout the 19th century, as recent immigrants wrote to friends and relatives in the Old Country urging them to relocate to predominantly German communities in the New World. Propaganda from various Midwestern states, as well as from the railroads and other industries, also played a role in attracting German immigrants.

Although Germans in the United States were more highly urbanized than their counterparts back in Germany, German immigrants tended to live in cities only temporarily before relocating to small towns or rural communities. Nevertheless, compared to the national average, German Americans continued to be underrepresented in the agrarian sector throughout the 19th century. They owned more land than the Irish, who remained highly urbanized, but German Americans as a group were equaled or surpassed in rates of land ownership by Scandinavians, Swiss, Dutch, and Czech immigrants.

Scandinavians were heavily concentrated in the states along the Canadian border from Michigan to North Dakota. The 1860 census recorded 72,000 people of Scandinavian birth, the majority of them Norwegians, living in the United States. Over half of them lived in Wisconsin, but within a short time, Scandinavians quickly established new communities in Minnesota and the Dakotas.

German Neighborhoods

In urban areas, German Americans tended to cluster in neighborhoods that were predominantly German. The following letter excerpt describes one such community and also shows the centrality of the parish to German-American life. The letter is by Angela Heck, wife of a tailor named Nikolous Heck. The German Catholic couple left their home in southwest Eifel, a few miles from the Luxembourg border, in 1854. After 14 years in crowded neighborhoods in Manhattan, they moved across the East River to the lower-middle-class neighborhood of Williamsburg, which was populated primarily by German immigrants, especially small tradesmen and skilled craftsmen like Nikolous.

Williamsburg, Jan 24, 1869

My dearest Anna and Johannes,
*   Since the 1st of August we've been living for over a year in Williamsburg, a town very near New York. [. . .] It is much healthier here than in New York, just like in Germany. All of the small shops are German, 7–8 German-Catholic churches and each one has a Catholic school. We don't have to go further to church than you do at home. There is a church, it's like a cathedral, with three spires on top. Next to it is a small one like in Germany. There's a big school there, with 8–9 teachers, and also that many nuns. The nuns teach the girls and also the little boys until they are grown up. Then they go to the high school until the age of 14. Our little Nikolaus also goes there. We pay 15 cents a week. In the school there are 1,500, all with German parents and all Catholic; the priests visit the schools every day and are very strict. We also belong to this parish. We have a pew in the church. For that we pay one taler every three months. My husband belongs to the St. Joseph's society. If he gets sick, he gets 4 talers a week sick pay. And if he dies, he will be collected from the house and taken to the churchyard by the members of the society. The society covers all the expenses. [. . .] There is confession every Saturday. They are much stricter with confession and sermons here than in Germany. In all of the churches there are lovely organs and four-part choirs, all German singers. My dear Johannes and Anna, you mustn't think so, we won't lose our religion even though we are in America. [. . .] You can keep up your religion just as well here as in Germany. For there are Catholic churches everywhere now. In New York alone there are 42 Catholic churches, English and German. . . . We receive the church newspaper every Sunday and see everything that's happening in Rome.*

Thanks in large part to the Homestead Act, the decades following the Civil War brought an upsurge in Scandinavian immigration, which peaked in the early 1880s. By 1890, 400 Minnesota towns had Swedish names. As a group, Scandinavian Americans were largely agricultural; the Danes in particular established

This Swedish church in Indiana was built in 1880 during a peak period of Scandinavian immigration.

themselves as leading experts in dairy farming. Even so, Chicago and Minneapolis contained large Scandinavian communities that boasted newspapers, churches, fraternal societies, clubs, and schools. Danes, whose mass migration to the United States began a generation later than the other Scandinavian groups, were more likely to settle in urban areas. At the end of the 19th century, at least 33 percent of Danish immigrants in the United States lived in cities.

Between 1855 and 1920, 3 million Irish immigrants joined the 1.5 million who had fled to the United States during the great Irish Famine. Although significant numbers of middle-class Ulster Protestants had settled in the United States earlier in the century, the mass immigration of the famine years (and subsequent developments in the Irish-American experience) ensured that from mid-century onward, Irishness in America was equated with Catholicism. It was the Irish immigrants' Catholicism, together with their poverty and their reputation for drunkenness and criminality, that made them the targets of nativist prejudice and vilification throughout much of the 19th century.

Despite their rural background, Irish immigrants were the most urbanized of the "old immigrant" groups. Because they often lacked the capital to buy land and equip modern farms—and perhaps because they saw advantages in settling where Irish neighborhoods and strong ethnic networks already existed—Irish immigrants in this period lived in urban areas at twice the rate of the population as a whole. In many northeastern cities, especially, the Irish quickly came to dominate the building trades, municipal politics, and the Roman Catholic Church.

WORK, HOME, AND FAMILY

The families of Dutch and German immigrants tended to be large and strongly patriarchal. As with many immigrant groups, the family was regarded as an economic unit. Children began work at a young age, often helping out with farm work or in a family business. Older children typically worked outside the home to supplement the family income. Relatively few German-born women joined the labor force, but those who did were concentrated in domestic service and the clothing trades. Often, if a woman worked outside of the home, she did so in a small business belonging to her family or that of a friend. In addition to farming, German men were heavily represented in the food and brewing industries. Skilled craftsmen and artisans found work in such areas as ironworks, furniture making, upholstery, jewelry making, and glassblowing. German Americans tended to marry within their immediate community, and it was not unusual for several generations of a family to live under one roof, or at least in close proximity to each other. Scandinavians also tended to marry within their ethnic group, although Danes opted for out-group marriages more frequently than Norwegians and Swedes.

Rates of out-group matrimony were low among immigrant and second-generation Irish Americans as well, and they married less frequently overall than other Americans. Those who did marry typically opted to do so late in life. The average age of marriage for Irish Americans during this period was 31 for women and 35 for men. The relatively late marriage age gave Irish-American females an opportunity to enter the labor force, often sending a large portion of their earnings to family members back in Ireland. Domestic service was the occupation of choice for most female Irish immigrants; in 1900, over 60 percent of Irish-born women who worked in the United States did so as

An Irish-American mother pins a cloverleaf on her son as her daughter watches a street parade from the window on St. Patrick's Day in 1872. While single Irish-American women worked in large numbers, especially as domestics, married women and mothers tended to stay home.

Rural Isolation

A good deal has been written about the difficulties that immigrants faced in the tenements and slums of 19th-century American cities. Less attention has been paid to the hardships experienced by rural immigrants who helped to settle the Midwestern prairies. This excerpt from an 1863 article that appeared in *Atlantic Monthly* discusses the isolation of life on the prairie farms of Nebraska and the Dakotas, which the author suggests accounted for the high incidence of insanity among the Scandinavian population in those regions.

If there be any region in the world where the natural gregarious instincts of mankind should assert itself, that region is our Northwestern prairies, where a short hot summer is followed by a long cold winter, and where there is little in the aspect of nature to furnish food for thought. On every hand the treeless plain stretches away to the horizon line. [...] When the snow covers the ground the prospect is bleak and dispiriting. [...] The silence of death rests on the vast landscape, save when it is swept by cruel winds that search out every chink and cranny of the buildings, and drive through each unguarded aperture the dry, powdery snow. In such a region, you would expect the dwellings to be of substantial construction, but they are not. The new settler is too poor to build of brick or stone. He hauls a few loads of lumber from the nearest railway station, and puts up a frail little house of two, three or four rooms that looks as though the prairie winds would blow it away. Were it not for the invention of tarred building-paper, the flimsy walls would not keep out the wind and snow.

In this cramped abode, from the windows of which there is nothing more cheerful in sight than the distant houses of other settlers, just as ugly and lonely, and stacks of straw and unthreshed grain, the farmer's family must live. In the summer there is a school for the children, one, two or three miles away; but in the winter the distances across the snow-covered plains are too great for them to travel in severe weather; the schoolhouse is closed, and there is nothing for them to do but to house themselves and long for spring. Each family must live mainly to itself, and life, shut up in the little wooden farmhouses, cannot well be very cheerful.

domestic servants, and women of Irish birth constituted over 40 percent of all white servants. Irish females were also heavily represented in textile mills and in the garment industry.

Wives and mothers seldom worked outside the home in Irish-American communities. In fact, female Irish immigrants and their American-born daughters had among the lowest rates of employment after marriage of any ethnic group in the United States. Because of late marriages and a high rate of industrial accidents among Irish males, however, widowhood was more common among Irish Americans than among the population at large. Higher-than-average rates of male desertion among the Irish also contributed to an unusually large number of households run by females. In cases of widowhood or desertion, Irish women reentered the labor force, often taking in laundry or sewing if they still had young children to care for at home.

Irish immigrant males initially took unskilled positions as longshoremen or as laborers with the railroad, in factories, or in mining communities. Wages were low, and unskilled Irish workers faced many of the same hardships that the "new immigrants" from southern and eastern Europe would later face. Within a generation or two, however, the Irish took advantage of their concentration in urban centers and their hold on municipal politics to dominate the building trades. In 1870, nearly 20 percent of the building contractors in the nation were Irish-born, and they tended to hire Irish subcontractors and employees. Irish Americans, male and female, took on leadership roles in the nascent labor movement of the 19th century.

ETHNIC ASSOCIATIONS AND THE IMMIGRANT PRESS

As European immigration continued unabated throughout the 19th century, immigrants and their American-born descendants established a number of voluntary associations such as mutual aid societies, fraternal orders, temperance lodges, cultural groups, and charitable organizations. The purpose of these associations was to assist new immigrants in adjusting to life in America and to help preserve the culture of the homeland. While some were purely social in character, others functioned as labor unions, self-help societies, or political clubs. Networks established through ethnic associations such as Irish America's Ancient Order of Hibernians could prove valuable in facilitating employment opportunities for members. At times, these associations were organized along religious lines; the Irish Catholic Benevolent Union and the Knights of Columbus, for example, were both tied to the Catholic Church. In other cases, the associations were based on occupation or, as in the case of the Irish county clubs, village or county of origin.

The German-American community built this bank headquarters in Missouri in 1889.

While the Irish Americans of the mid- to late-19th century were a fairly homogeneous group in terms of religion and class status, the social framework of German Americans was considerably more complex. For one thing, many German immigrants identified themselves not with Germany per se, but rather with their province of origin (such as Bavaria or Prussia), thus making a unified group identity difficult to achieve. This was particularly the case prior to German unification. The class structure of German Americans was also quite diverse, including large numbers of middle class and professional men in addition to farmers, artisans, and unskilled workers. Religion was also a source of division among German Americans: in addition to numerous Protestant sects, both Calvinist and Lutheran, there were also significant Catholic and Jewish populations, as well as a small but outspoken minority of German freethinkers who eschewed all institutional religion.

The competing and, at times, overlapping identities among the German-American population led to a wide assortment of voluntary organizations. These *Vereine* included literary, musical, and theatrical societies as well as mutual aid societies organized on the basis of occupation, religion, or province of origin. Turner Societies, first established in the United States by political refugees from the 1848 revolution, emphasized gymnastics and physical education and also offered lectures and ethnic celebrations. Informal social institutions such as beer halls also served as gathering places for German-American families. Sunday gatherings at beer halls, picnics, and festivities helped to reinforce familial and community ties, but also gained for Germans the disapprobation of Anglo-American reformers who sought to legislate the Continental Sunday out of existence.

The Gilded Age also witnessed the proliferation of ethnic newspapers. These served a dual purpose of maintaining communal ties among members of a given ethnic group and of keeping those individuals apprised of events back in their homelands. On a pragmatic level, foreign-language newspapers also advertised job openings and played an important role in fostering chain migration. By the 1880s, at least one Irish-American newspaper could be found in nearly every major city in the north and the Midwest. Germans led the way, however, with regard to ethnic newspapers: at its height in 1894, the German-American press published 800 German-language newspapers, including 97 dailies.

THE CALL TO ARMS

When the Civil War broke out in 1861, ethnic Americans signed up by the thousands to serve in the military. Approximately 200,000 German Americans and nearly 150,000 first- and second-generation Irish Americans served in the Union army during the Civil War. Smaller numbers served with the Confederate forces, in large part because European immigrants were more concentrated in the north. Several Swedish communities in the Midwest fur-

Enamored of the style and flair of the French uniforms, a number of Civil War units adopted variations on the baggy pants and turbans of the Zouaves, like these men of the 114th Pennsylvania Infantry.

nished predominantly Swedish units, while other companies, such as the 15th Wisconsin Infantry, contained a large proportion of Swedish, Danish, and Norwegian volunteers.

Not all European immigrants who served did so in ethnic regiments. In the case of German Americans, approximately one in five soldiers served in German or mostly German regiments; the rest served in mixed units. Even within non-ethnic or mixed regiments, however, it was not unusual to find a company of Swedes or Germans or Irishmen. Recruiters played upon ethnic considerations and cultural pride in appealing to European Americans. Recruitment posters and rallies in ethnic neighborhoods were delivered in the native language of the audience, and communities in northeastern cities held parades to celebrate the formation of ethnic fighting units.

Several reasons motivated these men, many of whom had been in the country only a short time, to volunteer for military service. For some it was the recognition that, however difficult their plight in the United States might be, their new home offered opportunities denied to them in Europe. It was, therefore, with a sense of patriotism—coupled with a desire to preserve the same opportunities for future immigrants—that they volunteered for service. In addition, certain ethnic groups (most notably Irish and German) sought to counter nativist stereotypes and demonstrate their loyalty as

Americans. There was a widespread hope, especially in the early years of the conflict, that patriotic service would raise the status of ethnic minorities in the aftermath of the war. Still others saw military service as an opportunity for a steady income that was otherwise difficult to obtain. Irish Americans

Anti-German Prejudice in the Military

Many ethnic soldiers who volunteered to serve during the Civil War did so with the hope of improving their status in American society. The following passage suggests, however, that anti-German prejudice did not entirely disappear with the coming of the war. This excerpt is taken from a letter written by a Union soldier of German birth.

The treatment or rather mistreatment of the Germans in the army has recently demanded the attention of the German press more than usual. My experience with people close to me enables me to speak competently about this subject. There may be about 600 Germans in my brigade. They make up five all-German companies, the remainder are scattered over the different regiments and companies. If a full company is needed for some easy service, for example, Provost-Guard, a German company is never taken. If an entire company is required for rough service, for example, several days or several weeks as Train-Guard, a German company will be ordered whenever possible. As this happens on a company basis, so it happens to individuals in the mixed companies. As a rule the German has to wade through the mud, while the American walks on the dry road. The German is a "Dutch soldier" and as a "Dutchman" he is, if not despised, disrespected, and not regarded or treated as an equal. . . . A colonel once said that he could not understand why so many Germans volunteer so readily for the army, after all, as foreigners they could not be interested in it. This opinion is mainly represented by Americans from the North.

I have already heard many crude jokes made about one of the best known generals for the Union, not because he is not up to his high position, every Know-Nothing will argue the opposite, but rather because he is a German . . . Let me return to the German soldiers, and state another fact, i.e., that the German soldier is generally far more faithful, conscientious and zealous than the native-born American. This is part of the German nature, which is our reason to be proud of our nation. One more thing: The German soldier is obedient and loyal to duty without regard to reward or punishment. The American generally considers only reward, or—the Guard-House. This is caused by the national education on either side, in the broadest sense of the word. Because of the situation as mentioned, you may possibly draw the conclusion that the mixing of Germans and Americans in the Army may be beneficial to both parties, but such conclusion is in error.

also wanted of wanting to gain military experience for an anticipated fight for Irish independence.

In some important respects, the Civil War did help to integrate immigrants and ethnic minorities, particularly Germans, into mainstream American society. Irish Americans were still not warmly received after the war, in part because of their involvement in the 1863 Draft Riots. For many Irish Americans, more complete acceptance into mainstream society would have to await the arrival of masses of new immigrants from southern and eastern Europe near the end of the century.

THE NEW IMMIGRANTS

While older migrant streams continued to flow into the United States, the overall composition began to shift in the final decades of the 19th century. Immigrants from southern and eastern Europe came to dominate the influx of new arrivals, with Italians and eastern European Jews accounting for 17 percent and 14 percent, respectively, of total immigration from 1880 until World War I. Various Slavic populations including Ukrainians, Poles, Czechs, Slovaks, Lithuanians, and others also migrated to the United States in significant numbers at the close of the century. Overwhelmingly poor, the new masses of immigrants were also largely Jewish and Catholic. Many Americans of older stock reviled the new immigrants and considered them backward and incapable of assimilation.

Nearly 1 million Italians arrived in the last two decades of the 19th century, most of them unskilled male laborers from the south of Italy. These were not the first Italians to arrive: between 1860 and 1880, nearly 68,000 Italians arrived and began to establish Italian colonies in several major cities including New York, Chicago, New Orleans, and San Francisco. The early immigrants had set up foreign-language newspapers, mutual aid societies, and other ethnic organizations. Italian immigration reached its height in the decades between 1880 and World War I.

Eastern European Jews also began migrating to the United States in significant numbers during the 1880s. Faced with repressive anti-Semitic legislation and government-sponsored pogroms at home, Jews who left the Russian Empire regarded themselves as permanent exiles there rather than as temporary "birds of passage." Whereas 60 percent of the southern Italians who migrated to the United States ultimately returned to their homeland, only 3 percent of eastern European Jews returned. Because they expected the move to be permanent, Jews were more likely to migrate as a family unit: nearly half of the Jewish immigrants were women (compared to only one in five among Italians), and children represented one out of four Russian Jewish immigrants.

Unlike Jewish immigrants from eastern Europe, Greek immigrants were overwhelmingly single and male. For every 11 Greek men who immigrated to the United States, only one Greek woman made the journey, and children

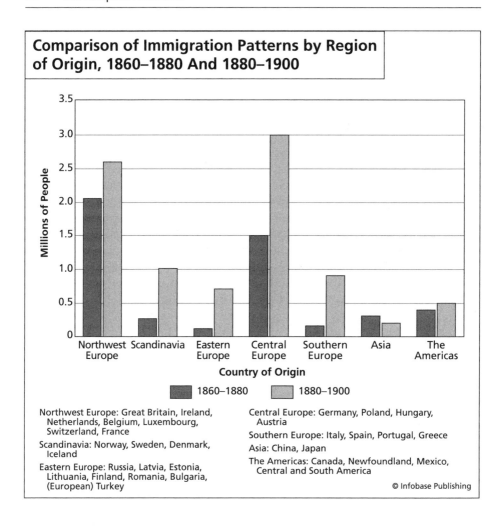

Comparison of Immigration Patterns by Region of Origin, 1860–1880 And 1880–1900

Northwest Europe: Great Britain, Ireland, Netherlands, Belgium, Luxembourg, Switzerland, France

Scandinavia: Norway, Sweden, Denmark, Iceland

Eastern Europe: Russia, Latvia, Estonia, Lithuania, Finland, Romania, Bulgaria, (European) Turkey

Central Europe: Germany, Poland, Hungary, Austria

Southern Europe: Italy, Spain, Portugal, Greece

Asia: China, Japan

The Americas: Canada, Newfoundland, Mexico, Central and South America

© Infobase Publishing

comprised only four percent of Greek immigrants. Most Greeks settled in the mill towns of the northeast or in large urban centers such as New York and Chicago. Like Slavic and Italian immigrants, young Greek men tended to arrive in the spring to take jobs in mining or construction, and then to return home for the winter months. Polish and Slavic Americans were fairly widespread geographically, but concentrations could be found in the industrial cities of the Great Lakes region and the mining communities of Pennsylvania. The most influential Polish and Slavic settlements were in Pittsburgh, Cleveland, Detroit, and Chicago. Given their similar histories and common religious faith, Poles and Lithuanians occasionally joined together to establish Catholic parishes or joint benefit societies. For Polish Americans in particular, the parish was the center of their communal life.

Immigrant laborers at the close of the century overwhelmingly took unskilled positions at the bottom rungs of the workforce, filling the need for cheap labor in factories and mines during a period of rapid industrial expansion. Of the 14,000 unskilled laborers employed by Pittsburgh steel plants, for example, 11,000 were from southern and eastern Europe. Slavic immigrants frequently found jobs in railroad and construction work, as did many Italians. Housing conditions were far from ideal for the new immigrants. Slavs and Greeks who worked in the mines or on construction sites often lived in overcrowded shacks in nearby shanty towns.

CONCLUSION

Like the earlier European ethnic groups who had come before them, the "new immigrants" of the late 19th century worked to maintain communal solidarity while facilitating the adjustment to urban-industrial America. In both urban and rural settings across the country, European Americans organized a vast array of churches, schools, shops, and businesses for their communities. These institutions served their own people and, at the same time, helped them to become acculturated to American society—something that would become of even greater importance in the Progressive Era.

KATHLEEN RUPPERT
INDEPENDENT SCHOLAR

Further Reading

Bruce, Susannah U. *The Harp and Eagle: Irish-American Volunteers and the Union Army, 1861–1865.* New York: New York University Press, 2006.

Burton, William L. *Melting Pot Soldiers: The Union's Ethnic Regiments,* 2nd ed. New York: Fordham University Press, 1998.

Cashman, Sean Dennis. *America in the Gilded Age: From the Death of Lincoln to the Rise of Theodore Roosevelt,* 3rd ed. New York: New York University Press, 1993.

Daniels, Roger. "The Immigrant Experience in the Gilded Age." In *The Gilded Age: Essays on the Origins of Modern America.* Ed. by Charles W. Calhoun. Wilmington, DE: Scholarly Resources, 1996.

Diner, Hasia. "Erin's Children in America: Three Centuries of Irish Immigration to the United States." In *Origins and Destinies: Immigration, Race, and Ethnicity in America.* Ed. by Silvia Pedraza and Rubén G. Rumbaut. Belmont, CA: Wadsworth, 1996.

Ewen, Elizabeth. *Immigrant Women in the Land of Dollars: Life and Culture on the Lower East Side, 1890–1925.* New York: Monthly Review, 1985.

Friedman-Kasaba, Kathie. *Memories of Migration: Gender, Ethnicity and Work in the Lives of Jewish and Italian Women in New York, 1870–1924.* Albany, NY: State University of New York Press, 1996.

Furer, Howard B., ed. *The Scandinavians in America, 986–1970: A Chronology & Fact Book.* Dobbs Ferry, NY: Oceana Publications, 1972.

Helbich, Wolfgang, Walter D. Kamphoefner, and Ulrike Sommer, eds. *News from the Land of Freedom: German Immigrants Write Home.* Ithaca, NY: Cornell University Press, 1993.

Kamphoefner, Walter D. "German Americans: Paradoxes of a 'Model Minority.'" In *Origins and Destinies: Immigration, Race, and Ethnicity in America.* Ed. by Silvia Pedraza and Rubén G. Rumbaut. Belmont, CA: Wadsworth, 1996.

Kenny, Kevin. *The American Irish: A History.* London and New York: Pearson Education Ltd., 2000.

Kraut, Alan M. *The Huddled Masses: The Immigrant in American Society, 1880–1921.* Wheeling, IL: Harlan Davidson, 1982.

Lee, J.J. and Marion R. Casey, eds. *Making the Irish American: History and Heritage of the Irish in the United States.* New York: New York University Press, 2006.

Lindaman, Matthew. "*Heimat* in the Heartland: The Significance of an Ethnic Newspaper." *Journal of American Ethnic History,* v.23/3 (Spring 2004).

Lovoll, Odd S. *The Promise of America: A History of the Norwegian-American People,* rev. ed. Minneapolis, MN: University of Minnesota Press, 1999.

Miller, Kirby A. *Emigrants and Exiles: Ireland and the Irish Exodus to North America.* New York: Oxford University Press, 1985.

Nelli, Humbert S. *From Immigrants to Ethnics: The Italian Americans.* Oxford: Oxford University Press, 1983.

Pula, James S. *Polish Americans: An Ethnic Community.* New York: Twayne Publishers, 1995.

Reinhart, Joseph R., ed. *Two Germans in the Civil War.* Knoxville, TN: University of Tennessee Press, 2004.

Takaki, Ronald. *A Different Mirror: A History of Multicultural America.* Boston, MA: Little, Brown, 1993.

Thernstrom, Stephan, ed. *Harvard Encyclopedia of American Ethnic Groups.* Cambridge, MA: Harvard University Press, 1980.

Tolzmann, Don Heinrich. *The German-American Experience.* Amherst, NY: Humanity Books, 2000.

Van Vugt, William E. *Britain to America: Mid-Nineteenth Century Immigrants to the United States.* Urbana, IL: University of Illinois Press, 1999.

CHAPTER 5

The Progressive Era and World War I: 1900 to 1920

MOST HISTORIANS DEFINE the Progressive Era as those highly eventful years beginning in 1900 and lasting until 1920. These decades symbolized a time of tumultuous political and social change. A wide variety of intriguing people gave life to these changes and many of these characters were Americans of European ancestry. The period's multicultural diversity and its many separate strands of endeavor remain a rich field for investigation. Furthermore, the tenets of Progressivism touched upon all levels of societal development, and continue to offer insight into the beginnings of modern America.

The America that emerged was an increasingly urban and industrial state that operated according to free-market laissez-faire capitalism. However, a direct consequence of this transformation were imbalances and injustices that threatened what some saw as the fabric of older American ideals and values. The nation's political forces, from the nation's presidents to local reformers, struggled throughout the era to find acceptable solutions.

These challenges also received national exposure through the efforts of writers such as Frank Norris, whose book *The Octopus* (1901) explored monopolistic railroad practices in California. Other business investigations such as Ida Tarbell's "History of the Standard Oil Company" published in *McClure's* Magazine in 1904 examined the unfair practices of J.D. Rockefeller's Standard Oil Company, which stifled competition; this would eventually lead the drive

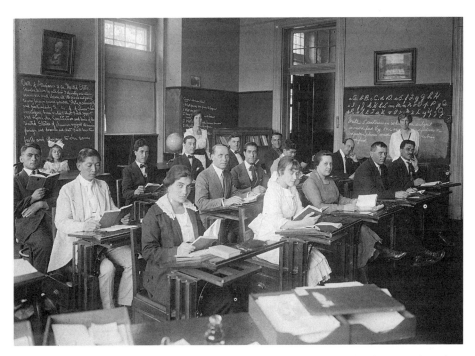

During the Progressive Era, anxiety over immigration led to a growing emphasis on acculturation and Americanization in education. In the photo, men and women of various ethnicities read in an Americanization class in 1920.

to break up the trusts. Lincoln Steffens's *Shame of the Cities* (1904) looked at the state of corruption in municipal government. Such corruption, often driven by money and power brokers, undercut and perverted democratic practices. Upton Sinclair's *The Jungle* (1906) uncovered the industrial practices and terrible hygiene found in Chicago's meatpacking industry.

These muckraking efforts stirred the popular reform spirit, particularly in America's old-guard middle class who felt that their position was undermined by the era's march toward mass industrialization. The rich became richer and the poor became poorer, and the middle class felt threatened from above and from below. The political campaigning of middle America shaped many of these reform drives and led to a range of significant changes, including at the urban level, where city commissioner and city manager government plans took shape. These endeavors were geared toward ending the often-corrupt control of ward bosses in the running of municipal administrations.

THE CHANGING FACES OF AMERICA

The era was also a time of rapid population growth spurred by both immigration and internal migration. The U.S. population grew from 76 million in 1900 to over 106 million in 1920. Industrialization changed the American landscape and this growth stimulated the need for a variety of jobs in all sectors of the production process. Europeans formed the major force behind this wave of immigration as they left the Old World and came to the New World. They looked for work and higher wages in the booming industries that transformed urban America.

The decade from 1900 to 1910 produced population increases that were truly historic. Now immigrants composed 15 percent of the general population. The degree of this growth was best reflected, between 1900 and 1910, in the over 1 million immigrants who arrived each year. All of Europe contributed to this exodus, including increasingly eastern and southern European countries.

At the beginning of the century, the Italians were the main group that entered the United States, with over 655,000 coming between 1890 and 1900. They left an overcrowded land of little opportunity for the United States, which represented great promise. Between 1900 and 1910, a further 2.1 million Italians came. Most of the Italians arrived without skills and, therefore, were absorbed into the industrial expansion that created a multitude of unskilled laboring jobs. They settled in the cities where these jobs were being created such as New York, Philadelphia, Chicago, Boston, Baltimore, and Detroit. They also arrived without the capital to start a business or to buy a farm. This was particularly the case since the free-land opportunities of the 19th century had passed.

European Jewish immigration to the United States also increased dramatically in the late 19th century and continued into the 1920s. Many came as a result of systematic persecution in areas of eastern Europe. In particular, a wave of Yiddish-speaking Ashkenazi Jews came from rural Russia and the Pale of Settlement (a region in Russia where Jews were allowed to establish permanent residence). Over 2 million Jews arrived during this period and settled primarily in New York City and its neighboring regions, eventually establishing one of the largest Jewish communities in the world.

Although Italian and European Jewish immigration was particularly significant during these years, there were other European immigrants contributing to the overall pattern of arrivals. In sta-

These Italian boys were selling bananas from a pushcart in Indianapolis, Indiana, in August 1908.

This September 1911 photograph captured an extended family of 17 French immigrants in Winchendon, Massachusetts. Most of the family, including the older children, worked in a textile mill.

tistical terms, over 10 million immigrants arrived in the country during the decade of 1890 to 1900, as recorded by the 1900 census. Of these, almost 9 million came from Europe. According to the 1910 census, over 13 million new immigrants came in the previous 10 years and, of this total, almost 12 million were European. The 1920 census, which reflected the decade that included the years of World War I, revealed that of nearly 14 million immigrants, 12 million came from Europe.

These figures were further subdivided and revealed that over 3 million of the overall total in 1900 and 1910 came from the various countries of western Europe, with the British Isles, Ireland, and Germany being most prominent. However, this number slipped to fewer than 3 million in 1920, following World War I.

Yet as the years passed, southern and eastern Europe replaced the previously dominant western European immigrant orientation. The great immigrant influx from southern and eastern countries rose from less than 2 million immigrants in 1900 to over 5 million in 1920. Italy, Poland, Austria-Hungary, and what became the Soviet Union after 1917 contributed the largest numbers.

This tidal wave of people whose labor was vital to America's growth nevertheless produced rising anxieties within the native population. Established Americans became worried about the cultural and religious pressures these strangers brought to America. As opposed to earlier immigrants from the

British Isles and western Europe, these new arrivals were more foreign in behavior, customs, looks, and religion. For some, these differences posed a threat to the traditional sense of America's identity. This fear became a critical motivator in certain Progressive circles that produced reforms to deal with native anxieties over this immigrant presence. Aspects of these concerns led to educational reforms geared to acculturation and Americanization drives. However, for some Progressives, the only lasting solution for America's identity was through tighter immigration control.

SETTLEMENT PATTERNS

Progressive Era immigrant settlement largely followed patterns established in the 19th century. For the most part, new arrivals lived in the mid-Atlantic region. In addition, what was most observable during this period was a migration shift from northern and western Europe to southern and eastern Europe. By the beginning of the 20th century, the majority of these immigrants— some 3 million Italians, 3 million Slavs, as well as 2 million eastern European Jews—formed core immigrant communities. However, precise immigrant identification was further complicated by a state of administrative confusion surrounding those ethnic groups from the Austro-Hungarian Empire. Often these arrivals were simply catalogued by officials as Germans, Austrians, or Hungarians. In addition, Poles did not get a separate ethnic classification until after 1918—previously they were seen as Russians.

New York City was the national port of entry and many immigrants joined the city's burgeoning population. This was particularly the case for Italians and east European Jews, but there were plenty of other ethnic communities within the city. With factory and manufacturing growth, many immigrants moved to outlying states such as New Jersey, Connecticut, and Massachusetts. Pennsylvania attracted immigrant miners, and unskilled jobs in heavy industry drew Poles, Slavs, and Italians to Cleveland, Buffalo, and Chicago. By 1920, Chicago had large numbers of Jews, African Americans, and numerous varieties of Slavs, which broadened the city's diversity from a 1900 base that was heavily German, Scandinavian, and Irish.

Estimates suggest that in 1906 Cleveland, one in six residents had Slavic origins and one in five claimed a German heritage. This gave the city a clearly foreign feel. Even cities farther west and north such as Milwaukee, Omaha, and Minneapolis experienced a considerable influx of eastern and southern Europeans looking for industrial jobs. These newer immigrants supplemented the 19th-century Scandinavian and German influx. In terms of the widest national dispersal, Germans led the way, and by the beginning of the Progressive Era, Germans made up the largest single ethnic group in 30 states. Germans were also a leading presence in eight of the 10 largest cities, with the exception of Philadelphia and Boston, where the Irish were more numerous.

Ellis Island

For many European immigrants arriving in New York Harbor, Ellis Island served as an introduction to their new home. Since more affluent passengers were usually directed to Manhattan, arrivals at Ellis Island, known as the "Isle of Tears," were often poor and desperate. Whether or not the tired and often overwhelmed immigrants filing past the stone eagles guarding the entrance to officialdom were allowed to enter the country was decided by examiners employed by the Bureau of Investigation and physicians working for the Marine Hospital Service. As part of the processing routine, potential immigrants were required to walk up a designated staircase to weed out those with physical infirmities. Entrants deemed to need further examination were labeled according to an established code, including such designations as E (eye diseases), H (heart conditions), Pg (pregnancy), L (lameness), S (senility), and X (possible mental problems).

Those who passed initial tests were then required to provide officials with information about their current finances and potential and employment status. They were also required to own up to radical political views. Through word-of-mouth, immigrants learned to offer only information that was considered acceptable. Those who failed physical tests or whose answers were considered unacceptable were denied entry, often languishing at Ellis Island for weeks on end. Overworked immigration officials sometimes separated families through haste, misunderstandings, or lack of compassion, leading to major disruptions in family life.

Over 75 percent of Italians settled in New York, New England, and Pennsylvania, and New York City absorbed similar percentages of eastern European Jews. Many found work in the city's garment district and cigar factories or as street merchants, all appreciative of the escape from Russian pogroms and Slav nationalism. Many of the other eastern Europeans and southern Italians who arrived also hoped to eventually return home, once their earnings provided them with the means. Some estimates suggested that within Slavs and Hungarians, perhaps 50 percent returned home. However, this back-and-forth flow was seriously contained by the coming of World War I and by the growing drive for immigration restriction.

RESTRICTING IMMIGRATION

During the Progressive Era, immigration anxiety produced a steady stream of controls that became law. Following the assassination of William McKinley in 1901 by a Polish anarchist, immigration fears became linked to radical politics and the Anarchist Exclusion Act followed, supposedly ending entry of those immigrants who had extreme political beliefs. In addition, further restrictions

Not all new immigrants found industrial jobs when they moved west. These Hungarian immigrants working in the beet fields of Corunna, Michigan, were part of a group of several hundred who moved on from New York City by train in spring 1916.

were added that made entry more difficult for criminals, lunatics, idiots, and vagrants. In 1907, an Expatriation Act was passed that theoretically stripped an American woman of her citizenship if she married a foreigner. Also during this time, following a gentleman's agreement with Japan, Japanese immigration was restricted through passport labor controls, although Hawaii was excluded from the U.S. continental ban.

For Asian immigrants already residing in the United States, laws such as California's 1913 Alien Land Law affected them by restricting their right to own land. Other states followed suit with similar discriminatory laws. Immigrant curbs continued and, in 1917, Congress instituted a literacy provision to further restrict the unskilled and uneducated from entering the country. The law also increased prohibitions on Asian immigration, although with certain exceptions for Japan and the Philippines.

The Progressive Era ended with the introduction of the quota system as represented in the 1921 Quota Act, which from that date limited immigration to 3 percent of the nationality groups as defined by the 1910 census.

NATIVISM: IMMIGRATION BACKLASH

Previous nativist movements during the 19th century, such as the mid-century Know Nothing Movement, were opposed to the influx of primarily Irish immigrants. The American Protective Association (APA), with their anti-Catholic sentiments, also reached their height in the 1880s and 1890s. The APA's influence declined with the increasing labor demands during the Progressive years.

However, the rise of the Ku Klux Klan during the era kept anti-immigrant sentiment alive and well. Around 1890, the term *hyphenated American* began to be used as an epithet, and its use became even more common after the turn of the century and as tensions increased before World War I. Presidents Theodore Roosevelt and Woodrow Wilson both used the expression to question the patriotism of various groups of immigrants, such as those with ties to European countries, who did not fully assimilate.

There was widespread concern regarding the impact of European immigration that extended beyond nativist organizations. This was particularly the case with the arrival of more and more southern and eastern European immigrants, who seemingly grew more threatening as their numbers increased. They were viewed as less skilled, less educated, less desirable, and more clannish than other immigrants, and this made them appear to be potentially dangerous to American social development. These conclusions were reached in a 1911, 42-volume government report on immigration and motivated the Bureau of Naturalization and the Bureau of Education to guarantee that the Americanization process would be more fully implemented to ensure the fuller integration of immigrants.

Immigration increasingly became seen in some supposedly Progressive quarters as a force that weakened the nation's racial strengths as an Anglo-Saxon state. These beliefs were given philosophical and scientific support in the form of Sir Francis F. Galton's late-19th-century eugenics theories that divided races into superior and inferior stocks. According to this movement, nature had far more influence on a nation's destiny than nurture, and biology could, over time, produce substandard types that undermined a country's strength.

During these years, many Progressives linked the nation's social and political ills to what they imagined was the mass influx of genetically inferior immigrants. Those concerned with such issues, such as John Henry Kellogg, made racial improvement a goal worth pursuing. In 1906, he organized the Race Betterment Organization and promoted the organization's ambitions through conferences held at his Battle Creek, Michigan, home. In 1910, the Eugenics Record Office was founded to argue for not only immigration control, but also control over marriages and the sterilization of those deemed inferior. The popularity of the movement was seen in its extensive media coverage and in its several associations such as the Galton Society, created in 1918. Eugenics remained an influential force until the 1930s, when the brutality of Nazism discredited ideas of racial superiority.

WORLD WAR I TENSIONS

The coming of World War I created new issues and raised new tensions in an already-fragmented immigrant culture. After the United States joined the Allies in 1917, becoming an enemy of Germany and the Central powers, it was not long before "100 percent Americanism" was demanded of the public. The situation became heated and many German Americans were suspect, particularly those who argued for neutrality or promoted German-American cultural institutions.

The situation caused some German Americans to panic, mainly over concerns for property and wealth confiscation. Other, more vocal German Americans resisted, with defenses of the German cause attacking the pro-war press and accompanying government propaganda. In addition, a sizable number of German Americans viewed the growing Prohibition crusade as vindictively aimed at the German populace. The National German American Alliance worked to avoid the road to war at the same time as it proclaimed total American loyalty. Most German-American newspapers also advocated war avoidance, but offered loyalty once war was declared. However, there were those in the German press who argued that the war was without principle and was motivated by financial forces.

With war, many German Americans felt a wave of intimidation, especially after Attorney General Thomas Gregory called for surveillance of suspect German-American aliens and others seen as potential threats. Such investigations were led by organizations like the American Protective League, founded in Chicago in 1917, as well as by the National Security League, which was devoted to identifying subversion on the home front. From the initial search for suspect aliens, they soon turned to searching for German spies in the nation's midst. This vigilante activism was reinforced by government bodies such as the Creel Committee, which promoted patriotic values. Patriotic values were eventually introduced into German-language teaching by means of specially prepared patriotic texts.

As the war progressed, suspicions grew stronger, and much of the public became intolerant of dissent of any kind and made patriotism synonymous with anti-German feeling. What soon followed was a hatred for

This German sailor, who worked aboard American ships until October 1917, was detained at Angel Island in San Francisco during World War I.

ENLIST TO-DAY
— IN —
THE 69TH INFANTRY
JOIN THE FAMOUS IRISH REGIMENT
THAT FOUGHT IN ALL THE GREAT
BATTLES OF THE CIVIL WAR,
FROM BULL RUN TO APPOMATOX
GO TO THE FRONT
WITH YOUR FRIENDS
DON'T BE DRAFTED INTO SOME REGIMENT
WHERE YOU DON'T KNOW ANYONE
MEN WANTED FROM 18 TO 40
APPLY AT THE ARMORY
LEXINGTON AVENUE and 25th STREET

This 1917 poster urged Irish men to enlist in the 69th Infantry, or the "famous Irish regiment."

anything remotely German. Free speech suffered along with freedom of association. Threats of violence increased and some acts of actual violence occurred inside this toxic atmosphere.

Some critics soon attacked German schools, churches, newspapers, and associations without reflection or balance. By June 1917, the anti-German spirit was widespread and threatened the full spectrum of German Americans. German-American newspapers were denounced and some even called for the imprisonment of German Americans in concentration-style camps. Congress also responded to the patriotic mood by producing the Espionage Act, which, among other provisions, required English translations of the German-American press to guarantee that no negative comments were expressed that challenged the American government. The U.S. Post Office became an intervening censor during the war. Persecution was sometimes directed at those with German names, leading individuals to name changes, and evidence existed that employers were criticized for employing German Americans.

German music did not escape patriotic attention, and by the autumn of 1917, Beethoven was even banned in Pittsburgh. Dr. Karl Muck, conductor of the Boston Symphony Orchestra, was for a time sent to an alien detention camp, and the Philadelphia Orchestra refused to play German music. In addition, California's Board of Education attempted to eliminate German folk songs from textbooks. By 1918, half of the states had ended the teaching of German and many communities demanded that German not be spoken in public.

Many Irish Americans joined with those German Americans as opposition voices to America's entry into the war on the side of the British. New York City's Fenian Brotherhood, founded in 1858, was a movement long associated with the end of Irish union with Great Britain. Anglophobia was an established Irish cause and, on occasion, an embarrassment to U.S. relations with Great Britain.

By the early 20th century, in both the United States and Ireland, nationalists supported Home Rule, and for a growing minority, total independence replaced parliamentary representation as the goal. The use of force was becoming acceptable in the struggle, especially if it could more speedily deliver the desired ends.

With the coming of war in 1914, many Irish-American organizations sympathized with the Central powers. Further, Irish Americans frequently complained of the pro-Allied bias found in the American popular press. Following the Easter Rebellion of 1916, especially after the execution of many rebels, Irish-American nationalism turned more heated and emerged as a mass movement against British rule. In support of the nationalist cause during the war, and in the years immediately thereafter, Irish Americans raised millions of dollars for Irish independence.

As the drumbeat of war increased in 1917, Irish Americans were perhaps the most effective force against U.S. entry into the conflict. During the 1916 election, Irish Americans became increasingly doubtful of President Woodrow Wilson's pledge to keep America out of the war, and many city political machines failed to deliver votes as in the past. Irish-American Catholics developed a uniform approach: no help for the British Empire without Irish independence. Unlike many other urban ethnic groups, by the Progressive Era, Irish Americans exerted a considerable influence within the Democratic Party that could affect election results. This put considerable pressure on Wilson to pursue war goals that stood outside those of Great Britain, and provided a degree of independence to American aims such as a postwar settlement based on the self-determination of nations.

EUROPEAN AMERICANS IN WORLD WAR I

Although many Irish Americans and German Americans felt serious reservations concerning the Allied cause, the United States during World War I drafted a half million troops comprised of over 40 nationalities, including over 18 percent who were foreign born. A further 3 million potential soldiers were ineligible because they were not, at the time, naturalized. In addition, there were many thousands who were second-generation Americans.

German- and Austrian-born troops created a potential conflict of interest. Some feared that they wouldn't reliably fight against fellow countrymen; yet most from these backgrounds chose loyalty to their new country and remained in the military. New York's 69th Infantry, dominated by Irish Americans, joined the Rainbow Division and fought with distinction during World War I, avoiding any reservations about being an ally of the British. However, this enormous foreign presence made for serious problems for the army, which needed a uniform fighting force.

The array of different languages, religions, and customs presented training obstacles to the officers charged with the creation of a modern fighting force.

In general, the War Department attempted to develop policies that forged loyalty and patriotism and that, at the same time, considered ethnic differences and traditions. To aid in this initiative, many foreign-community leaders were recruited to offer their services to the military. These advisers hoped that military conformity could be achieved without imposing practices that discriminated against these foreign troops. Progressive social welfare organizations and ethnic associations were also brought into the training process to improve overall efficiency and to prevent negative moral influences from corrupting the troops. The fact that venereal disease had disabled some army divisions made this involvement extremely useful in preparing soldiers for combat in foreign lands.

Other benefits of having ethnic leaders on board included the contributions they made in translating and teaching English and clarifying the purpose of the war in terms that the foreign troops could understand. English lessons fell under the general Americanization process, along with lessons in government and citizenship, but English also was essential for communication purposes, particularly for taking orders; with this reality in mind, new English-instruction programs were introduced in July 1918.

There was also community pressure to persuade the military to employ multifaith chaplains, to honor leave for religious holidays, and to acknowledge specific cultural beliefs. Another contribution of ethnic leadership was to relay intelligence concerning wartime sympathies of specific communities. Ultimately, for most European Americans, World War I provided an opportunity to demonstrate patriotism and formed another part of the Americanization process. This was in direct contrast to the xenophobia found in immigration restriction and nativist propaganda.

EUGENICS AND IMMIGRATION CONTROL

Charles P. Davenport (1866–1944), a Harvard-trained biologist and member of the National Academy of Sciences, became one of America's leading eugenicists during the Progressive Era. After becoming director of the Cold Spring Laboratory in 1910, he worked to establish the Eugenics Record Office to spread his particular ideas of human heredity. His 1911 book *Heredity in Relation to Eugenics* was extremely popular and widely used for many years as a teaching text.

He used his quantitative knowledge to argue against miscegenation, which he saw as a contributory factor in biological and social harm. His *Race Crossing in Jamaica* (1929) reputedly studied the population damage caused by interbreeding. His "scientific," biased racism led him to be identified with similar theories in Nazi Germany, where he was later linked to several Nazi racial theorists.

Lothrop Stoddard (1883–1950) was a Harvard-trained historian, Ph.D. 1914, who emerged as a leading eugenicist during the Progressive Era. He

Margaret Sanger and
Progressive Reform's Other Directions

Margaret H. Sanger (1879–1966) provided an interesting example of the Progressive Era's many cultural incongruities. Sanger manifested the moral reform fervor of this generation, but outside a purely religious context. The Progressive movement was overflowing with many women reformers who hoped to make American life better. Sanger was different from the Anglo-Saxon Protestant mainstream—she came from a Roman Catholic family where she was one of 11 children. Sanger was deeply affected by her mother's deteriorating health, which led to an early death. This led Sanger to conclude that her death was the result of having such a large family.

After her mother's death in 1899, Sanger trained as a nurse in White Plains, New York, and in 1902 married architect William Sanger. She and her husband moved to New York City in 1912, but her marriage soon floundered and eventually ended in divorce. In the 1920s she married again; this time to oil baron Noah Slee.

Sanger's nursing took her initially to New York City's Lower East Side, where she witnessed how family size was interrelated to poverty and the generally poor living conditions of the city's immigrants. She came to believe that women had a choice in family size and began to defy the 1873 Comstock Law that defined contraceptive advice as a form of obscenity. Sanger disregarded such authority and opened her first birth control clinic in Brooklyn in 1916. This deed led to a 30-day jail sentence, but upon appeal, the law was modified.

By 1918, doctors gained the right to prescribe contraception. To further her birth control cause, Sanger published *What Every Girl Should Know* and *What Every Mother Should Know*. Both publications were important steps toward the distribution of useful sexual and birth control information. Her work led to the establishment of the American Birth Control League in 1921, which eventually became Planned Parenthood.

Although Sanger embraced socialist politics as a solution to America's capitalist injustices, she was also a eugenicist who saw the immigration of inferior races as a problem that upset the Progressive drive for reform and human advancement. Her belief in racial hygiene made her an advocate of segregation, sterilization, and euthanasia as practical solutions to unwelcome population growth. She particularly did not want to see genetically unfit children growing up in unfit environments. Regardless of her beliefs, Sanger's clinics were open to all, including New York's cross-section of poor and unfortunate.

Sanger's mix of reform and racial reaction made her a prime example of the incongruities of the Progressive movement.

campaigned against the rising tide of immigration, which he saw as a threat to the nation's development and ultimate survival. His racial theories were outlined in his popular *The Rising Tide of Color against White World Supremacy*, which defined the growth of non-white populations as a force that challenged the very existence of Western civilization. Stoddard's racial definitions of white were broader than some other eugenicists' and, as such, he argued for a form of pan-Aryanism. Therefore, he did not automatically exclude Mediterranean peoples from his white classifications. He also avoided the extreme expressions of racialism as taken up by the Nazis in the 1920s. Stoddard served on the boards of several notable Progressive organizations such as the Birth Control League, which later evolved into Planned Parenthood.

Madison Grant (1865–1937), educated at Yale and Columbia, was a lawyer by vocation. Grant became the most widely known eugenicist of the period. He embodied many of the era's attributes such as concern over the impact of massive immigration and, in particular, the perceived negative racial makeup that resulted from it. He was equally well known as a conservationist, an extremely important Progressive preoccupation. Grant saw the nation's population as racial stock that he believed was being steadily corrupted and weakened by the growth of an undesirable gene pool.

In the early 20th century, America grew more urban and diverse. This photograph captures the mix of people in New York City's densely populated Lower East Side around 1900.

According to Grant's eugenics-based racial theories, the dominant and superior Nordic European peoples were being eroded by the presence of so many inferior peoples. He outlined his views in his widely known *The Passing of the Great Race* (1916), which defined his views and fears. Grant believed that only through immigration control, the elimination of miscegenation, and the practice of racial segregation and racial hygiene could the demise of the Nordic people and, by implication, the decline of American and other European societies be prevented.

Grant's influence was widespread and it impacted the development of the hereditary branch of American anthropology. However, his views were greatly opposed by other scholars. Horace Kallen and Randolph Bourne were among those who developed the idea of "cultural pluralism," or the coexistence of many separate groups maintaining their own traditions and identities. Kallen's essay "Democracy versus the Melting Pot" (1915) argued for resisting assimilation and influenced Bourne, who followed up with a now famous essay, "Trans-National America" (1916). In it, Bourne foresaw a future in which the United States could become a "trans-national" nation whose ties to many other cultures would be a strength, not a weakness.

In the face of criticism, Grant went on to establish the Galton Society in 1918 to propagate his particular anthropological views. His influence spread outside the United States, and *The Passing of the Great Race* was translated into German in 1925; it seemingly confirmed many aspects of Nazi racial thinking. However, Grant's work as a conservationist put him in the midst of another important and contradictory avenue of Progressive reform. He helped a number of well-known projects and was instrumental in the creation of the Bronx Zoo and Glacier National Park. In addition, he headed and was a benefactor of the New York Zoological Society from 1925 until his death. Grant personified important aspects of Progressivism, which was in many ways best understood as an elitist-driven reform movement that promoted change and improvement in terms that later generations would find largely unacceptable.

THE IMPLICATIONS OF SOCIETAL CHANGE

These new European-American immigrant arrivals found themselves in a society of many dark contrasts, including a glaringly unequal distribution of wealth that placed massive economic control in the corporate hands of relatively few large industries. Industrialization created great wealth for a few and delivered poverty for many. For example, steel magnate Andrew Carnegie received $23 million in untaxed profits in 1900, while a steel worker received $450 annually to feed his family, and women garment workers in New York's sweat shops made only $5 per week.

In addition to low wages, these workers found that there were no safety nets to protect them. They faced long hours, poor wages, and dangerous working conditions in the factories that employed them. These conditions were also faced by many women and children who worked in the factories. In modern terms, the workers lacked a minimum wage, social security, workers compensation, and unemployment insurance. Employment was insecure and dependent on frequent downturns in the business cycle such as those of 1900, 1904, 1908, 1912, 1914, and 1919.

Nevertheless, industrial growth continued unabated—gross domestic product doubled in the era, and manufacturing volume increased by a factor of six. The growth of the motorcar, led by Henry Ford and the Ford Motor Company, symbolized this transformation. In 1907, there were 44,000 cars nationally, but by 1916, there were over 1 million cars on American roads. Henry Ford also innovated in hiring and training large numbers of immigrants. The Ford Motor Company established the Ford English School for its foreign-born workers, who represented as many as 33 nationalities in the school, in 1914. The school taught English at different levels depending on the workers' previous education, while also instructing them in American manners and values.

For many Americans, industrialization and immigration were forever changing the nature of American life. America was becoming urbanized and by 1900, 40 percent of the population lived in cities that also housed the overwhelming majority of new immigrants. By 1920, this figure had risen to 50 percent. In combination, these economic, social, and political forces were affecting democratic government and economic opportunities. In addition, American industrial production was in the hands of relatively few firms. Between 1897 and 1904, 4,227 businesses combined to form 257 corporations. The largest merger consolidated nine steel companies to create the U.S. Steel Corporation controlled by Andrew Carnegie. By 1904, 318 companies controlled about 40 percent of America's manufacturing output. This consolidation put power into the hands of a small number of industrialists whose influence was seen by many Progressive reformers as a corrupting blight on American values and independence.

WORKING CONDITIONS

The working conditions that accompanied this industrial growth were oppressive. Yet immigrant workers were generally willing to put up with the long hours, hard work, and bad conditions if they had steady employment. In Chicago and New York, Italian women home workers did their finishing for the garment trade for as little as 5 to 7 cents per coat. The income of immigrant wives and children was essential to the survival of many families.

In Carnegie's steel industry, immigrants were usually stuck with the dirtiest, hottest, and most hazardous jobs. Steelmaking was a dangerous business for even the most seasoned workers, but was truly hazardous for newcomers, many of whom came from peasant agricultural backgrounds. From 1906 to

This March 28, 1911, edition of the Italian-American newspaper Il Progresso lists the names of the Italian women lost in the Triangle Shirtwaist fire (last column at right).

The Triangle Shirtwaist Fire

The most famous industrial disaster of the Progressive Era that best symbolized the poor working conditions found in the nation's factories was the March 25, 1911, Triangle Shirtwaist fire in New York City. The factory occupied the top three floors of a building at Greene Street and Washington Place, and it employed approximately 500 women, many of whom were European immigrants. These women worked 14-hour days for $6–$7 a week. Triangle factory working conditions were poor, with floors piled with textile scraps and paper. Light came from open gas lamps.

The fire started on the eighth floor, possibly by a discarded match, although the actual cause remains unknown. It quickly spread and engulfed all floors, trapping the mostly women workers. Escape proved impossible— exit doors were locked and the fire escape collapsed. In the end, 148 workers died, many jumping to their deaths from windows or down the elevator shaft. The publicity resulting from the disaster spurred health and safety reforms including workers' compensation; it also boosted the organizing efforts of the International Ladies' Garment Workers Union, which had campaigned for years to improve workers' conditions. Ultimately, the owners were not held responsible by the courts and the compensation dispensed was a meager $75 per victim.

An Italian-American mother doing piecework at home with the help of her children in Framingham, Massachusetts, in November 1912. Fresh macaroni is also spread out to dry on the table.

1910, the accident rates for immigrants at Chicago's South Works steel plant were double those for English speakers. During these years approximately one-fourth of immigrant workers were killed or injured on the job.

The seriousness of the problem provoked many companies to examine safety practices and moved some companies toward an acceptance of workers compensation programs. In 1906, U.S. Steel officials began meeting annually at company headquarters in New York to review the situation and this led, in 1908, to the creation of a U.S. Steel Committee of Safety with the power to improve safety in order to reduce accidents in all plants. New rules and procedures followed, as well as new safety technologies. Other industries improved safety as they came to see the economic benefits that resulted from such improvements. There were even company-initiated accident compensation programs.

Progressive politicians also noticed the need for health and safety legislation to protect workers if they were injured or killed. From private and state investigations it was discovered that most large corporations saw the benefits of such schemes, as did the unions. What followed was the establishment of state workers compensation programs. In May 1911, Wisconsin became the first state to establish a workmen's compensation system. Within that year, nine other states passed compensation laws, followed by three more states in 1912, and eight more in 1913. By 1921, 46 states out of 48 had workmen's compensation laws in force.

LABOR UNREST, RADICALISM, AND SOCIALIST MOVEMENTS

During these years, European-American workers were sometimes accused of bringing "socialist" ideas to the American workplace. European Americans whose politics or union activities were deemed too radical could face persecution and deportation, as labor unrest and the "Red Scare" at the end of the era witnessed.

The rise of mass industries had changed the make up of labor unions. In response to industrialism, in 1905, the International Workers of the World (IWW, the Wobblies) were founded in Chicago by groups of radical socialists and anarchists. The leaders included important names in American radicalism: Daniel De Leon, William (Big Bill) Haywood, Eugene Debs, Mary Harris Jones (Mother Jones), and many others. Their ambition was to overthrow capitalism with an industrially based and organized mass working-class movement. Their appeals combined many of the socialist and anarchist goals of the times, such as ending the wage system, as well as the promotion of continuous class conflict.

To be most successful, the Wobblies believed, workers should be organized into one enormous industrial union, run by the rank and file, that could dominate all industrial production. The IWW also had an open recruitment policy that welcomed everyone to the movement, including immigrants, women, and African Americans. In Philadelphia, the Longshoremen Local 8 branch was headed by Ben Fletcher, an African American. Given the racial climate of the period, this made the Wobblies highly unrepresentative of the times.

In 1906, the IWW gained national attention with its mining strike at Goldfield, Nevada, and with numerous other vocal, and at times violent, actions that spread across the country. However, the IWW's opposition to World War I proved to be its most damaging policy. This position severely damaged its recruitment and growth as a union force. Although some in the union argued for a more low-key anti-war position, the Wobblies failed to dampen their criticism sufficiently, and came to be viewed as a potential threat to the war effort. Accordingly, the Justice Department no longer tolerated their actions. In September 1917, the government launched cross-country raids that hit the IWW's offices and led to the arrest of over 100 of its leaders for violating the Espionage Act. Many were sent to trial in 1918, and the punishments delivered included 20-year sentences in some instances. This convinced Wobbly leader William Haywood to flee to the Soviet Union, where he lived until his death.

The 1920 Palmer raids that occurred at the end of the Progressive Era also continued the government's vendetta against the IWW, as well as other radical threats. Attorney General A. Mitchell Palmer used his powers to round

Six members of the IWW displaying newspapers such as Il Proletario. This photo was collected as evidence against the men when they were arrested in San Francisco in July 1918.

up many of the IWW's foreign-born members and deport them for seditious activities. By the mid-1920s, internal political splits had seriously weakened the union, and membership fell steadily, removing the IWW as a force in American unionism. This was particularly the case when America's newly formed Communist movement attempted to dominate union affairs.

Besides the IWW's radical stand, the rise of other socialist movements in this period reflected another aspect of Progressive reform. Although much middle-class reform rested easily within the Democratic and Republican parties (and after 1912 in the breakaway Bull Moose Progressive Party), there were also more radical alternatives. By 1912, the growing popularity of socialist presidential candidate Eugene V. Debs, who drew 6 percent of the 1912 presidential vote, suggested that the movement had a definite and influential following in the general population.

The American Socialist Party was essentially moderate and social democratic in its approach to ending capitalism, yet socialism had many interpretive directions that became even more pronounced after the Bolshevik Revolution in Russia in 1917. The excesses of the Russian Revolution bred fear at home and divided the socialist movement, especially after the creation of an American Communist Party in 1919.

By 1920, much of the old socialist rhetoric and programs had become so reformist that capitalism was accepted as permanent in the American context with only its monopolistic edges clipped. Many of the Progressive Era's European-American populations, who were familiar with socialist and anarchist ideals, gave their support to a variety of radical positions. However, a suspicious federal government alarmed by the Russian Revolution and the actions that followed the postwar Red Scare of 1919–20 did much to intimidate those who believed in socialist or radical solutions. In this way, Progressivism re-

Jane Addams and the
Social Settlement Movement

The new European immigrant poor who clustered in the city slums through-out America were a stain on the American conscience and some reformers looked for ways to improve the situation and to offer a means to change current circumstances for the better. One such idea that gained enormous popularity during this period was the social settlement movement.

The driving spirit behind the movement was the need to bring culture to the masses so that class divides and antagonisms could be dissolved. The social settlement was to be an urban oasis for university-trained and religiously inclined persons to live in in order to better the conditions of the poor. It was believed that by having a visible physical presence, such good people could inspire change and stand as an example for the less fortunate.

The idea itself was a European creation imported to New York's Lower East Side by Stanton Coit. London's Toynbee Hall founded in 1883 by Canon Barnett provided Coit with an ideal model for adaptation. The move-ment was a kind of practical socialism where settlement workers per-formed good works and, in the course of their activities, made politicians aware of the extant slum conditions needing amelioration.

The settlement movement quickly spread to other cities in the United States, where, through self-help and a commitment to social justice, improvements in living conditions and opportunities could occur. Young university reformers were drawn to the movement through organizations such as the College Settlement Association. The message was best spread by establishing ever more numerous settlement projects, which rose from six settlements in 1891 to over 400 in 1910.

The most well known of these settlement missions was the work of two young Rockford College classmates, Jane Addams and Helen Gates Starr, who in 1889 founded Hull House in an old Chicago mansion on South Halstead Street at the corner of Polk. Jane Addams and her follow-ers believed that they were creating an oasis that would be an instrument for social, educational, civic, and humanitarian reform. In turn, social unity would be promoted and democracy strengthened. The social settlement was to be a center for civic cooperation and a rallying point for reform in the city. In addition, the settlement was not simply a physical place but a way of life where cultured men and women made their home in order to bring help to those in need.

By showing local people the benefits of a good life based on strong principles, devotion to duty, and other middle-class virtues, the poor could be transformed. Redemption of the poor and an end to poverty came through learning the correct cultural lessons.

mained essentially a conservative reform movement that operated within the confines of America's established political parties.

CULTURAL INCONGRUITIES

In addition to their potential radical politics, the rising European urban working class were seen by many in the middle class as social threats. They appeared to be a growing industrial proletariat whose numbers could challenge life as it was known. Even with the restrictions on unionization, strikes were frequent during this period and often violent. In the first decade of the Progressive Era, the AFL's membership exceeded 2 million members. This, in combination with the rise of the IWW, made unionization appear to some to be a threat to traditional practices and beliefs.

Furthermore, the working-class culture enjoyed drinking and dancing and keenly showed off their enthusiastic nature in the city's parks and public spaces to the annoyance of many of the cities' "finer" citizens. Such entertainment also included the celebration of ethnic festivities and customs. Many in the working class often refused to be reformed and resisted schooling and labor laws for their children if these put family incomes at risk. Yet there were exceptions, as indicated by a New York City survey in 1911 that discovered that 16 percent of Jewish children were graduating from high school, the highest percentage of any immigrant group. In a few years this would translate into college enrollments. Education clearly contributed to the relatively rapid Jewish social mobility that was apparent by the second generation.

Irish Americans also experienced greater upward mobility in this era, with over two-thirds becoming citizens and over 40 percent achieving white collar jobs by 1900. In addition, Irish Americans exercised considerable influence in the skilled-labor market, which had an impact on unionization drives. Union leaders such as Terence Powderley, Mary Kenny O'Sullivan, and Mother Jones all came from Irish backgrounds. In addition, the Irish made significant inroads in higher education, and Irish Americans used their urban numbers to achieve political influence, controlling Democratic Party organizations in cities such as New York, Chicago, Boston, and San Francisco.

Skilled workers and old-style craftsmen also feared the consequences of mass industrial changes that undercut their position in society and their earnings. Skilled workers, and this included many of the older European Americans as well as new European immigrants, were losing out to production changes at the hands of the growing band of personnel managers and efficiency experts. Also during the Progressive Era, a change developed in understanding and explaining the roots of urban poverty. The poor were no longer viewed as simply the dangerous poor deserving of their plight because of indolence, sin, and criminality. There was still hostility toward pauperism, but new definitions appeared that characterized poverty as more the result of insufficiency and insecurity than simply of personal failings.

The poor became that part of the population best described as inadequately fed, clothed, and sheltered. Furthermore, poverty was no longer seen as an experience that strengthened character, stimulated incentives, or punished sloth. For many Christian Progressives, these times led them to the systematic reexamination of previously held religious assumptions.

Within a few years, such new religious viewpoints produced a trend in Christianity called the "social gospel." This doctrine was shaped by books such as Walter Rauschenbusch's *Christianity and the Social Crisis* (1907), which emphasized the debilitating effects of want on humanity. These liberal Protestant Christians, most of whom were drawn from America's old-line Anglo-Saxon and European base, believed poverty made the poor prone to moral decay. This was because the existing social system gave predatory wealth to the few. In contrast, vast numbers of the working poor fell into a corrupting destitution that undermined the social and moral fabric of society. Such reforming Christians were driven by a missionary zeal that called for society's ills to be addressed by an applied Christianity.

CONCLUSION

The Progressive Era represented a time of accommodation and adjustment for America's legions of European immigrants. The period also witnessed an important change in previous immigration patterns, with northern and western Europe replaced by the increasing and varied numbers of southern and eastern Europeans. The size of this influx was truly incredible, with well over 25 million immigrants arriving between 1880 and 1930.

However, these years also began a process that would lead to a system of immigration restriction in the 1920s that would last for decades. It was assumed that a discriminatory ethnic quota system could restore the desired European-American cultural balances, preserve national identity, and protect racial lines. This policy, shaped by eugenics and under pressure from nativists, reflected the concerns of sizable portions of the population who were alarmed by the changing ethnic face of America.

THEODORE W. EVERSOLE
NORTHERN KENTUCKY UNIVERSITY
AND UNIVERSITY OF CINCINNATI

Further Reading

Boyer, Paul. *Urban Masses and Moral Order in America, 1820–1920*. Cambridge, MA: Harvard University Press, 1978.

Burt, Elizabeth. *The Progressive Era: Primary Documents on Events from 1890 to 1914*. Westport, CT: Greenwood Press, 2004.

Chambers, John Whitecay. *The Tyranny of Change: America in the Progressive Era*. New York: St. Martin's Press, 2000.

Dinnerstein, Leonard, Roger L. Nichols, and David M. Reimers. *Natives and Strangers: A Multicultural History of Americans*. New York: Oxford University Press, 2003.

Ford, Nancy Gentile. *Americans All! Foreign-born Soldiers in World War I*. College Station, TX: Texas A&M University Press, 2001.

Frankel, Noralee and Nancy S. Dye, eds. *Gender, Class, Race and Reform in the Progressive Era*. Lexington, KY: University Press of Kentucky, 1994.

Gordon, Lynn D. *Gender and Higher Education in the Progressive Era*. New Haven, CT: Yale University Press, 1992.

Gould, Lewis L. *America in the Progressive Era, 1890–1914*. Harlow, UK: Pearson, 2001.

Higham, John. *Strangers in the Land: Patterns of American Nativism 1860–1925*. New Brunswick, NJ: Rutgers University Press, 2002.

Jones, Maldwyn. A. *American Immigration*. Chicago, IL: University of Chicago Press, 1992.

Lee, Mordecai. *Bureaus of Efficiency: Local Government Reform in the Progressive Era*. Milwaukee, WI: Marquette University Press, 2008.

Levine, Peter. *The New Progressive Era*. Lanham, MD: Rowman & Littlefield, 2000.

Link, Arthur S. *Woodrow Wilson and the Progressive Era, 1910–1917*. NY: HarperCollins, 1972.

Luebke, Frederick C. *Bonds of Loyalty: German Americans and World War I*. DeKalb, IL: Northern Illinois University Press, 1974.

McGerr, Michael. *A Fierce Discontent: The Rise and Fall of the Progressive Movement in America, 1870–1920*. New York: Free Press, 2003.

Mowry, George. *The Era of Theodore Roosevelt, 1900–1912*. New York: Harper and Row, 1958.

Painter, Nell Irvin. *Standing at Armageddon: A Grassroots History of the Progressive Era*. New York: W.W. Norton, 2008.

Takaki, Ronald. *A Different Mirror: A History of Multicultural America*. Boston, MA: Little, Brown, 1993.

Thomas, William H. *Unsafe for Democracy: World War I and the US Justice Department's Covert Campaign to Suppress Dissent*. Madison. WI: University of Wisconsin Press, 2008.

Woods, Thomas E. *The Church Confronts Modernity: Catholic Intellectuals and the Progressive Era*. New York: Columbia University Press, 2004.

CHAPTER 6

The Roaring Twenties and the Great Depression: 1920 to 1939

IN 1920, EUROPEAN Americans and those of European descent made up almost 90 percent of the total U.S. population of 105 million, a population that would rise to 122 million by the end of the decade, and reach over 131 million in 1940. America remained an overwhelmingly white country composed of many varieties of European Americans, both native and foreign born. These years presented the contrasting image of enormous economic growth and opportunity that soured in 1929 with the coming of the worst economic crash in American history. The 1930s aftermath signaled a decade of business depression and social misery in the form of declining production, poverty, and mass unemployment. European Americans would benefit from the 1920s boom years, but suffer the throes of the Great Depression.

The election of President Warren G. Harding in 1920 began a new, more conservative era in American society that lasted until the coming of the Depression in 1929, the congressional elections of 1930, and finally the 1932 election of President Franklin D. Roosevelt (FDR). Following Harding's death in 1923 his successor, Calvin Coolidge and later, Herbert Hoover, presided over a prosperity that stemmed from a system of laissez-faire economics and reduced taxes made possible by the 1924 Revenue Act. These and other policies stimulated growth and consumption as well as raised government revenues, allowing the repayment of part of the enormous war debt. During this period of economic expansion average growth rates of between seven and 10 percent occurred, with incomes rising from $74.3 billion in 1923 to $89 billion in 1929.

The Harding and Coolidge presidencies also oversaw the adoption of the Emergency Immigration Act of 1921 and the Immigration Act of 1924, which introduced quota systems that limited annual immigration to a small percentage of those who were resident first in 1910, and to those who were residents in 1890, respectively. This in effect excluded a vast range of potential immigrants and further excluded Asian immigration on any large scale. The act represented a Nativist political triumph.

The transforming quality of ethnically unregulated immigration had been an issue since the Progressive Era when many decried the rising tide of non-Nordic immigration. This tightening of the system reflected the sentiments of many eugenicists such as Madison Grant, who believed in the supremacy as well as the necessity of limiting immigration to only particular Nordic racial groups.

The immediate result of the new restrictions was that of the 150,000 annual quota, over 85 percent of those allowed in would come from northern and western Europe with Germany, the British Isles, and Ireland. Certain Euro-

Even with immigration restrictions, five million new immigrants arrived in the 1920s and 1930s and spread throughout the country. A Lithuanian-Russian immigrant built this trapper's cabin, which displays typical Russian-American craftsmanship, in Bristol Bay Borough, Alaska, in 1926.

peans would be favored, but those from eastern and southern Europe would be penalized. For example, Italians who previously came in large waves would see their numbers drop from 200,000 annual immigrants in 1900 to only 4,000 annually after 1924. These restrictions, when matched with the Great Depression of the 1930s and the coming of World War II in 1939, cut immigration to a fraction of its annual high in 1913.

However, immigration restriction did not end immigration entirely in this period. There were nearly five million additional immigrants who arrived during these decades, primarily from 1920 to 1924, who represented approximately 50 percent of the ultimate total. Before the end of the decade, a further 37 percent of this total arrived, falling to approximately 13 percent in the Depression years and World War II.

The effect of restriction as the 1920s progressed was essentially to end immigration in absolute terms. Surprisingly, Germany, America's World War I enemy, made up 20 percent of what European immigration remained by 1924. By the end of the decade German immigrants contributed 25 percent of the allowed total. The Germans joined with other favored groups from northwest Europe such as the Irish, British, and Scandinavians to form substantially all of those coming from Europe.

Even though German, Irish, and Scandinavian arrivals outnumbered British immigrants by over three to one during the 1920s, by the end of the 1920s, Great Britain had a quota greater than the total of all other countries in northwest Europe combined. Since the legislation's intent was to reduce southern and eastern European immigration, its impact seriously affected Polish and Italian numbers, reducing them to 28,000 and 46,000 a year, respectively, during this decade, and for groups like Hungarians their annual total became only 1,000.

The coming of the Depression further reduced immigration numbers to fewer than 350,000 for the entire decade, and in many cases conditions were so severe that emigration exceeded immigration, with more choosing to leave the country rather than to hold on and battle the economic tide. During the 1930s, FDR's New Deal did not provide an immigration reform alternative and the quota system from the 1920s stayed in place. There was also the additional social problem that the existing legislation, made clear with the outbreak of World War in 1939, did not differentiate between immigrants and refugees. This fact would have a major impact on many Europeans trying to escape Nazi and Fascist oppression during the 1930s. However, some exceptions were made for intellectuals such as the Hungarian physicists Leo Szilard and Edward Teller, who became instrumental in America's atomic research during World War II.

SETTLEMENT PATTERNS AND SOCIAL DEVELOPMENT

The 1920s were also a time of general urbanization, when Americans moved from the countryside to the town and city. Such urbanization marked a major

European-American Responses to Prohibition

The introduction of the Eighteenth, or Prohibition Amendment in 1919 that ended the manufacture, transport and sale of alcoholic beverages had an enormous social impact upon American lives in ways that were not anticipated. Prohibition, until the amendment's repeal in 1933, defined the entire era as no other factor did. The federal government's role in enforcement brought politics into the lives of common citizens in unprecedented ways.

The amendment came to be viewed as a failed political attempt to legislate morality. Prohibition also had a divisive effect upon European Americans. Those urbanized European Americans such as the Irish, Italians, and most Germans rejected the tenets of Prohibition completely. Yet many older European Americans, particularly those with Scots-Irish and English roots who had settled in the south and had embraced Bible Belt values generally endorsed Prohibition as morally uplifting.

To further the contrast, Republican Congressman Andrew Volstead of Minnesota, a man with Scandinavian roots, engineered Prohibition's enforcement legislation. In addition, one of the period's most well known Prohibition crime fighters, Elliot Ness, had a Norwegian-American background.

Throughout the 1920s, public resentment mounted over this increased intrusion into private lives, as well as the perceived ineffectiveness of enforcement. In addition Prohibition helped make large sections of the public criminals, and built extensive illegal fortunes for the bootleggers who supplied public demand. Prohibition made crime a highly profitable business and provided the basis for the permanent establishment of organized crime as a feature of American life. The criminalizing of society also filled federal prisons, with Prohibition violations accounting for one-third of the 12,000 inmates in federal jails.

The national prohibition of alcohol was originally seen as a noble experiment in the Progressive tradition that promised social, economic, and moral uplift. It was particularly promoted by certain Protestant religious groups and the Anti-Saloon League. In theory benefits would flow: crime would be reduced, workers would gain sobriety, family life would be revitalized, and healthy living would replace drunkenness. Tax burdens would fall and the need for prisons and public assistance would disappear. However in reality, Prohibition was a total failure on all these counts.

In addition Prohibition was viewed by many European Americans, particularly Catholics, as a cultural attack against social outlets that they valued and supported. This would eventually help forge a political momentum in the Democratic Party for repeal.

change in the nation's living arrangements. European-American immigrants during this period, particularly those from numerically dominant groups, such as the Irish and Italians, followed by recent arrivals after 1918 from war-torn countries in Eastern Europe, such as the Poles and Russians, overwhelmingly chose to live in urban areas.

This was an especially dramatic change for many of these immigrants, because they were often peasants and unfamiliar with not only America, but also city life. As to where to settle, the majority of these arrivals preferred to live in the large cities of the northeast and midwest as opposed to small towns spread across the nation's interior.

ITALIAN AMERICANS

Between 1880 and 1920, over 4.1 million Italians came to the United States and 97 percent of these migrated through the Port of New York. Italians overwhelmingly concentrated in New York City, with over 400,000 residents in 1920, representing a quarter of all foreign-born Italians. This settlement by 1920 also had shifted from Manhattan proper to other boroughs such as Brooklyn, the Bronx, and Queens. Other Italians also stayed primarily on the East Coast in New England and the mid-Atlantic states.

Although there was a large Italian population in Chicago in the 1920s, Italians were not heavily represented in the rest of the Midwest. However, in the 1920s there were a large number of Italians resident in California, making them the largest group of the foreign born living in that state. There was also a lesser Italian presence in New Orleans.

Italian settlement did not reflect a system of segregated urban ghettoes but a system of neighborhoods built primarily around local businesses, housing, and cultural institutions such as schools and churches. Occupationally during this era, many Italians were engaged in manual labor, which increasingly included construction work. Being tied to primarily unskilled or semi-skilled jobs, many Italians stood outside the era's various unionization drives, with the exception of the garment workers, where Italian unionization increased particularly during the 1930s.

Wages were low and living conditions in many crowded tenement neighborhoods were poor. High school education remained problematic, with large numbers of students leaving school to find work, including Italian girls. In addition, although Catholic, many Italians resisted the Irish- and German-dominated Catholic Church and attended with less regularity than other American Catholic groups. This sometimes ambivalent attitude to the church has been explained in the Italian case as reflecting resentment over the Catholic Church's opposition to Italy's 19th-century unification movement, known as the *Risorgimento*.

A significant number of the Italian immigrants of this era also brought with them not only regional identities and family values, but also radical socialist or anarchist politics. Such political inclinations created conflicts with mainstream America. As a consequence many Italians as well as a range of eastern European immigrants, enthused by the 1917 October Communist Revolution in Russia, became the focus of Attorney General A. Mitchell Palmer's Red Scare of 1919 to 1921. Palmer attempted to stamp out any form of radicalism before it could take root in American soil. Approximately 3,000 such radicals would be rounded up and deported in these years, and a climate of suspicion surrounded those who remained attached to radical politics.

Even in the face of this pressure, many Italians were prominent in radical politics such as Arturo Giovannitti, Augusto Bellanca, Salvatore Ninfo, Guiseppe Bertelli, and Luigi Antonini. During the 1920s and 1930s, they directed their attention to anti-Fascism. Anarchist editor Carlo Tresca, through *Il Martello*, continued this crusade until his assassination in 1943. With the rise of Mussolini and Fascism in the 1920s, some American Italians were initially enthusiastic and a Fascist League of America was organized in 1925, but was disbanded by 1930. With the coming of the Depression in the 1930s, the overwhelming majority of Italians began to identify with the Democratic Party.

The most famous symbolic event of these years was the Sacco and Vanzetti trial, which captured widespread public attention. The case signified the divisions found in American society and manifested the potentially serious ramifications that followed the competition between Americanism and radicalism.

Nicola Sacco (1891–1927) and Bartolomeo Vanzetti (1888–1927) were Italian immigrants and anarchists living in Massachusetts who were arrested in May 1920 for payroll robbery and murder. Their politics in the eyes of many shaped the evidence against them and challenged the idea of a fair trial in the face of the prejudices against them. In turn they became 1920s causes célèbres in liberal-left circles. However, their convictions were upheld and they were executed on August 23, 1927, in the face of worldwide, although primarily European-led protests.

Although the immediate Red Scare soon passed from the front pages, there remained in American society a deep suspicion of the radical menace that would grow larger in the 1930s with the rise of totalitarianism, to be repeated again after World War II. Xenophobia became part of the 1920s social landscape and recent

Anti-Communist U.S. Attorney General A. Mitchell Palmer around 1920.

Members of the American League for Peace and Democracy protesting Fascist and Nazi conquests in Europe outside the Italian Embassy in Washington, D.C., on April 8, 1939.

European-American arrivals were not immune from its effects, particularly those ethnic groups with a revolutionary tradition. Other organizations arose during the 1920s such as the American Legion and the Rotary Club (founded in Chicago in 1905), which became active promoters of "100-percent Americanism." Many European Americans, particularly those in the era's emerging second and third generations, saw the threat and enthusiastically responded through public displays of their American patriotism whenever called upon. Columbus Day and the many other community festivals provided opportunities for flag waving celebrations.

The economic boom of the 1920s benefited many Italians by offering prospects for mobility. Prohibition also gave rise to Italian criminals loosely labeled as "the Mafia," who saw the opportunity bootlegging provided. In Chicago, greater prosperity enabled an expansion into neighborhoods outside of the Near North Side, with successful families moving west and north. In addition, as the Italian population rose from 59,000 in 1920 to 73,000 in 1930, more local Italians moved into business, politics, and the professions, which contributed to an improving social status.

Those who engaged in organized crime remained attached to the old Chicago neighborhoods, even though huge financial profits from their illegal activities offered other residential options. Prohibition provided the means for an easy return on investment, a fact that attracted many of these new-style gangsters like John Torrio and Al Capone. In New York City, however, Mayor Fiorello La Guardia, who was of Italian and Hungarian-Jewish descent, had some success in targeting organized crime, most notably the Italian-American mafia bosses Frank Costello and Lucky Luciano. This period saw older Black Hand criminality giving way to larger organized Italian crime syndicates.

Greater assimilation throughout the era also reduced the dependence on the Italian language press, with 10 local Italian papers between 1920 and 1930 ceasing existence. *La Italia,* the oldest and most respected paper, saw its circulation decline from 38,000 in 1921 to 27,000 in 1930. This reflected greater integration with mainstream culture as more Italians became comfortable with English. Decline was also seen in 19th-century social and mutual aid associations geared for both Italians and Sicilians whose work was absorbed by other groups such as Sons of Italy in America and the Italo-American National Union.

IRISH AMERICANS
During the 1920s, the Irish remained one of the most dominant European-American ethnic groups, whose immigration history stretched back to the 1820s. They had by the 1920s established deeper American associations and settlement histories. In 1900, two-thirds of the Irish were citizens by birth. The Irish, like the Italians, maintained urban residential settlement patterns primarily in the northeast, where 90 percent of Irish Americans had settled.

Of 11 large urban areas with many Irish residents, 10 were in the northeast, and seven of those were in New England. The 19th-century pattern of male-dominated immigration was also more gender balanced after 1880 with an increase in single women coming to America. By the 1920s, there were established families already resident, which made the move to America considerably easier. There was also a well-developed infrastructure of schools, workers' organizations, and social clubs that further eased the transition to American life.

By the 1920s, many Irish Americans had gained a modest degree of economic mobility, and advanced to skilled positions in the building trades, such as plumbers and pipefitters, often becoming overseers of many other immigrant construction crews. By the 1920s, many Irish daughters were becoming educated, avoiding domestic service, and moving into careers such as teaching. In northern cities, they held as much as a quarter to a third of all teaching posts. The Irish also continued to be represented in the police and fire departments of the northeastern cities, and they built strong political links through union activity and through urban political machines, allowing them to become extremely influential in urban politics. In the early decades of the 20th century, the Irish had also reached a stage were they were attending college in greater proportions than mainstream Anglo Protestants.

During the 1920s and 1930s, Irish-American assimilation was well advanced, particularly when compared to other immigrant groups, as symbolized by St. Patrick's Day becoming part of the American events calendar after 1900. Further intermarriage fostered additional moves into the American mainstream. By 1924, Irish-American politicians gained national recognition as symbolized by Al Smith (1873–1944), a governor of New York and the first Catholic presidential candidate in 1928. During this time, the Irish also started to achieve great success in theater, film, sports, business, and the professions.

For most Irish Americans, the family unit remained central into the second, third, and even fourth

Al Smith, the first Catholic candidate for U.S. president, speaking to supporters and media, possibly during his 1928 campaign.

generations, and the parish became the key community unit. The church gave structure to the American-Irish family, and gave dogma to its members. Kinship remained important, and the rituals such as marriages and wakes gave additional weight to family life, perpetuating identities. If marriages over time came to involve those outside the Irish community, particularly for non-Catholics, church instruction and conversion were expected of these new family members.

GERMAN AMERICANS

The height of German-American immigration occurred like that of the Irish in the 19th century; they represented 30 percent of all foreign born in 1900. These numbers were stopped by World War I, but grew again after the war, albeit at a slower rate because of the 1920s restrictions. German immigration was reduced further by the rise of Nazism during the 1930s.

German immigration and settlement patterns had also been more varied than that of the Irish. German immigrants represented complex national regions and varying religious groupings including Protestants, Catholics, and Jews. These divisions were additionally complicated by concepts of ethnicity

A small number of German Americans supported Hitler before the war, while other German Americans saw this support as anti-American. A Nazi flag is clearly visible in this October 30, 1939, parade by the anti-Semitic German-American Federation (or Bund) in New York City.

as opposed to purely national origins. Therefore, most German Americans had an established immigrant history by the 1920s. German settlement patterns also contrasted with that of Irish and Italians in that only a minority chose initially to settle in the larger cities and there was a higher percentage of Germans who took up agriculture.

Beside New York, Germans attracted to urban areas often also moved to midwestern cities such as Chicago, Cincinnati, St. Louis, and Milwaukee. In states like Wisconsin and Minnesota, people of German ethnicity came to make up over 16 percent of the total population base. The Midwestern

Protestant Fundamentalism

Fundamentalism spread to a range of Protestant denominations and affected the whole of American society in the 1920s and 1930s. This drive was shaped by many with European-American ancestry, particularly those with English, Welsh, and Scots-Irish roots in the rural south and Appalachia. The basis of the movement was a belief in the literal accuracy of the Bible in all cases, including the resurrection, virgin birth, and the second coming, as well as the geologic age of the earth. Fundamentalism stood in opposition to the encroachment of modern science and philosophy in society, particularly when science challenged any Biblical certainties.

The name *fundamentalism* gained currency after 1920, taking its origins from the slogan: "doing battle royal for the fundamentals." The World Christian Fundamentals Association was founded in 1919 to spread the message with leaders such as A.J. Gordan, William Jennings Bryan, C.I. Scofield, A.T. Pierson, and J. Gresham Machen carrying the word across the nation. Highly influential with Baptists, Presbyterians, and Disciples of Christ, other Protestant groups resisted the trend and held to more liberal religious principles.

Organizations such as the Fundamentalist Fellowship (formed in 1921), and the Baptist Bible Union (created in 1923) successfully led the charge in many churches and helped shape seminary teaching and the ordination of new preachers. These beliefs were not contained to one region such as the south or Midwest, but were found everywhere. New denominations were created to reflect fundamentalist's values, such as the Presbyterian Church of America (1936), the General Association of Regular Baptist Churches (1932), and the Bible Presbyterian Church (1938), as well as other offshoots. The stridency of the cause led to a lasting schism in American Protestantism.

The most significant sign of this increasing spiritual divide was revealed in the *Scopes Monkey Trial* in 1925. John T. Scopes was a 25-year-old high school teacher who was charged with teaching Darwinism in his lessons in a Dayton, Tennessee, school. These lessons were derived from a locally required school text, *Civic Biology*. The basis for his prosecution was the 1925 Butler Act, a law passed by the Tennessee legislature that banned the teaching of any theories that contradicted biblical creation.

Scopes was represented by the famous defense attorney Clarence Darrow, who saw the case as a clear violation of academic freedom and freedom of speech. The prosecution was led by a leading fundamentalist, William Jennings Bryan, a former secretary of state and frequent presidential candidate. Scopes's guilt was a foregone conclusion and he was fined $100. The decision was appealed, and the fine was eventually dismissed because of a legal technicality. The case left the impression that Tennessee was a fundamentalist backwater that stifled free expression and denied modern viewpoints their place in American culture. The anti-evolutionary teaching law remained on the books until 1967.

strength of German Americans enabled them to assert cultural influence in education and religion, often struggling with the Irish over the appointment of Catholic priests and archbishops. German Americans also benefited occupationally, arriving with more capital and greater skill levels than many other immigrant groups. These advantages often translated into easier social mobility and entrée into middle class professions, as well as greater cultural involvement in both theater and music.

The negative consequences stemming from World War I made attempts to expand a specific and separate German ethnic identity more difficult in the 1920s. Revival was made harder with the sizably reduced flow of German immigration. Mainstream America maintained political reservations in light of Germany's recent past, and preferred that German Americans keep a low profile, which stressed the American identity more than the German. There was also a resentment of German cultural elitism, which fell out of favor with Americans and with many German Americans during these years.

The rise of Nazism, which propagated ideas of a German identity based on blood and racial superiority, became increasingly distasteful to the majority of German Americans who wanted to avoid associations that could engender a return to wartime hostility. In the 1930s, many German intellectuals such as Albert Einstein, Thomas Mann, Walter Gropius, Paul Tillich, and Mies Van Der Rohe arrived in America as refugees, and this stimulated an awakening within the larger public as to what of Nazi ideology meant in practice. Such refugee arrivals also gave America the benefit of 12 Nobel Prize winners.

EUROPEAN-AMERICAN FAMILIES

By the 1920s and 1930s, many European-American families of all ethnic bases found themselves moving into the second and even third generations. As such, the general process of Americanization and the exposure to different cultural forces had been firmly established. In addition many families had adopted a multi-generational structure, with grandparents and great grandparents part of the extended family arrangement.

Furthermore, the greater American society and its institutions had become more familiar, including schools, health authorities, policing, and government services. These institutions formed part of the assimilation process, provided social control, and helped in societal integration, often in the face of ethnic resistance to change.

The local European-American immigrant establishments of stores, butchers, taverns, and other services often were places where native languages could be maintained. However, by this era English had become the language of communication for most, and this in itself often became a subject for generational conflict. Many in the new generation saw Old World languages as a burden that alienated their sons and daughters. Such distinctions could undercut confidence and hinder the assimilation process.

American Cinema in the 1920s and 1930s

The film industry established in the Progressive Era reached new heights during the 1920s. The industry was principally created by European Americans, including many Eastern European Jews whose arrival preceded the 1920s immigration quotas. Joseph Kennedy, a prominent Boston Irish American, also invested in 1920s film production, which enlarged his fortune considerably during these years.

Additional European immigrants also greatly affected America's film development. Directors Alfred Hitchcock, Fritz Lang, Ernst Lubitsch, and Jean Renoir arrived during this period, along with actors such as Rudolph Valentino, Marlene Dietrich, Greta Garbo, Ronald Colman, and Charles Boyer.

By mid-decade, $2 billion had already been invested in film. Cinema attendance expanded from 40 million weekly ticket sales in the early 1920s to over 100 million weekly sales in 1929. This decade also saw the greatest number of film productions in U.S. history, with over 800 releases a year.

During the 1920s, silent films remained the dominant product but technical advancements were made in lighting, make up, costumes, and studio scenery. While many immigrants could not read, write, or understand English, they could relate to the universal themes found in silent films. Different film genres emerged, offering a wide range of entertainment products such as historical features, melodramas, comedies, westerns, and even films about the immigrant experience itself.

One film that drew on immigrant life in America was Charlie Chaplin's *The Immigrant* (1917). In the film, Chaplin plays his famous Tramp character, who has just arrived in the United States by steamship from an unnamed country. A penniless newcomer, his misadventures include being mistaken for a thief, struggling with American customs and manners, and meeting with cruelty and intimidation before his circumstances improve.

Film production changed with the arrival of the big five studios. These studios integrated production and distribution and built the initial Hollywood star system that tied key performers to long-running studio contracts. The big studios soon controlled 90 percent of all films produced, including national and international distribution. The big five studios included Warner Brothers, incorporated in 1923 by Jack, Harry, Albert and Sam Warner, which merged with First National Pictures in 1925. Paramount Studios arrived on the scene through a series of company mergers in 1927. Controlled by Adolph Zukor and Jesse Lasky, the studio produced silent films starring Mary Pickford and Douglas Fairbanks, among others. RKO Pictures formed in 1928 and became home to the popular Fred Astaire and Ginger Rogers musicals in the 1930s. In 1924, the Marcus Loew Studio became Metro Goldwyn Mayer Pictures. The other member of the big five was Fox Films, started by William Fox in 1912, which merged in 1935 with Darryl Zanuck's Twentieth Century Films to form 20th Century Fox.

A Polish-American miner listens to the radio at home in Westover, West Virginia, in 1938. The spread of radio brought American entertainment, news, and music to national audiences.

The freer American environment also had an impact on institutions like marriage, which could undercut extended family income if sons or daughters moved away. Life in urban America also extended the range of prospective brides and grooms. The choice of a potential mate expanded and became freer from family influence and selection; by the 1920s, this represented a major change from traditional patterns.

The growth of industry in the 1920s created an additional demand upon European-American families. Besides the internal transfers when families were uprooted and moved to new cities in the search for employment, those already settled also saw the rise of suburbanization as streets were paved and highways built. Streetcars, buses, and affordable cars and the construction of workers' apartments and homes led to moves away from the older central city neighborhoods in order to be closer to places of employment.

This in itself could divide families and create a greater cultural and ethnic mix in living arrangements.

NAME-CHANGING AND IMMIGRANT IDENTITY

Upon arriving in the United States, many European immigrants changed their names to make them seem more Americanized or to fit into preconceived notions about what was needed to achieve the American dream. For instance, famed piano maker Charles Steinweg, who immigrated to the United States from Germany, changed his name to Steinway to comply with the notion of English superiority within his field. Italian-born actress Anna Maria Louisa eventually became Oscar winner Anne Bancroft. Chinese Tong leader Wong Ah Ling, who established himself as the unofficial mayor of New York's Chinatown, changed his name to Tom Lee. The practice of Americanizing foreign-sounding names continued until the late 20th century.

Efforts to display credentials as true Americans often surfaced as attempts to combat discrimination against particular ethnic groups such as Jews, Italians, and the Irish. In the 1920s and 1930s, both European Jews and Italians were considered non-white by most Americans, despite a legal designation of White. Eventually, reaction to extensive African-American migration into northern cities, which had become havens for European immigrants, provided them with the opportunity to become assimilated into the white immigrant community. However, it also frequently placed them at odds with African Americans, who blamed immigrants for standing in the way of their own economic and social progress.

Many European immigrants who came to the United States during the 1920s and 1930s did so in response to events taking place in their own countries. Russian immigrants, for instance, came to the United States to escape the political and social upheaval that followed the Russian Revolution. They came from all walks of life, but they were united in rebelling against Communism. In the late 1930s, some 14,000 Russians arrived in the United States to escape the invasion of German and Japanese armies. These Russian immigrants were generally determined to establish themselves as Russian Americans, a classification that allowed them to hold on to cherished elements of their own cultures while rejecting imposed cultural dictates.

Even though they hailed from the same country, many new Italian immigrants in this period spoke different dialects and had different traditions. Despite these differences, they found common ground as they acknowledged their shared position as outsiders in an American society reacting to the widespread fear that the influx of Italian immigrants would mean the loss of opportunity and status for others. Even labor unions initially shunned Italians because they felt their willingness to accept low salaries undercut the fight for workers' rights. Over time, as they became more acclimatized to American society, many Italian families began to prosper.

While the majority of immigrants remained fairly close to their points of disembarkation, fanning out over northeastern cities, others migrated to American cities where foreigners were less common and more noticeably "different." In the Connecticut River valley, for instance, all eastern European immigrants became locally known as "Poles." Despite differences of language, religion, and culture, these immigrants soon established common bonds. In turn, eastern European immigrants exerted their influence on the developing culture of the area. This same pattern was repeated throughout the United States.

CONCLUSION

America's combined white population during the 1920s and 1930s remained the overwhelmingly dominant ethnic groups in American life and society. The major European-American nationalities were further supplemented by numerically smaller groups such as Scandinavians, Czechs, Poles, and Hungarians, whose settlement and contributions to American life had definite impacts. These influences were particularly felt regionally, as these groups followed employment opportunities to America's industrial cities such as Cleveland and Chicago, as well as states such as Wisconsin and Minnesota.

All aspects of American culture were influenced or governed by this complex assembly of peoples often with different religious, social, political, and economic backgrounds and tastes. The wide-ranging European-American base continued to shape the nation's identity during these years. The coming of the immigration quota system in the 1920s asserted a strong north and west European immigration bias that reversed the broader American population trends that were reflected in the waves of mass immigration before 1890.

Nevertheless, by this period, the ethnically complex European nature of American society had expanded considerably with the arrival of so many southern and southeastern European immigrants, as well as eastern Slavic immigrants. The impact of these differences was particularly clear in the Progressive Era. These new immigrants and their children came of age, many as second-generation Americans, during the 1920s and 1930s. Although outside the preferred racial lines of the eugenicists, the large numbers of Italians, Greeks, and others would make major contributions to the development of the United States during the 20th century as they became Americanized and absorbed into the wider mainstream culture.

Theodore W. Eversole
Northern Kentucky University
and University of Cincinnati

Further Reading

Barfield, Ray. *Listening to the Radio, 1920–1950*. Westport, CT: Praeger, 1996.

Best, Gary Dean. *The Dollar Decade: Mammon and the Machine in 1920s America*. New York: Praeger Publishing, 2002.

———. *The Nickel and Dime Decade: American Popular Culture During the 1930s*. Westport, CT: Praeger, 1993.

Braeman, John et al., eds. *Changes and Continuity in Twentieth-Century America: The 1920s*. Columbus, OH: Ohio State University Press, 1968.

Cogdell, Christina. *Eugenic Design: Streamlining America in the 1930s*. Philadelphia, PA: University of Pennsylvania Press, 2004.

Daniels, Roger. *Coming to America: A History of Immigration and Ethnicity in American Life*. New York: Harper Perennial, 2002.

Dumeril, Lynn. *The Modern Temper: American Culture and Society in the 1920s and 1930s*. New York: Hill and Wang, 1995.

Egan, Timothy. *The Worst Hard Time: The Untold Story of Those Who Survived the Great American Dust Bowl*. New York: Mariner Books, 2006.

Goldberg, David J. *Discontented America: The United States in the 1920s*. Baltimore, MD: Johns Hopkins University Press, 1999.

Gourley, Catherine. *Rosie and Mrs. America: Perceptions of Women in the 1930s and 1940s*. Breckenridge, CO: Twenty-First Century Books, 2007.

Grant, Robert and Katz, Joseph. *The Great Trials of the Twenties: The Watershed Decade*. Cambridge, MA: Da Capo Press, 1998.

Hicks, John D. *Republican Ascendancy, 1921–1933*. New York: Harper & Row, Publishers, 1960.

Karl, Barry D. *The Uneasy State: The United States from 1915 to 1945*. Chicago, IL: University of Chicago Press, 1983.

Kennedy, David M. *Freedom From Fear: The American People in Depression and War*. New York: Oxford University Press, 2001.

Kempton, Murray. *Part of Our Time: Some Ruins and Monuments of the 1930s*. New York: Simon and Schuster, 1955.

Kyvig, David E. *Daily Life in the United States, 1920–1939: Decades of Promise and Pain*. Westport, CT: Greenwood Press, 2002.

Lee, J.J. and Marion R. Casey, eds. *Making the Irish American: History and Heritage of the Irish in the United State*. New York: New York University Press, 2006.

Leuchtenburg, William E. *The Perils of Prosperity, 1914–1932*. Chicago, IL: University of Chicago Press, 1958.

McCoy, Donald R. *Coming of Age: The United States in the 1920s and 1930s*. Baltimore, MD: Penguin, 1973.

McElvaine, Robert S. *The Great Depression America, 1929–1941*. New York: Three Rivers Press, 1993.

Mindel, Charles H., Robert H. Haberstein, and Roosevelt Wright, Jr. *Ethnic Families In America: Patterns and Variations*. Upper Saddle River, NJ: Prentice Hall, 1998.

Nash, Roderick. *The Nervous Generation: American Thought, 1917–1930*. Chicago, IL: Rand-McNally & Co., 1970.

Nelli, Humbert S. *Italians In Chicago: 1880–1930*. New York: Oxford University Press, 1970.

Ogren, Kathy J. *The Jazz Revolution: Twenties America and the Meaning of Jazz*. New York: Oxford University Press, 1992.

Parrish, Michael E. *Anxious Decades: America in Prosperity and Depression, 1920–1941*. New York: W.W. Norton, 1994.

Roberts, Sam. "New Life in U.S. No Longer Means New Name." *New York Times*. Available online, URL: http://www.nytimes.com/2010/08/26/nyregion/26names.html?_r=1. Accessed September 2010.

Rothbard, Murray N. *America's Great Depression*. Auburn, AL: Ludwig Von Mises Institute, 2000.

Schlesinger, Arthur M., Jr. *The Crisis of the Old Order, 1919–1933*. Boston, MA: Houghton Mifflin Co., 1957.

Shindler, Colin. *Hollywood in Crisis: Cinema and American Society 1929–1939*. New York: Routledge, 1996.

Sowell, Thomas. *Ethnic America: A History*. New York: Basic Books, 1981.

Wallace, Mike. "The Ellis Island Immigration Museum." *Journal of American History*. Vol. 78. No. 3, December 1991.

CHAPTER 7

World War II and the Forties: 1939 to 1949

FOR EUROPEAN AMERICANS, who constituted the overwhelming majority of America's population of 132 million in 1940, history was shaped by the Depression and its New Deal legacy as well as by crises abroad. Over the next decade the most pressing problem that Americans faced was a deadly, destructive, and costly World War II, with origins in Europe but with dimensions that enveloped the globe. The rise of fascism and militarism in the 1930s, as well as the consolidation and expansion of communism in the Soviet Union, cast a dark specter over the American people.

Although President Franklin D. Roosevelt's New Deal created a degree of optimism in the midst of much misery, economic problems were still not overcome in 1939. Economic recovery was incomplete, and poverty was far from abolished, with approximately 40 percent of Americans living in hardship. Almost eight million workers' wages fell below the minimum wage, and a further eight million were still unemployed or underemployed. For all of the New Deal's rhetoric, and for all the promises made and programs initiated, the nation remained in poor economic straits. The median national income was but $2,000 per year with an average annual income of only $1,299. These realities affected the American psyche in profound ways, producing a nation that was fearful and cautious. For the 1940s generation, even as World War II stimulated recovery in ways that the New Deal never did, the nation's worldview was uncertain and reflected a timorous view of the future.

IMMIGRATION RESTRICTION

In population terms, the immigration quota system that was introduced in the 1920s and the Great Depression of the 1930s combined to reduce immigration to a trickle. The country's historic roots remained overwhelmingly European. However, by 1940, out of a population of over 132 million, 120 million were native born and thus products of a more purely American cultural process. To further cement Americanization, of the over 11 million who were foreign born, and who were almost universally European given immigration quota restrictions , over 7 million or 67 percent had become naturalized citizens. Between 1930 and 1950, the percentage of foreign born declined from 11.6 percent of the total population to 6.9 percent, which meant a significant change in the country's cultural composition.

The European-American immigrant experience was being steadily absorbed into a general American consciousness. It was in the large, urban areas that a non-native feel remained—for example, in New York City, over

This photo shows an Italian produce market in the Bronx in 1940. Italians and other groups resumed a process of moving out of their traditional urban ethnic neighborhoods in the 1940s.

2 million or 28 percent of its population were foreign born. Likewise, cities such as Philadelphia, Detroit, and Cleveland still posted figures suggesting that as many as one-fifth of their residents were foreign born. One had to look to the larger cities to discover the European immigrant core; yet this core was equally concerned with successful Americanization and a return to prosperity.

However, residence patterns were changing, even in the large cities where high ethnic concentrations remained. For example, in New York City Italians continued a migration process that began in the 1920s, slowed during the 1930s, but underwent renewal in the 1940s. Italians moved from older neighborhoods such as those on the Lower East Side, Brooklyn, and Queens to suburbs such as Westchester and Long Island. By 1940, this trend reduced New York's older Italian neighborhoods to less than half their former size. This phenomenon toward greater dispersal also affected the Irish in Boston, Poles in Cleveland, and Germans in Cincinnati. Suburbanization opened these second- and third-generation European Americans to middle-class lifestyles, and in the process, reduced ethnic ties by broadening exposure to other aspects of American life.

WORLD WAR II DRIVES THE NATURALIZATION PROCESS

The war years also stimulated a major drive toward naturalization for European Americans. More people became naturalized between 1941 and 1945 than in any previous five-year period, and comprised 25 percent of all those aliens naturalized from 1907 to 1945. The majority of these people—numbering over 1.5 million—were civilians, and an additional 112,000 became naturalized while serving in the military. Since many came from Great Britain, the Soviet Union, Italy, Germany, and Poland—all nations at war—these European Americans wanted desperately to clarify their residence.

This became more pressing after the passage of the Smith Act in 1940, which called for alien registration and fingerprinting. The act also defined enhanced deportation procedures. Since 75 percent of these aliens had married and many had families, it became doubly important to clarify their commitment to the United States. It was reported that immigrant women were particularly motivated to be naturalized, and their rate of naturalization increased from 39 percent in 1936 to 59 percent in 1942. There previously had been a naturalization lag for alien wives that the war years helped correct. The rush toward naturalization acknowledged the importance of assimilation in wartime. For others, such as Japanese Americans, the quota system made the naturalization process impossible because they were classified as ineligible for citizenship along national ethnic lines.

The rise of Nazism in the 1940s with its accompanying racial doctrines brought about a period of reflection and examination of America's past racial attitudes. This growing awareness began a slow process of change in regard to European-American thought on racial matters. Ashley Montague's *Man's Most Dangerous Myth: The Fallacy of Race* (1942) and Gunnar Myrdal's *American Dilemma* (1944) were major steps toward a critique of past racial beliefs, particularly as the war came to be redefined as a war against racial intolerance

The Assimilation Process: A German-American Case Study

This account of the assimilation experience of a German-American family through several generations was published in *Ethnic Families in America: Patterns and Variations* by Charles H. Mindel, Robert W. Habenstein, and Roosevelt Wright, Jr. in 1998.

Gustav and Anne, immigrants arrived in Cleveland, Ohio in 1880 and moved into the city's major German settlement. Gus was a skilled craftsman, a cooper. His wife was all her life a housewife. The couple had three children. Two sons went through grade school, as did the daughter. All three became skilled workers in the steel wire mill. The daughter's husband also worked there, and the daughter became a housewife, as did the marrying-in wives.

The two sons and daughter of Gustav and Anne had a total of three spouses, and later ten children, all of whom were German on both sides of the family. As the second generation descendents married and started families, two moved to rural suburbs and one further east from the German settlement, almost to a suburb.

Of the ten children in the third generation, three were female, two of whom became skilled in service and business; the third earned a college degree and became a professional. Three males became skilled workmen and went through high school, and four became professionals. The husbands of the three females became skilled service or businessmen. The wives of the seven males all had work careers, mainly in skilled services or business. Two became professionals.

In the fourth generation, all 16 descendents and spouses have had advanced careers based mainly on college and graduate school training. Since the third generation, no females became "housewives only": one became a skilled craftsperson, one worked in sales, six were or are in skilled service or business, and the other eight were or are professionals. Gus and Anne would have been proud. But their pride may have been tempered by the fact that although their sons and daughters married Germans, none of the third generation "marrying in" were Germans. Rather, the spouses from the outside were Polish, Italian, Irish, English-American, and one half German. Gus and Anne would have been more than satisfied by the fact that all those descendents became professionals and/or skilled service and businesspersons, even if the trade of cooper got lost among the generations.

and for greater democracy. In many ways this period marked the beginnings of a postwar drive toward better multicultural understanding that eventually produced greater equality for America's minorities.

The period between 1945 and 1953 revealed a slow evolution away from past thinking toward a more liberal viewpoint. This development meant that previous immigration restrictions were moderated to a degree, as demonstrated during the postwar years when the United States admitted almost 400,000 World War II survivors, initially under the Displaced Persons Act of 1948; this act was extended in 1953 to include another 200,000 European refugees. This was done despite the McCarran-Walter Immigration Act of 1952, which continued the earlier restriction philosophy of 1924. Furthermore, the attitudes of many Americans changed in the face of Holocaust discoveries that made earlier American anti-Semitism seem shameful. In addition, the ongoing Cold War revelations of Communist brutalities in Europe and Asia had a dramatic impact on changing national attitudes toward peoples fleeing totalitarianism.

ISOLATIONISM

During the 1930s, American fear of involvement in European conflicts became more widespread. With the outbreak of war in 1939 and the subsequent fall of France in 1940, many became convinced that Franklin Roosevelt would ignore his promises to avoid war and drag the United States into the conflict. In order to exert political pressure against such external entanglements, the America First Committee (AFC) was formed. Organized in Chicago in September 1940, the AFC was dedicated to enforcing the 1939 Neutrality Act. The committee had many supporters, which soon resulted in 650 AFC branches and nearly 1 million members throughout the United States.

Many European Americans—as diverse as Walt Disney and Yale Law student and future president Gerald Ford—were attracted to the movement; the appeal was strong in many European-American population groups. General Robert E. Wood, head of Sears & Roebuck, served as the AFC's nominal leader, but its most influential and visible spokesperson was Charles Lindbergh, a national hero.

Lindbergh believed that the Atlantic and Pacific oceans created the only barrier the United States needed to keep it from being attacked. The movement became incensed by the introduction on March 11, 1941, of the Lend-Lease Act, and by the proclamation by Roosevelt and British prime minister Winston Churchill on August 14, 1941, of the Atlantic Charter. Between 1941 and 1945, the amount of Lend-Lease aid came to $31 billion in exports to Great Britain and an additional $11.3 billion in aid to the Soviet Union. Given such an investment, neutrality was soon forgotten.

The AFC thought both measures were clear steps toward full-scale involvement that made participation in the war on the side of the Allies inevitable. The movement's influence ended when the Japanese Navy attacked

U.S. forces at Pearl Harbor on December 7, 1941, resulting in a declaration of war. A few days later the German government declared war on the United States, ending any talk of isolation.

ECONOMIC AND SOCIAL CHANGES

World War II had an immediate economic effect on the labor force, which rose from 56 million in 1940 to over 65 million in 1945. The jobs that were created contributed to rising average yearly earnings, and within a short time reduced the percentage of the American population living at poverty levels. In addition, a third of those working received wages that gave them increased disposable incomes for the first time since 1929.

The war was a stimulus that ended the worst effects of the Great Depression. Furthermore, it set the stage for a revitalized U.S. economy that would establish degrees of cooperation involving the federal government, private business, and organized labor that had not previously been seen. At the end of the war in 1945, the United States found itself physically secure, undamaged

U.S. and British officials meet the first American Lend-Lease food delivery to Britain at the beginning of the program in 1941. By 1945, Lend-Lease aid to Great Britain had totalled $31 billion.

from wartime attacks, and in possession of considerable economic advantages over other countries in the world.

In 1945, America's economy was richer and more developed than any in the world, which gave it the ability to influence world events in unprecedented ways. The United States was in a position to dictate worldwide postwar recovery through the Marshall Plan (Economic Recovery Program) that delivered $13 billion in aid to Europe and $1.8 billion in aid to Japan between 1947 and 1951. This aid stimulated reconstruction, strengthened Europe and Japan against communist subversion, and tied international economic affairs to American trade goals that were further shaped by new institutions such as the World Bank and the

This Norwegian-American farmer in traditional costume worked as a guide at a "Little Norway" amusement park in Wisconsin in 1942.

International Monetary Fund. This was a decidedly different outcome than existed in 1919 or 1930 when international trade collapsed because of protectionism and reduced demand.

The 1930s and 1940s also witnessed additional demographic changes following the rapid mechanization of American farming. The result was the greatest internal movement in the nation's history. During this period as many as 15 million people of European-American extraction left the countryside for urban jobs. This included the arrival of many Appalachians from the border and southern states whose Scot-Irish and English heritages stretched back for generations. A further 1.5 million African Americans also joined this migration to the nation's northern and western industrial centers.

WORLD WAR II

The 1940s were shaped by global conflict and the fighting of a multifront war. The entire American economy was geared to war production in order to supply the world with the materiel needed to defeat the Axis powers. General Dwight D. Eisenhower became Allied Commander of the European theater after 1944. General Douglas McArthur and Admiral Chester Nimitz led the American Pacific campaign after 1941, which took a secondary role to the campaign in Europe. Such wartime leadership, although stemming from varied and established European-American roots (most were drawn from the

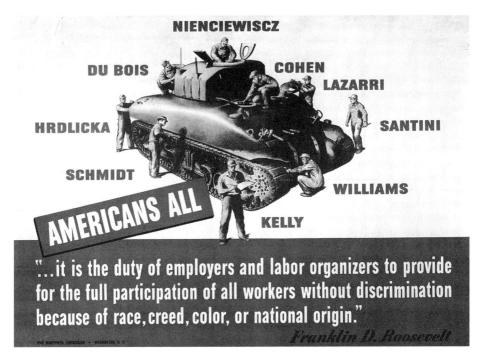

NIENCIEWISCZ

DU BOIS

COHEN

LAZARRI

HRDLICKA

SANTINI

SCHMIDT

AMERICANS ALL

WILLIAMS

KELLY

"...it is the duty of employers and labor organizers to provide for the full participation of all workers without discrimination because of race, creed, color, or national origin."

Franklin D. Roosevelt

This 1942 U.S. government anti-discrimination poster promoted the acceptance of defense laborers from diverse origins by listing a wide variety of surnames, including Irish, French, German, Italian, and Polish names.

white Anglo-Saxon Protestant elites), nevertheless stressed America's common values and unity, not its ethnic divisions.

The war not only revealed an American commitment at the highest levels to victory, but also transformed the population. Those whose origins lay in the great waves of immigration from 1880 to 1930 reached maturity as children of immigrants during the Great Depression, and now found themselves after 1940 in a war that threw them together with the widest regional and social mix of Americans.

From lives previously shaped by local and perhaps ethnic communities, 15 million men and hundreds of thousands of women were thrown together with other Americans of all shapes, backgrounds, and regions through military service. The war exposed America to previously unknown world geographies and cultures, changing the lives of many Americans accustomed only to their own comfortable localities and customs. This exposure was intellectually and socially eye-opening, making a postwar return to old neighborhoods and ways of life difficult, if not impossible. Horizons were widening for many European Americans, breeding new ambitions and creating greater confidence. This in turn allowed distance to be placed between this generation and the hyphenated worlds they left behind.

HOMELAND SAFETY

Although there was increased concern over homeland security and the potential for Axis espionage, generally those Europeans of German or Italian extraction were not given special consideration by the authorities unless they were classified as "enemy aliens." However, instances of intolerance did occur. These negative circumstances affected some German and Italian residents, as well as aliens from other belligerent countries and ultimately created a hidden history of World War II.

There were Nazi-inspired espionage attacks, such as the Duquesne spy ring and the U-boat landings of saboteurs, but none of these proved effective. However, they did create a general climate of fear. The matter became much worse for the Japanese, many of whom were second generation. The sneak attack on Pearl Harbor had so incensed the majority of Americans that those of Japanese heritage were subjected to an unprecedented reduction in civil liberties.

This came in February 1942, when President Roosevelt issued Executive Order 9066, which ordered that 120,000 Japanese Americans on the West Coast be resettled in 10 internment camps in several western states. In Hawaii, which had a large Japanese population, the internment policy affected far fewer individuals. What was particularly alarming was that two-thirds of

European-American women made up the majority of the six million female defense workers. This woman checked electrical assemblies at the Vega Aircraft Corporation in Burbank, California, in 1942.

these people were U.S. citizens and half were children and infants. The conditions in the camps were poor and, although legal challenges were made to end this most discriminatory treatment, the Supreme Court upheld the confinement during the war.

The only way out was for the men, and later some women, to enlist in the armed services. Eventually, second-generation Japanese were given the opportunity to enlist and over 20,000 chose to serve. The 442nd Regimental Combat Team served with particular distinction in Italy and Germany, becoming the most highly decorated regiment in World War II. The internment situation did not change until 1944, and all camps closed in 1945 at the end of the war.

WARTIME INTOLERANCE OF GERMANS AND ITALIANS
Presidential proclamations issued in January 1942 required certificates of identification for all those deemed "enemy aliens" aged 14 and older. These orders restricted freedom of movement and in some cases curtailed property ownership rights. These requirements affected approximately 1 million enemy aliens, including thousands of Italians, and 300,000 German-born aliens—the second-largest immigrant population of this era. Executive Order 9066 (famed for its impact on Japanese Americans) affected Italians and Germans living in military zones, and could involve internment and relocation.

These restrictions affected many Italians and Germans, and during 1942 and 1943, over 50 internment camps were established; the largest were located in Crystal City and Seagoville, Texas; and Ft. Lincoln, North Dakota. There were also direct exchanges with Germany in 1942 of around 2,000 alien internees that involved transfers of American-born children and U.S. spouses, who were often greeted in Germany with suspicion and hostility. In addition, over 4,000 Germans from Latin America between 1942 and 1945, including German and Austrian Jews, also faced internment for the course of the war.

Conditions in camps could be harsh. They had armed guards and barbed wire and were located in remote areas. Mail was censored and internee life brought about much personal anguish, and in some cases psychological and physical suffering. Appeals were generally ignored, and the small number released were subject to parole conditions; many were pressured to emigrate. Some of those deemed reliable were allowed outside the camps to find work on the Northern Pacific Rail Road or with the U.S. Forest Service.

Many Italians faced the same fate as the Germans. In February 1942, some 10,000 Italians living along the Pacific coast were forcibly relocated. Many had their radios confiscated and their fishing boats seized, destroying their livelihoods. Some Italian newspapers were suppressed, and even scientist Enrico Fermi and the parents of baseball great Joe DiMaggio faced restrictions, although the worst of these intrusions ended after six months.

Some 250 Italians underwent internment for two years, and by 1942, as many as 1,500 Italians aliens had been arrested, although they were usually only held for short periods. In San Francisco, many were taken to a facility at Sharp Park, now in the city of Pacifica, where Italian prisoners of war were also held. Some internees were later transferred to Fort Missoula, Montana, where over 1,000 Italians were held since 1941. Most of these were members of the Italian merchant marine.

What made matters worse for a number of these internees was the fact that they were *Combattenti*, Italian-American veterans of World War I. In some cases, their crime was sending money to Italy for the benefit of families of war dead. Italy's surrender in 1943 brought about the release of most internees, but still, many were held for up to two years. Given the loyalty of many German and Italian Americans who served with distinction in the military throughout the war, this treatment left a mark. During the 1980s, a Commission on Wartime Relocation and Internment of Civilians (CWRIC) was formed, but German and Italian testimonies were restricted and the situation was generally underplayed or dismissed as acceptable under wartime realities.

COURSE OF THE WAR

American participation in the war was vital to victory, although full combat readiness did not come until 1942 with the North African Campaign. Nevertheless, millions of European Americans from all quarters, both volunteers and conscripts, became the core of America's military presence and a factor that evolved through the course of the war to become a major determinant of victory. Furthermore, military service introduced a more equal footing for all soldiers that underplayed ethnic differences in order to forge a common American identity.

In Europe, the United States remained initially a junior partner supporting the combined British Empire forces that had been fighting against German advances since 1939. General Bernard Montgomery's defeat of General Erwin Rommel at El Alamein stopped Germany's march toward the Suez Canal and began a German retreat that ended in May 1943 with surrender in Tunisia.

In the Pacific, the June 1942 defeat of the Japanese by U.S. Navy forces during the Battle of Midway reversed a string of Japanese military successes that enabled Japan to occupy much of the Pacific Islands and Asia. The U.S. victory at Guadalcanal in 1943 stopped any further Japanese advances. From this time on, the war in the Pacific became a series of island-hopping invasions leading to the 1944 Philippines offensive that steadily dismantled the Japanese navy and army along the way. The Japanese were pushed back from their earlier conquests as American forces closed on the home islands in preparation for a formal invasion of Japan. In addition, American and

The Manhattan Project and the Nuclear Bomb

The Manhattan Project was the name given to a massive World War II engineering and scientific program undertaken by the United States, Canada, and the United Kingdom to develop an atomic bomb. The project ran from 1941 until 1946; it was commanded by army general Leslie R. Groves and overseen by the U.S. Army Corps of Engineers. The scientific research section was supervised by American physicist Robert Oppenheimer. The need for such a devastating weapon arose out of fear that Nazi nuclear physicists were working on a similar bomb, which could doom Allied efforts in the war. The eventual success of the project depended upon the contributions of an extensive array of European émigré and other talent. This group included, among others, Enrico Fermi, Albert Einstein, Leo Szilard, Eugene Wigner, Hans Bethe, Edward Teller, Lise Meitner, Egon Bretscher, and a British team led by James Chadwick. Initial research was undertaken as early as 1939, and the full program eventually demanded a massive commitment of money and resources. Ultimately, the atomic bomb project cost over $2 billion and employed over 130,000 scientists, engineers, and technicians spread around 30 sites across the country.

Uranium enrichment occurred at Oak Ridge, Tennessee, and the primary experimental laboratory was at Los Alamos, New Mexico. The development of a successful bomb depended on mastering nuclear fission, which physicists had been working on throughout the 20th century. Scientists such as Albert Einstein, Ernest Walton, Sir John Cockcroft, Enrico Fermi, and Leo Szilard made tremendous contributions. In the late 1930s, prominent German physicists such as Otto Kahn, Werner Heisenberg, and Fritz Strassmann were also experimenting with ways to split the atom and create a chain reaction. Einstein and Szilard, out of concern over Nazi intentions, wrote President Roosevelt, warning him that such an alternative bomb project was necessary.

In 1942, Robert Oppenheimer recruited numerous top scientists to work on the project and made use of facilities at the University of Chicago and the University of California to accelerate bomb research. After 1943, cooperation with Canada and the United Kingdom lessened as the project took on a more American composition. Different techniques were explored to discern the best way to make fissionable material reach the critical mass necessary for an explosive device. Bomb designs rested on the use of U-235 (uranium) or processed enriched plutonium, and finally on July 16, 1945, a bomb was successfully tested at Alamogordo, New Mexico.

Upon the death of President Roosevelt in April 1945, Harry Truman assumed the presidency, and he decided to use the atomic bomb against the Japanese in late July. On August 6, 1945, Colonel Paul Tibbetts, flying a B-29 bomber, the *Enola Gay*, dropped the first atomic weapon on Hiroshima with devastating results. Japan finally accepted the terms of surrender on August 15 and thus ended World War II.

British forces in east Asia pushed back the Japanese in Burma while maintaining a supply line for the Chinese, who were fighting Japanese occupation on the Chinese mainland.

In Europe, the war started to turn with the February 1943 Soviet victory at Stalingrad in what was the bloodiest battle of the war. Stalingrad provided an early indication of Germany's ultimate fate on the eastern front. The successful July–August 1943 amphibious and airborne assault on Sicily by combined British and American forces resulted in Mussolini's overthrow and Italian surrender. The fall of Sicily was followed by an invasion of southern Italy that started a slow and costly advance northward, where German resistance proved

Italian scientist Enrico Fermi in a photograph dated in the 1940s.

very effective. Rome fell in June 1944, but fighting over rugged terrain in northern Italy continued until April 1945, with German surrender finally coming on May 2, 1945.

A second western front was repeatedly called for by the Soviet Union's Joseph Stalin throughout 1943, which meant an invasion of France. However, Allied troop strength and materiel for such a difficult task were not sufficiently available until 1944. The western Allies, now led by General Eisenhower as supreme commander, reflected America's position as the dominant Allied partner in 1944. The critical second front came in June 1944 with the massive Normandy invasion. The Nazis were now in full retreat and occupied western Europe was slowly liberated as the Germans were pushed back toward the Rhine.

Although the Germans launched an offensive in December 1944, the Rhine was crossed in the winter months of 1945, and the Allies speedily advanced across Germany, stopping at the Elbe River as the Soviets closed on Berlin from the east. As they drove the Nazis out, Soviet forces occupied all of eastern Europe except Yugoslavia. With defeat staring Nazi leadership in the face, Hitler committed suicide on April 30, 1945; in his final testament, he appointed Admiral Karl Doenitz as the new German leader. Unconditional German surrender came between May 7 and May 8, 1945, ending the war in Europe.

THE HOLOCAUST

European Americans were geographically distanced from the crimes of the Nazi Holocaust, and because of the immigration limitations that were in place, few knew how far German anti-Semitism had progressed from the 1930s to the systematic murders of World War II. This was largely because between 1942 and 1944 the U.S. Department of State and the Office of War Information kept knowledge of German genocide limited to a few individuals in government. There was a fear that the public might sense that Nazi crimes were only directed at the Jews and not against all those in occupied Europe, lessening support for the war. However, as early as December 1942, the United States joined with the other Allies in denouncing Nazi actions against the Jews and threatened postwar prosecution for such crimes.

Reactions were strengthened after 1944 with the creation of a War Refugees Board to help those fleeing and displaced by Nazi persecution, the majority being Jews. A few hundred even made it to the United States, but with the Red Army's advance west, more and more concentration camps were liberated that provided the press with information on gas chambers, crematoria, and,

Defendants at the Nuremberg Trials in 1945 or 1946. In the front row at the far right sits the Nazi leader Hermann Wilhelm Göring, who was sentenced to death, but committed suicide in his cell.

through the victims' ashes, direct evidence of murder. In November 1944, news of the existence of death camps like Auschwitz was released by the War Refugees Board based on information provided by some escaped detainees.

As the Allied armies marched into the German heartland, more and more camps were found and liberated, confirming previous accounts and suspicions. Almost 2 million Jews were exterminated at one camp alone: Auschwitz-Birkenau in Poland. By the end of 1944, most Americans believed that the Germans had committed far-reaching atrocities in the camps. This indicated a sizable shift in public awareness from 1943, when less than 50 percent thought that the Germans were systematically murdering detainees.

By May 1945, over 80 percent of Americans accepted that the Nazi crimes were massive and that Germans were responsible for the deaths of millions. The evidence found in the liberated camps proved the degree of Nazi culpability, yet the direct connection with a specific program of extermination, as opposed to a multinational persecution, was not yet established or connected to years of Nazi anti-Semitism. The particular Jewish dimension did eventually become clear. By September 1945, President Harry Truman was fully aware of the extent of damage done to the entire European Jewish population. In addition, this awareness initiated pressure to increase Jewish settlement in Palestine, which was still under British control, as well as to increase immigration to the United States.

With the Nuremberg Trials, which began in November 1945 and continued until 1949, the American public became even more aware of the nature of German crimes against humanity, which specifically in counts 3 and 4, proved that the Jews were the victims of a systematic genocide. Subsequent postwar publications examined the direct ties between Nazi philosophy and the elimination of Europe's Jews. This evidence built tremendous public sympathy for the Jewish plight that would, after 1948, lead to a U.S. commitment to an independent Israel. Questions would also be raised as to why more was not done to close the camps through the use of Allied strategic bombing, particularly after long-range missions became more feasible.

THE TRUMAN ADMINISTRATION: 1945–53

Harry Truman's succession to the presidency followed the death of President Roosevelt and placed him at the center of the final actions of World War II and the numerous postwar difficulties that followed peace. Domestically, the end of the war meant the end of a wartime economy. Many Americans feared that peace could return the United States to economic depression and unemployment as troops were rapidly demobilized. Wartime controls over management and labor were also cancelled, which meant a return to the old levels of confrontation and strife.

In addition, Truman in the immediate years after the end of the war faced demands by the American Legion, Daughters of the American Revolution,

War Brides

After World War II, many soldiers brought home "war brides"—women they had met while serving abroad, including some 70,000 British women and great numbers of German and Italian women they met while occupying those enemy countries. Italian war brides constituted a significant part of the Italian population in Los Angeles, a city new enough to have missed most of the immigrant influx before quotas were instituted in 1921 and that had become home to a wide range of Italian refugees after World War I.

Many war brides resulted in interracial marriages, such as between European Americans and Filipino or Japanese women, which could result in legal complications when soldiers returned to states that did not recognize such marriages. In other cases, European brides faced discrimination when trying to settle into their new homes, either because of their association with a defeated enemy nation, or simply because of their foreign names, accents, and clothing.

One place where this was less true was in the Midwest, where there had long been large German and Scandinavian populations and where European accents and traditions were alive and well, albeit in modified form. For instance, although there is a strong myth that Midwestern American speech is unaccented or neutral, the speech of the Upper Midwest—particularly the Dakotas, Wisconsin, Minnesota, and the Upper Peninsula of Michigan—is strongly inflected by Scandinavian influences.

and Veterans of Foreign Wars among others to enforce further restrictions on immigration for a period of five to 10 years. Yet Truman resisted such pressure. He worked through Congress, and through executive directives, to enable many displaced Europeans to enter the United States. Truman knew that in the heightened Cold War atmosphere, American immigration policies could be exploited by the Communists.

Truman saw a more open door as a necessary response because of the growing Communist menace in eastern Europe. Furthermore, America had a moral duty to reduce such suffering. Changing public attitudes and the nation's continuing postwar prosperity created a climate in which objections to new arrivals declined and world affairs made Americans more willing to accept ethnic differences. Initial acts including the War Brides Act of 1945 enabled 120,000 wives, husbands, and children of American service personnel to immigrate. Truman also issued directives to consulates to favorably process the applications for entry of displaced Europeans. The Displaced Persons Act of 1948 followed, which had limitations particularly for displaced Jews. Restrictive immigration law continued into the 1950s, but proponents of liberalization were becoming more numerous and discriminatory policies were becoming less popular.

OTHER CULTURAL DEVELOPMENTS

During World War II and in the immediate postwar period, European Americans responded to the racial ideology of the Nazis by rejecting theories of white supremacy and the idea of a superior race dominant over all others. The 1940 Alien Registration Act promoted the notion that those of foreign backgrounds should become naturalized citizens as a show of their full-hearted acceptance of America. The operating policy, supported by propaganda during the war, encouraged the idea that America was a melting pot of nationalities where different ethnic groups blended into singular Americans, all sharing common values. General national differences and cultural identities were becoming less important. Though these beliefs were being applied more evenly to the broad cross-section of whites in the postwar period , non-whites were still treated and perceived somewhat differently.

During the 1940s, American society also faced steadily increasing marriage rates, as many couples entered rushed marriages due to the prospects of war and male overseas military service. The birth rate increased accordingly from 19.4 births per thousand in 1940 to 24.1 births per thousand in 1946. This created a situation in which mothers were left to raise the children on their own while husbands were away at war for long periods of time. In addition, teenagers became more noticeable as an identifiable group. With greater employment opportunities, teenagers brought in wages that contributed to family earnings. Furthermore, the extra money transformed many teenagers into potential consumers, which, in turn, attracted specialized advertisers. After the war, marriage rates and birth rates rose even more significantly, creating what has come to be known as the baby boom. The social impact of this generational change is still felt in the United States.

With marriages, children, and increased earnings, American life looked forward to a new domestic age of prosperity, marked by new homes, automobiles, and appliances. Life became an exercise in consumerism once the immediate postwar economic duress had passed. New suburban communities were built throughout the nation, offering pleasant and uniform landscapes for living.

In each year from 1945 to 1949, one million new homes were constructed. To get to these homes, new roads were built and over 21 million cars were produced to provide the necessary transportation. To furnish further comfort, 20 million refrigerators and over 5 million stoves were manufactured. Higher education became accessible for those with ambition and ability. Between 1940 and 1949, college attendance increased by a factor of three. Helped by the GI Bill, more Americans gained the necessary qualifications to become professionals and to enter an increasingly white-collar business world.

A Mennonite teacher with a class of Amish, Mennonite, and Pennsylvania Dutch children in Lancaster County, Pennsylvania, in 1942. While the country underwent rapid cultural change during and after World War II, enclaves following older European traditions continued to exist.

The future was also shaped by major technical and scientific changes that affected America at every level. Television, which was first demonstrated at the 1939 New York World's Fair, was more fully established by 1947, with 13 stations in operation. TV's growing importance in American life was reflected in 1952 by annual sales of 17 million TV sets. The arrival in 1945 of the massive, vacuum-tube driven ENIAC computer revealed the first steps toward the computer age. The computer would shape companies like IBM and soon change every aspect of society and the very nature of modern life.

ENTERTAINMENT AND THE ARTS

During the 1940s, entertainment was still largely defined by the radio, and performers like Kate Smith, Arthur Godfrey, Red Skelton, and Abbott and Costello were tremendously popular. By the end of the decade, although big bands still produced their jitterbug music, solo performers such as Bing Crosby and Frank Sinatra along with many other recording artists had made popular music even more popular. Other aspects of American music and American art were enriched by the many European refugees who had fled a war-torn Europe for the safe haven of America.

Movies during the 1940s steadily increased their mass audiences and were deemed vital to America's war effort—a propaganda tool that offered a host of Japanese and German villains. Movies also boosted America's morale with tales of unity, sacrifice, and triumph over adversity. Popular actors included Gary Cooper, Humphrey Bogart, Bette Davis, Katherine Hepburn, Joan Crawford, Judy Garland, Mickey Rooney, Ginger Rogers, and Fred Astaire. After the war, Jimmy Stewart and Tyrone Power returned to the big screen, joining a new generation of stars such as Montgomery Clift, Marlon Brando, Elizabeth Taylor, and Lana Turner. Betty Grable became a wartime pinup, Veronica Lake and Rita Hayworth played femme fatales and brought a sexual desirability to their 1940s film roles. The 1940s also launched Walt Disney's rise in popular culture with his cartoon features such as *Fantasia* (1940), *Dumbo* (1941), and *Bambi* (1942).

During the 1940s, American theater became more experimental, reflective, and expressively modern with successes such as Thornton Wilder's *The Skin of Our Teeth* (1942). Tennessee Williams's *Glass Menagerie* (1945) and *A Streetcar Named Desire* (1947) made serious impressions on audiences with tales of family dysfunction. Musical theater also delivered great hits during the period with a stream of popular songs and dance routines. *Oklahoma* (1943), *Carousel* (1945), and *Annie Get Your Gun* (1946) stood out as prime period examples.

American literature furnished further evidence of the country's growing importance on the world stage. The 1940s and the postwar period saw the rise of a more diverse literary scene with African-American and Jewish-American writers gaining greater footholds in the popular imagination. However, even in the face of growing ethnic diversity, European-American writers continued to make major literary contributions in large numbers. John Hershey, William Saroyan, and Gore Vidal established reputations in

Gore Vidal in 1948, the year his groundbreaking The City and The Pillar was published.

this period. Vidal's *The City and the Pillar* (1948) became one of the first works to deal explicitly with homosexuality, marking a major literary departure. Robert Lowell's poetry in works such as *Land of Unlikeness* (1944) revealed America's continuing poetic presence. The publication of John Crow Ransom's *The New Criticism* (1941) set an influential model for subsequent American literary criticism in the 1940s and 1950s and reflected the general impact of the southern literary renaissance.

The 1940s also witnessed the emergence of what would become a major American and world cultural form in the 1950s, Abstract Expressionism. The New York School, as it came to be known, featured a number of European exiles such as Arshile Gorky, Hans Hoffman, and Willem de Kooning who enriched the movement and influenced many young American painters. But native-born American artists such as Jackson Pollock and Alexander Calder also made considerable marks in the abstract movement.

SPORTS IN THE 1940s

America's enthusiasm for all types of sports continued unabated in the 1940s. However, the war affected professional sports as players entered the military. In major league baseball, by 1943, half the players were in the service. This meant that the game had to rely on older players and younger prospects brought in to fill rosters. For instance, Joe Nuxhall of the Cincinnati Reds made his big league debut in 1944 at age 15. The New York Yankees' Joe DiMaggio set his record 56-game hitting streak in 1941, and Ted Williams of the Boston Red Sox batted over .400 in 1941, becoming the last Major Leaguer to do so for an entire season. Williams served as a Marine Corps pilot during the war. Most dramatically, the segregated white-only (European-American) major leagues changed in 1947, when Jackie Robinson became the first African American to play baseball for the Brooklyn Dodgers.

American football continued to develop at both the college and the professional levels. Free substitutions came in 1941, which opened the game to more player specialization; penalty flags were introduced, and play books became more complicated and strategic. Basketball also grew increasingly popular and the professional game took its modern form in 1949 when the National Basketball Association came into existence. The Women's Professional Golf Association was formed in 1949, which revealed the general move in more and more sports from amateur to professional. In addition, auto racing was revived in the postwar era. "Indy" car racing made a comeback and, in 1947, the National Association for Stock Car Racing (NASCAR) was organized and offered competitive races at several national venues by the late 1940s.

Boxing continued its popularity in the 1940s with many great boxers competing in all weight divisions. However, with 4,000 professionals in the military, including the African-American heavyweight champion Joe Lewis, the overall quality of the competition diminished. Peace saw a return to the weekly fight action, and gambling helped promote even greater interest in the sport. At the featherweight division, Willie Pep dominated the decade, and the middleweight division produced colorful European-American champions such as Tony Zale, champ from 1940 to 1947; Rocky Graziano, who won the title in 1947 from Tony Zale; and Jake LaMotta, who defeated Mercel Cerdan of France in 1949 to become middleweight champion.

CONCLUSION

Since 1940, the U.S. population showed a 14.5 percent increase, reaching over 150 million in 1950 even in the face of a devastating world war that took many lives. Of this total, approximately 135 million were classified as white and of these, 125 million were native born compared to 10 million who were foreign born. The older European-American national divisions had been combined into a general classification system that suggested that out of many, there was but one type of white American. What was now most important was a sense of common identity and purpose. This remained true for European Americans, but for non-whites, particularly African Americans, segregation was still present in many areas of society including the military throughout World War II.

For the European-American majority, the 1940s changed lives completely, and at decade's end, America had become more urban and suburban, as well as more prosperous and powerful. Domestically, the United States emerged virtually untouched by war, while Europe and Asia faced massive destruction and turmoil. The breakdown of the wartime alliance with the Soviet Union after 1946 introduced a Cold War American psyche that would dominate future generations. This was made more complicated by the arrival of the atomic age in weaponry.

Demobilization also signaled a new age of consumerism, with a baby boom producing the next generation of consumers. Science and technology were changing the way the American economy worked and white collar industries were replacing the old blue-collar world of manufacturing and heavy industries. Nevertheless, during the war American industry made the nation an "arsenal of democracy" that ensured Allied victory. From 1945 on, the United States was a world leader, replacing old imperial powers and facing emerging threats in the form of the Soviet Union and its many Communist satellites.

The era also witnessed ethnic European Americans taking on a fuller role in American life. Besides the already established Irish-American and German-American political progress, the newer immigrants from eastern and southeastern Europe began to have a political impact and joined more fully in the complete American experience. As the second and third generations came of political age, many changed past party attachments and became Democratic Party activists, strengthening that party's broad New Deal coalition base.

Furthermore, these generations started to make significant inroads into the major political landscape. Czech Anton Cermak's election as mayor of Chicago in 1930 was a first step. After 1945, Joseph Mruc was elected the first Polish-American mayor of Buffalo, and Rhode Island's John Pastore became the first Italian-American senator. In areas where Italian Americans were concentrated such as New Jersey, more political power was transferred their way. Italian Americans after the war even became a dominant force in New York's traditionally Irish-controlled Tammany Hall.

For Jewish Americans there were also sizable political gains during the era: Abraham A. Ribicoff became governor of Connecticut, and Jacob J. Javits became New York's attorney general from 1947 to 1954. For all European Americans, past barriers were steadily decreasing and new experiences were reducing old ethnic loyalties and ties. Differences persisted, but primarily these were of a religious nature and, in many cases, intermarriage reduced the religious divide, particularly as society evolved during the postwar years. Fiorello La Guardia of mixed Italian and Jewish heritage was a New York City mayor and wartime director of civil defense; his success symbolized the changing face of America.

THEODORE W. EVERSOLE
NORTHERN KENTUCKY UNIVERSITY
AND UNIVERSITY OF CINCINNATI

Further Reading

Adams, Michael C. *The Best War Ever: America and World War II.* Baltimore, MD: Johns Hopkins University Press, 1993.

Alpers, Benjamin L. *Dictators, Democracy and American Public Culture: Envisioning the Totalitarian Enemy, 1920s–1950s.* Chapel Hill, NC: University of North Carolina Press, 2002.

Astor, Gerald. *The Greatest War: America in Combat, 1941–1945.* New York: Presidio Press, 1990.

Bell, Jonathan. *The Liberal State on Trial: The Cold War and American Politics in the Truman Years.* New York: Columbia University Press, 2004.

Blum, John M. *V was for Victory: Politics and American Culture During World War II.* New York: Harvest, 1977.

Bogel, Lori. *Cold War Espionage and Spying.* New York: Routledge, 2001.

Cooke, Alistair. *America Observed: From the 1940s to the 1980s.* New York: Knopf, 1989.

Dinnerstein, Leonard and David M. Reimers. *Ethnic Americans: A History of Immigration.* New York: Columbia University Press, 1999.

Erenberg, Lewis A. and Susan E. Hirsch, eds. *The War in American Culture: Society and Consciousness During World War II*. Chicago, IL: University of Chicago Press, 1996.

Gaddis, John L. *The Cold War: A New History*. New York: Penguin, 2006.

Gerdes, Louise I., ed. *America's Decades: 1940s*. San Diego, CA: Greenhaven Press, 2000.

Gitler, Ira. *Swing to Bop: An Oral History of the Transition to Jazz in the 1940s*. New York: Oxford University Press, 1987.

Gourley, Catherine. *Rosie and Mrs. America: Perceptions of Women in the 1930s and 1940s*. Breckenridge, CO: Twenty-First Century Books, 2007.

Honey, Maureen. *Creating Rosie the Riveter: Class, Gender and Propaganda during World War II*. Amherst, MA: University of Massachusetts Press, 1984.

Jones, Maldwyn A. *American Immigration*. Chicago, IL: University of Chicago Press, 1992.

Kaledin, Eugenia. *Daily Life in the US, 1940–1959: Shifting Worlds*. Westport, CT: Greenwood Press, 2000.

Kennedy, David. M. *Freedom from Fear: The American People in Depression and War, 1929–1945*. New York: Oxford University Press, 2001.

Koistinen, Paul A. *Arsenal of World War II: The Political Economy of American Warfare, 1940–1945*. Lawrence, KS: University Press of Kansas, 2004.

McFarland, Keith D. *Louis Johnson and the Arming of America: The Roosevelt and Truman Years*. Bloomington, IN: Indiana University Press, 2005.

Mindel, Charles H., Robert W. Haberstein, and Roosevelt Wright Jr. *Ethnic Families in America: Patterns and Variations*. Upper Saddle River, NJ: Prentice Hall, 1998.

O'Brien, Kenneth and Lynn A. Parsons. *The Home Front War: World War II and American Society*. Westport, CT: Greenwood Press, 1995.

O'Neill, William. *A Democracy at War: America's Fight at Home and Abroad during World War II*. Cambridge, MA: Harvard University Press, 1998.

Rees, Richard W. *Shades of Difference: A History of Ethnicity in America*. Lanham, MD: Rowman & Littlefield, 2007.

Reimers, David M. *A Land of Immigrants*. New York: Chelsea House, 1996.

Schatz, Thomas. *Boom and Bust: American Cinema in the 1940s*. Berkeley, CA: University of California Press, 1999.

Sickels, Robert. *The 1940s: American Popular Culture Through History*. Westport, CT: Greenwood Press, 2004.

Townsend, Peter. *Pearl Harbor Jazz: Change in American Music in the Early 1940s*. Jackson, MI: University Press of Mississippi, 2006.

Tuttle, William M. *"Daddy's Gone to War": The Second World War in the Lives of America's Children*. New York: Oxford University Press, 1995.

Wills, Charles A. *America in the 1940s*. New York: Facts on File, 2005.

CHAPTER 8

Postwar United States: 1950 to 1969

BY THE 1950s and 1960s, large numbers of European Americans were, by now, two or more generations removed from their home country. Many of these Irish Americans, German Americans, and Italian Americans were moving away from urban ethnic enclaves and assimilating into the homogeneity of the suburbs as simply Americans. The desire to assimilate was increased by the heightened nationalism that followed World War II, and by the paranoia of the Cold War. Under Senator Joseph McCarthy's direction, the Senate Permanent Subcommittee on Investigations investigated thousands of individuals as Communist sympathizers from 1953 to 1954. People were frequently targeted for McCarthy's attacks because of their leftist views or nontraditional lifestyles (such as homosexuality), and many of them lost their careers and their freedom despite questionable evidence. Most verdicts were later overturned or declared unconstitutional. World War II had also evoked strong patriotic feelings among immigrants, especially German and Italian Americans, many of whom had played critical roles for the Allies during the war. Avoiding postwar discrimination made these families even more eager to become Americans. The message of assimilation was also reinforced by the tales of American happiness told from the clean, white conformity of television.

Throughout the 1950s and into the 1960s, most European Americans rode one of two currents: assimilation or rebellion. The conservative establishment grew as more European Americans achieved middle-class status and moved to suburbia (both physically and spiritually). However, the seeds of the social unrest that would blossom in the 1960s were being planted by disaffected youth and demographic groups who were kept outside the flow of affluence.

As the civil rights movement gained momentum in the 1960s, African Americans, Native Americans, Chicanos, and others began to fight for their rights and to assert their cultural identities. This increasing awareness of non-white ethnic identities also resulted in a clearer understanding of what was included in white ethnic identity. For example, when Americans, especially in predominantly white areas of the country, commented on the black vernacular speech they heard on television, on the radio, or in the movies, they became aware of, and implicitly broadcast, the idea of there being a "white" way to speak. At the same time, that awareness of whiteness often brought with it a desire to distinguish finer differences—the difference between Irish-American identity and German-American identity, for instance.

In the 1950s and 1960s, European-American ethnic identity went through the following phases in a brief period: immigrant identity for the offspring and perhaps grandchildren of immigrants (though not for those European Americans who could date their first American ancestors to the colonial era); assimilated "white American" identity, in which whiteness was more important than country of ancestral origin; and finally rediscovered ethnicity, in which the descendents of immigrants who assimilated re-embraced aspects of their ethnic heritage.

THE GI BILL

The GI Bill was the final component of President Franklin D. Roosevelt's New Deal reforms and entitlement programs that helped pull the country out of the Great Depression. With the Depression a recent memory, the GI Bill was intended not only as a reward for the unusually large number of enlisted men who had been needed for World War II, but also to avoid a return to economic stagnation now that the war was over. The bill provided funding for higher education (or vocational education) for returning World War II veterans, low-interest no-down-payment housing or small business loans for veterans and their families, and a generous unemployment package. Despite a lack of segregation in the wording of the GI Bill, discrimination and segregation meant that the nation's thanks to its military for service overseas was more likely distributed to European Americans than to those who did not fit this demographic.

The success and popularity of the original GI Bill led to the Veterans' Adjustment Act of 1952, which offered similar benefits to veterans of the Korean War. The first result of these bills was a highly educated group of veterans entering the workforce; 51 percent of World War II veterans and 43 percent of veterans of the Korean War utilized their education benefits under the GI Bill. By the time the education benefits expired on the 1952 act, in 1965, approximately 2.4 million of the 5.5 million eligible Korean War veterans had used their education benefits. Half of those who utilized those benefits—1.2 million—used them for higher education at a college or university. Again, this benefit applied mainly to European Americans because returning African-American GIs and other minority veterans found that they had fewer educational opportunities available to them. The majority of colleges and universities still employed segregationist tactics in their admissions policies. Education results in a longer-lasting difference than most other forms of assistance: the children of parents with college educations are the most likely group to attend college, not simply because their parents are more likely to be able to afford it, but also because they have grown up with college as an expectation. This is the sort of change that most forms of assistance cannot purchase.

Though the GI Bill was instrumental in bridging American class boundaries and helping to integrate European-American immigrant groups—eroding differences in educational and income levels within the European-American population—it has been criticized in retrospect as essentially an instrument of white privilege, doing more to bridge the gap between poor and middle-class whites than between whites and non-whites. Just as the grandfather clause of the Jim Crow south had intentionally elevated whites above blacks without needing to specifically invoke race—by giving the vote only to men whose grandfathers had been able to vote—the GI Bill unintentionally provided benefits that were primarily enjoyed by whites, by making educational funding available without increasing educational opportunities for non-whites (through increased funding to predominantly non-white schools, for instance, or literacy and tutoring programs, or affirmative action).

The other critical benefit of the GI Bill was housing. The government insured loans to servicemen at up to 95 percent of the value of the home, and the Federal Housing Administration (FHA) simplified the process for builders to borrow capital to provide homes for GIs. The terms under the GI Bill were low interest, no down payment, and 30 years to pay; this enabled servicemen returning from both World War II and the Korean War to stop renting apartments in the cities and join the home-owning middle class in suburbia. However, despite the best efforts of the American Legion and Warren Atherton, who made certain that the GI Bill as written applied to all Americans, women and non-whites were limited in their ability to collect benefits from the GI Bill because banks and mortgage agencies still often refused to give them mortgages. As with educational benefits, the housing benefits of the GI Bill principally smoothed differences between European-Americans, bringing many of them to a new level of prosperity.

WHITE FLIGHT

That prosperity left many young men looking for ways to demonstrate their new-found status, and perhaps the greatest symbol of status of the era was a luxurious automobile. While the home ownership that the GI Bill made possible had always been part of the American dream, the 1950s mainstreamed the ambition of car ownership. In addition to the growing European-American middle class, the auto industry was bolstered by the interstate highway system and the growth of suburbia.

As American motor vehicle statistics have consistently shown, automobile owners did not live in urban areas, they lived in the surrounding suburban areas. As the number of automobiles on the road grew, traffic planners saw the need to replace America's haphazard, predominantly non-freeway system of roads with an interstate system of high-speed highways. Another exigency for a nationalized system of expressways was the Cold War threat of nuclear war. The idea was that to avoid the easy decimation of the American population in the event of an attack by the Russians, the dense urban living conditions should be done away with and the people dispersed into smaller, low-density suburban villages. This thinking, coupled with the highway system, also encouraged industry to move farther away from urban centers, perpetuating the growth of urban sprawl.

The interstate highway system came into being when the Federal-Aid Highway Act of 1956 (also known as the National Interstate and Defense Highways Act of 1956) was signed into legislation by President Dwight D. Eisenhower. The downside of this was that while the affluent, mostly white, European-American suburbanite escaped from urban living, these families took their tax base to the suburbs. The resulting shift in wealth meant that the quality of government services was better in wealth areas, not necessarily in the areas that most needed them.

Desegregation of public schools in urban areas, combined with the influx of African Americans and other minorities into the cities during the war years to look for work in war-related industry, meant that the housing market became very tight, urban rents inflated rapidly, and racial tensions increased in urban schools. Because of the advantages discussed above, European Americans were better able to leave urban centers in favor of newly developed and predominantly white suburbs.

LEVITTOWN LEADS THE WAY TO SUBURBIA

Prior to the 1950s, suburbs were a refuge from the city reserved primarily for the wealthy. However, the postwar social and economic pressures jump-started the housing industry and builders, led by New York's Levitt & Sons, began mass-producing a new style of home in a new kind of suburb. The "General Motors of the housing industry" built the first major modern suburb, Levittown, filled with quality, affordable houses.

William Levitt and his brother Alfred favored ranch homes, small single-floor plans built on a concrete slab that could be sold for between $7,900 and $9,500, thanks to mass-production. The floor plan was standardized, and many of the components were prefabricated at a central warehouse. Levitt bought timberlands, a sawmill, and a nail factory to lower costs, avoid shortages, and sell surplus material to competitors. This vertical integration gave Levitt the leverage to force manufacturers to sell supplies directly to him and thus reduce his overhead. By the start of the 1950s, Levitt & Sons was building four out of every five new homes in the United States—one every 15 minutes. This housing boom was fueled by the sudden growth of suburbia and made possible by Levitt's cost-saving measures, which also included a simplification of the construction process so that only 20 percent of the labor needed to be done by skilled workers, thus avoiding labor unions. The first "Levittown," with 17,400 homes, was built on Long Island farmland 25 miles east of New York and quickly became the archetype for the 1950s European-American suburb, with the neat square lawns and well-lit streets seen in TV shows like *Leave it to Beaver*.

Financing from the GI Bill and the development of low-cost construction techniques led to a mass exodus to the suburbs beginning in the 1950s. These children played jacks on a quiet suburban street in the 1950s or early 1960s.

Institutionalized racist practices such as redlining kept this American dream a principally white domain. Redlining is the practice of refusing services or increasing the cost of services (such as, real estate, banking, insurance, employment, and healthcare) to individuals who live in a certain, usually racially determined, geographic location. The name comes from the practice of drawing a red line on a map around neighborhoods in which a bank would not invest (generally because of the income, credit history, and racial makeup of the neighborhood's residents). The Federal Housing Authority's 1938 *Underwriting Manual*, still in use in the 1950s, stated that zoning covenants and ordinances should include provisions such as "Prohibition of the occupancy of properties except by the race for which they are intended" and that schools should not "be attended in large numbers by inharmonious racial groups." Between redlining and zoning, minorities were again effectively excluded from reaping the economic benefits offered by the GI Bill. As a consequence, the suburbs were essentially sorted by race, religion, and economic status. William Levitt explained the situation when he said, "We can solve a housing problem, or we can try to solve a racial problem. But we cannot combine the two." Even as late as 1960, there were no African Americans in the original Levittown. This was commonplace nationwide as segregated and stratified development became institutionalized and European Americans separated themselves economically and culturally from the rest of the country.

ETHNIC ENCLAVES: THE CASE OF NEW ENGLAND

Despite the desire to conform, not all European-American ethnic groups were part of the move to the suburbs in the 1950s, and older types of European-American ethnic enclaves could still be found. Initially one of the least diverse parts of the country—thoroughly WASP (White Anglo-Saxon Protestant)—New England gradually became home to pockets of ethnic communities, including the Italians of Boston's North End and later the Cambodians who settled in Lowell, Massachusetts. The 1950s were a period of significant growth and development for three major European-American groups in New England: the Irish, the Quebecois, and the Portuguese.

Irish immigrants had been coming to New England in large numbers since the potato famine of the 1840s, and a century later had become a significant political and cultural force, especially in Boston ("the next parish over," as the Irish called it). Honey Fitz—as John Francis Fitzgerald was better known—died in 1950, after a political career that had begun on Boston's Common Council in 1891 and had included a stint in Congress and as Boston's first American-born Irish Catholic mayor. Honey Fitz was the textbook example of how the public saw Irish-American politicians: a charismatic man of the people who loved to talk and was more than happy to thank his supporters with cushy jobs once he'd been elected. Even when he was not holding office, he was the public face of Irish Americans in Massachusetts politics, while

Irish-American Patrick Kennedy worked behind the scenes. Fitz and Kennedy had clashed at first, but soon came to terms, in an alliance that was solidified in a very old-country way when Kennedy's only son Joe married Fitzgerald's eldest child Rose.

Honey Fitz's funeral was one of the largest in the city's history and was widely commented on in the national press, a symbol of how the Irish had come to power in the self-proclaimed "Hub of the Universe." His pallbearers included Speaker of the House John McCormack, future speaker of the House Tip O'Neill, and Massachusetts Senators Leverett Saltonstall and Henry Cabot Lodge, Jr., whose grandfather Henry Cabot Lodge, Sr., had defeated Honey Fitz in Fitz's run for the Senate in 1916. In 1952,

John Francis Fitzgerald, the Irish Catholic mayor of Boston, early in his career in 1906.

Lodge Junior was defeated in his run for reelection by John Fitzgerald Kennedy, the son of Joe and Rose, and was again defeated by Kennedy in 1960, when he was Richard Nixon's running mate on the Republican presidential ticket.

The symbolic victory here represented more than just the recurring clash between the families. The Cabot and Lodge families were among the most esteemed of the "Boston Brahmins," the English Protestant families who had long held power in New England's political, cultural, and religious institutions, and who were the oldest and most deeply entrenched of the northern United States' powerful families. The "Boston toast" by John Collins Bossidy said much about Boston and the Brahmins:

And this is good old Boston,
The home of the bean and the cod,
Where the Lowells talk only to Cabots,
and the Cabots talk only to God.

Thus the union of two powerful immigrant families defeated the union of two powerful English Protestant families, and the public political power of those old aristocratic families has been shaky ever since.

French-Canadian children in Maine in the mid-20th century. The many Quebecois communities in northern New England were able to retain their native language longer than many other groups.

The Irish had established power in crime as well. In Boston in particular the Irish mob became quickly entrenched. The 1950s were a transitional period in New England's organized crime, the 1931 death of mob boss Frank Wallace having created a power vacuum that would continue to cause problems. The conflicts between the McLaughlin Gang of Charlestown and the Winter Hill Gang of Somerville would escalate into the Irish Gang War at the end of the decade.

The Quebecois, meanwhile—French-speaking immigrants from Quebec, Canada—had been immigrating to the United States since the previous century, and had settled in numerous communities in New England, especially near the border in Maine, New Hampshire, and Vermont (the name of which comes from the French *Vert-mont*, "green mountain"). A similar climate and geography—right down to the wild blueberry bushes and plentiful sugar maples, common to both Acadia and northern New England—made it easier for the French-speaking immigrants to adapt. While most of the Catholic influx in Boston came from the Irish, throughout northern New England a Catholic church was more likely to be named after St. Louis than St. Patrick.

Quebecois families kept their French dialect alive for more generations than most immigrant groups (and in northern New England, continue to do so today), creating bilingual households while other groups abandoned their native language as the generations born in the United States became native Anglophones. By the 1950s, New Hampshire had become the state with the largest percentage of French population, despite Louisiana's stronger historical ties to France. The mills in Manchester, New Hampshire, relied heavily on Quebecois labor, and the diners serving those millworkers—many of them open all-night and offering menus written in French—served up poutine, salmon pie, tourtiere, ployes, and other French-Canadian dishes. Such neighborhoods, scattered across New England and upstate New York, were often called "Little Canada" or "Little Quebec." Even smaller cities with significant Quebecois populations had French-language newspapers, and a handful of Francophone radio stations served the area.

Although Portuguese sailors and fishermen had been visiting New England since the colonial era, Portuguese immigrants did not come to the United States in large numbers until the early 20th century, when economic troubles in Portugal and the demand for factory labor in New England brought several hundred thousand Portuguese to the area, especially to Fall River and New Bedford, Massachusetts (where many whalers from the Portuguese Azores in the mid-Atlantic Ocean had already settled), and to Rhode Island. By the 1950s, Rhode Island had become a demographic oddity in New England, with the country's largest Portuguese population and consequently its only majority-Catholic population.

In the 1950s, these communities were thriving. Providence, New Bedford, and Fall River had a number of Portuguese restaurants and supermarkets, as well as the associated businesses (importers, and so on) that supported them, and Portuguese Americans had established themselves in the region's manufacturing, agricultural, and fishing industries. In these cities and in small fishing towns like Provincetown, Massachusetts, both American and New England culture were shaped by the Portuguese population: hot dog vendors carried chourico and linguiça sausage, for instance, while local clams were served not in a creamy chowder with potatoes, but in a tomato broth alongside mussels and salt cod.

Unlike most immigrant groups, Azoreans in particular were accustomed to farming in the hilly,

This tomato-based Portuguese stew features traditional salt cod, clams, and shrimp.

People of Portuguese descent dominated the town government of Provincetown, Massachusetts, by the mid-20th century. The photograph shows a group of Portuguese-American selectmen meeting in the town hall before a large painting of the Pilgrims signing the Mayflower Compact.

rocky, cramped conditions that New Englanders faced. Though new immigration slowed because of federal legislation, the existing population thrived and strengthened. When a series of earthquakes and volcanic eruptions on the island of Faial jeopardized the Azores in 1957 and 1958, then Senator John F. Kennedy of Massachusetts cosponsored—with Senator John Pastore of Rhode Island—the Azorean Refugee Act, which granted additional visas for Azoreans to relocate to the United States, most of whom came to the existing centers of Portuguese-American life in New England.

TELEVISION AND THE AMERICAN DREAM

By 1952, there were over 19 million television sets in U.S. households. As the nation transitioned away from radio, the situation comedy soon became the genre that painted the clearest picture of a new European-American vision of America. Sitcoms had developed as a radio genre and were dominated by the domestic comedy (such as *I Love Lucy*, 1951–60) and the workplace comedy (such as *Our Miss Brooks*, 1952–56). Lucille Ball's *I Love Lucy* was so popular that some businesses closed early on Monday nights to allow employees the opportunity to get home in time to see the show.

Ball had previously starred in the similar radio sitcom *My Favorite Husband*, co-starring Richard Denning. When CBS wanted to bring *My Favorite Husband* to television, Ball asked that the role of her husband be recast (as often happened in such transitions)—specifically, she wanted to costar with her real-life husband, Cuban-born bandleader Desi Arnaz. The couple had spent much of their marriage apart because of their careers. They dug in their heels when CBS refused to cast them as a couple because of their ethnic differences (and especially because Arnaz was foreign born). In 1950, they founded Desilu Productions to produce a vaudeville show that was meant to prove to CBS that the American public would have no problem with them as a couple. The eventual compromise was to produce a new show, which Ball developed alongside some of the writers from *My Favorite Husband*. Ball and Arnaz starred as Lucy and Ricky Ricardo in one of television's biggest successes. When Lucy Ricardo gave birth in 1953, 44 million viewers tuned in—twice as many as watched the inauguration of President Eisenhower the following day.

Although some of the humor of the show came from Lucy's making fun of Ricky's accent, the couple were careful to avoid explicit ethnic humor. Not only was Ricky not written as a Hispanic stereotype, but his ethnicity was not a source of tension or friction with other characters; nor was the Ricardos's marriage portrayed as anything unusual or difficult (that is, not for ethnic reasons). This portrayal of normalcy was groundbreaking in and of itself, particularly coming on the heels of decades of radio comedies that had used every ethnic stereotype under the sun.

While the boundaries between the reality of suburban life and the "realities" portrayed on television were fuzzy, television did reflect the value structure of the status quo through the lives of fictional, predominantly European-American characters. A 1954 study of race and gender roles on television showed that 85 percent of the characters who were portrayed in a show were

A boy displays his family's television set in 1952, by which time 19 million U.S. households owned sets.

either upper or middle class, and white males were portrayed on television dramas as higher on the social scale than either white females or any minorities. On television, women were more socially disadvantaged than even minorities. However, the same study showed that only four percent of black characters at the time were portrayed as "bad."

By the mid-1950s, television's portrayal of suburban life in America was an idealized, antiseptic land with no economic or class divisions and certainly no racial problems. In fact, the geographically generic suburban towns inhabited by families such as the Nelsons (*The Adventures of Ozzie and Harriet*, 1952–66) and the Cleavers (*Leave it to Beaver*, 1957–63) portrayed a culture that was free of African Americans, Jews, and even Italian Americans—instead they seemed to be inhabited by "only Americans, with names that were obviously Anglo-Saxon and Protestant; it was a world of Andersons and Nelsons and Cleavers."

Television was a world where no problem was so great that it couldn't be solved in 22 minutes. Where parents were fonts of wisdom and fathers worked hard at respectable, if somewhat vague, white collar jobs. Moms stayed at home to provide home-cooked meals and care for the children. This was an optimistic world where life was good and better times lay ahead and any real problems happened in other neighborhoods, far away. As David Halberstam explained, "These (television) families were living the new social contract as created by Bill Levitt and other suburban developers like him and were surrounded by new neighbors who were just like *them*. The American dream was now located in the suburbs."

ENTERTAINMENT AND REBELLION

At the same time, entertainment media saw the earliest seeds of dissent being sown for what would fully flower into social revolution in the 1960s. The Beat Generation poets and writers voiced their discontent with the status quo, many of them exploring the Eastern religions that soldiers in the Pacific theater had been exposed to. The term *Beat* comes from the street, specifically from the drug culture, and as Barry Gifford and Lawrence Lee write, it means ". . . cheated, robbed or emotionally or physically exhausted." Jack Kerouac later modified the meaning to a synthesis of the "beaten down" and the "beatific" as well as the musical association with the word *beat*.

The Beats were fascinated with all that was different or outside the "establishment." One thing with which they were especially fascinated was urban African-American culture, from which they borrowed a great deal of terminology ("dig," "cool," and "man"). They believed that blacks had somehow made themselves freer, that they had somehow escaped the suburban assimilation. The Beats also saw drugs as a means of escaping the mundane and opening the doors to the spiritual world. Their advocacy of nonconformity even extended to their literature, as their poetry did not conform to accepted style and much of their work used profane language and addressed topics such as drugs, sex, and anarchy—which were threatening to the establishment during these conservative times.

In the world of music, the raw sexuality of Elvis Presley made parents uneasy as the rhythms of African-American blues clubs were transformed into predominantly white rock music. Clubs in black and Hispanic neighborhoods were now evening destinations for some white urban couples and young people. While many whites had long associated looser standards of sexual conduct and propriety with other races, a greater degree of sexual openness and frank discussion was also introduced to white American culture in the 1950s. European Americans such as Alfred Kinsey (biologist and founder of the Kinsey Institute for Research in Sex, Gender, and Reproduction) and Hugh Hefner (founder of *Playboy* magazine) opened the boudoir for all to see, and changed the paradigm of sexual politics in the country.

Certain white-centric practices in the entertainment industry began to die out by the 1960s. By the end of the decade, it was more of a rarity for a white musician to cover an R&B or rock and roll song by a black artist, and when it happened, it was not in order to make the song acceptable for white audiences—which had been a common practice in the 1950s and propelled the careers of singers like Pat Boone. It was still common to see white actors playing non-white roles, sometimes for putatively comic effect (for example, Mickey Rooney as the Japanese landlord in *Breakfast at Tiffany's*, in which the character's stereotypical ethnic features are so exaggerated that no one could claim Rooney is trying to "pass" as Asian), and in other cases because of a supposed lack of available actors (as in the many cases of whites playing Native Americans in westerns, particularly when large numbers were needed). In still other cases, an actor's star power would "override" the racial character of the role, as when Nordic Audrey Hepburn played a half-Kiowa girl in 1962's *The Unforgiven*, or when Anglo-American Charlton Heston played a Mexican drug agent in Orson Welles's *Touch of Evil*.

ETHNIC FOOD AND ASSIMILATION

The United States has an interesting history with ethnic food. Early ethnic restaurants tended to cater to immigrants and ethnic communities, ranging from the tamale vendors of Texas to the noodle shops of Chinatown to the restaurants of Louisville's Little Bosnia to the pho houses of New Orleans's Little Vietnam. In time, customers came to these restaurants from other neighborhoods, particularly as immigrant groups adapted enough that English was spoken in most places, and menus typically included English descriptions. Eventually it became common for Americans—particularly in cities, where dining out is more common and more people live in homes with only rudimentary cooking facilities or no kitchens at all—to eat at restaurants serving cuisines to which they had no connection.

The Marked and the Neutral

There's an old riddle that isn't quite a joke, nor as hard to solve as it once was: "A father and son are in a car accident. The father dies, and the son is rushed to the hospital, where the doctor says, 'I can't operate on this boy, this is my son.' Who is the doctor?" The answer, of course, is that the surgeon is the boy's mother, and it depends on "female doctor" being a marked category of doctor—that is, especially when this riddle was more common, when the listener hears "doctor," he thinks "male doctor" and expects exceptions to be pointed out. This has been shown to be true in sociolinguistic studies of both gender and race—people hearing "pilot" or "lawyer" assume not only "male," but also "white."

Sociologists refer to maleness and whiteness in this context as neutral (or "unmarked") categories, while the exception—simply by virtue of the fact that they are referred to as exceptions—are marked. There are also cases where female or non-white is the neutral category, such as with "nurse" ("female nurse" is neutral, "male nurse" is marked) or in some cities, "gardener" or "cab driver" (where "white" or "Anglo-American" is marked).

What is interesting to the history of European Americans is the way that different groups of European Americans have been marked or neutral throughout history. Italians were not considered "whites" when they first arrived in the United States. Nor were Jews, of any ethnic background. Even the treatment in the 19th century of the French in parts of New England and the Irish in urban centers almost suggests that neither group was considered white—they were, in any case, definitely marked groups. An Anglo-German American was "normal," neutral; an Irish American, even third generation, was not.

Much has been written about the efforts of the Irish to prosper despite this treatment and about how Jews gradually came to be seen as white. By the 1960s, both of these things can more or less be considered true. "Jewishness" was still a marked trait, even to people who would have denied being bigots; "exclusive" country clubs that excluded Jews were not uncommon, even while the attendees of such clubs in the north scorned the south for its antiquated and intolerant practice of segregation. While "Irishness" was not similarly treated, Catholicism was. Some of the popularly distributed literature used against John F. Kennedy both during his campaign in 1960 and during his presidency can be shocking for the modern American. Kennedy's candidacy was derided because of the belief that, as a Catholic, he would be beholden to the pope, a foreign leader; he was not, as a result of his faith, a true loyal "American," but might owe fealty to foreign powers.

A defining characteristic of the 1960s is that in this decade in which most European Americans had been born in the country and spoke the language and could be considered neutral, having Polish, Romanian, Italian, or Hungarian grandparents was no longer a marked trait.

The earliest crossovers may have occurred simply because of proximity—for instance, early Jewish and Irish settlers in America shared a love of corned beef brisket. Though they prepared it differently, they benefited from relying on the same butchers, increasing the demand for brisket. In the case of Jewish cooks relying on an Irish butcher, this meant purchasing meat that had not been prepared in a kosher manner; but with the advent of Reform Judaism in the 19th century, this was less of a concern to some Jewish families as it might have been for others.

Consider three of the most common ethnic cuisines in the United States: Chinese, Italian, and French. Chinese restaurants became commonplace destinations for white Americans in the 1960s. Heavily Americanized Chinese-American dishes had developed in various regions. These included the chow mein sandwich (chow mein noodles with or without vegetables with brown gravy served hot on a hamburger bun) in the Portuguese-American regions of Massachusetts and Rhode Island; the St. Paul sandwich (an egg foo yong patty with bean sprouts and onions on white bread with pickles, lettuce, tomato, and mayonnaise) in Minnesota; the thick-skinned fried egg rolls of the northeast; General Tso's chicken, which originated in New York; fortune cookies, invented by Chinese Americans in San Francisco; and various salads for which there is no equivalent in indigenous Chinese cuisine. Furthermore, in New England "American chop suey" became common in European-American households, Italian and Greek restaurants, and school cafeterias—borrowing the term *chop suey* from Chinese cooking. American chop suey is a casserole of elbow macaroni, ground beef, vegetables, and crushed tomatoes or tomato sauce (sometimes seasoned with Lea & Perrins Worcestershire sauce, a New England kitchen staple), and is easy to make in bulk.

ITALIAN-AMERICAN CUISINE

Italian cuisine found in the United States is often Italian-American cuisine (a cuisine as well defined as the regional cuisines of Italy), generally characterized by a dependence on tomatoes (and particularly slow-cooked sauces), meat, and braising. Some of the most common Italian dishes in the United States—spaghetti and meatballs, red-sauce lasagna, and fettucine alfredo—are obscure or entirely absent in Italy. Meatballs in particular feature heavily in Italian-American cuisine—with pasta, in sandwiches, in soups, even as a side—and may be the subject of family heirloom recipes passed down from one generation to the next, but they are not nearly so common in Italy, especially not with pasta.

Italian-American cuisine also features a wide range of sandwiches entirely unknown in Italy: cold, leftover meatball sandwiches throughout the north; hot subs of meatballs or sausage and peppers with tomato sauce and provolone in the northeast; roast pork and broccoli rabe in Philadelphia; Italian beef with pickled vegetables in Chicago; and muffuletta, a two-to-four-serving sandwich invented by Italian immigrants in New Orleans, consisting of cold cuts, provolone, and olive salad (a mixture of olives and vegetables in highly seasoned olive oil).

But the most important characteristic of Italian-American food is the extent to which it has been assimilated into American cuisine. In the early 20th century, Italian Americans were not considered white and were the second most likely group (after blacks) to be lynched. During World War II, because of Italy's involvement in the war, many Italian Americans, most of them born in the United States, were sent to internment camps (albeit not in the more significant numbers of Japanese Americans). But by the 1960s, Italians were so mainstreamed that Italian food had become part of the standard repertoire of home cooking for all white Americans.

Furthermore, pizza—which has roots in Italy, but which in its most common American forms is a highly Americanized product—had become the quintessential American food, consumed with no thought to its cultural history. Indeed, in parts of central New England—overwhelmingly white, overwhelmingly English, French, and German in ethnic origin—pizza and Italian food had become so normalized that Greek immigrants found that they had more success opening pizza parlors or Italian restaurants rather than Greek restaurants, giving rise to the New England Greek style of regional pizzeria that was popularized in this decade. Featuring a crust thicker than Neapolitan thin crust but thinner than Sicilian thick crust, with a zesty sauce accented with Greek oregano, marjoram, and fennel, Greek-style New England pizza often featured "meatball" as a topping—really a beef-based gyro meat, shaved into strips. These pizzerias focused mainly on Italian items like pizza, spaghetti, baked ziti, and fried calamari, with a small selection of items like gyro sandwiches, Greek salad, and moussaka. Immigrants from Syria, Armenia, and elsewhere in the Levant followed the example of the Greek pizzaioli, typically offering a variant pizza made on pita bread instead of conventional pizza dough. The lesson learned was simple: to attract American customers, serve Italian food.

FRENCH CUISINE AND JULIA CHILD

The French arrived before either the Chinese or the Italians, part of the original colonial era ethnic mixture. And yet, French cuisine did not become an ordinary part of European-American culture until the 1960s. There had always been regional exceptions: the Cajun and Creole cuisines of Louisiana, for instance, and the Quebecois cooking of French-Canadian communities in New England. But like most immigrant cuisines, until after World War II these remained principally cuisines partaken of by those who included them as part of their heritage; the Quebecois restaurants in New England by and large served that ethnic community, not Anglo-Americans or other European Americans.

French cuisine, in fact, was not popularized by an immigrant group, by an American culture, or by restaurants—but rather by Julia Child, a military intelligence veteran who attended cooking school in postwar France when the State Department transferred her husband there. In 1961, Child published *Mastering the Art of French Cooking* in the United States. It was a mammoth work of almost 750 pages, presenting a thorough approach to the art with an American audience in mind—who, like Child, did not grow up with this food and who likely had not had it in many restaurants. Hands-on in nature, the book was filled with illustrations and in-depth discussions of preparation.

Two years later, Child became one of the earliest television chef successes when PBS affiliate WGBH in Boston premiered *The French Chef*. She remained on television for decades, but her impact in the 1960s cannot be overstated: she was the public face of French food, of the country's growing interest in trying new things, and in a very real sense, of populism. She turned a cuisine that had previously been available only at the most expensive restaurants in the country's largest cities into something that could be explained in a 26-minute television show and prepared in a home kitchen by anyone willing to practice a little. Even though a great deal of the white population could count

Julia Child signing one of her many cookbooks in 1989. Child's influence on European-American cooking changed the way many Americans thought about cooking and French cuisine in the 1960s.

the French among their ancestors, it took a French-trained chef on television to introduce them to cassoulet, bouillabaisse, béarnaise sauce, coq au vin, and boeuf bourguignon.

IMMIGRATION ACT OF 1965

The Immigration and Nationality Act of 1965 was one of the most significant pieces of legislation of the 1960s, irrevocably changing the character of the country in a decade of strong social change. It was the work of three influential legislators. Representative Emanuel Celler (D-NY), a Brooklyn native of German Catholic and Jewish heritage, proposed the bill near the end of what would be a 49-year career in the House of Representatives. Celler's first major speech to Congress had been in 1924, in opposition to the Immigration Act of that year, which limited immigration according to a formula designed to preserve a specific ethnic and religious ratio in the U.S. population. The formula, furthermore, was based on 1910 figures, and so was an attempt to turn back the clock to undo the demographic effects of World War I immigration.

Celler was outvoted, but would remarkably—after a career that included strong opposition to American isolationism and to McCarthyism, and collaboration on the drafting of the major civil rights legislation of the 1960s—manage to outlast his political opponents long enough to support the very bill that would undo that 1924 act. In the Senate, Celler's co-sponsoring counterpart was Philip Hart (D-MI), nicknamed "the Conscience of the Senate." The bill was also strongly supported by Senator Ted Kennedy (D-MA), and was later recalled as a significant part of Kennedy's legacy upon his death.

The bill proposed abolishing all of the national-origin quotas that the 1924 Immigration Act had established, and thus implicitly the idea that there was a particular ethnic mixture that was more or less American. Opponents feared that this would somehow make America "less American." Kennedy, known for his oratory, delivered a speech on the Senate floor that was widely publicized, putting fears to rest: "Our cities will not be flooded by a million immigrants annually . . . the ethnic mix of this country will not be upset . . . America [will not be inundated] with immigrants from any one country or area, or the most populated and deprived nations of Africa and Asia . . . it will not cause American workers to lose their jobs."

The act passed. Limits on immigration were still in place, but of a different nature: 300,000 total immigrants per year, 170,000 of whom could be from the Eastern Hemisphere, 120,000 of whom could be from the Western Hemisphere, on a first-come, first-served basis. Family reunification visas for family members of existing citizens or permanent residents were unlimited, which was a point of concern for the opponents because it had always been a typical feature of immigration patterns for a man to immigrate first, secure a job and a place to live, and then send for his family. It is not a coincidence that

Vatican II

The Second Vatican Council, or Vatican II, was the 21st ecumenical council of the Catholic Church, and the second such convened at the Vatican. Ecumenical councils are held among the bishops and cardinals of the Catholic Church to discuss matters of faith that go beyond the scope of ordinary church activity; the fact that there have been only 21 councils in the Church's 1,700-year history speaks to their significance. Held from October 1962 to December 1965, Vatican II was called by Pope John XXIII to discuss the Church and modernity. John announced his intention to hold the council almost immediately after his election to the papacy, to the surprise and in many cases disapproval of other Church leaders. Every future pope to succeed John (to date) was present at the council: Giovanni Battista Montini (who became Paul VI when John died before the close of the council), Albino Luciani (John Paul I), and Karol Wojtyla (John Paul II) who commemorated the Vatican II popes in their papal names, and Joseph Ratzinger (Benedict XVI).

Remembered now largely for the decision to allow mass to be conducted in vernacular languages rather than in Latin, Vatican II was actually deeply concerned with doctrinal points. While permitting a vernacular mass had the most effect on the weekly life of the world's Catholics, the most significant change to Catholic doctrine was its abdication of the Catholic Church's claim to be the sole valid church. Documents like *Lumen Gentium* produced by the council used very careful wording to affirm the Catholic Church's commitment to its beliefs, while also suggesting that there were sacred truths and paths to salvation that lay outside the Catholic Church—in other words, admitting the Orthodox, Anglican, and Protestant churches as "separate but valid," rather than the heretical institutions they had all at one point or another been accused of being. This flew directly in the face of centuries of Catholic tradition; after all, the very word *catholic* means "universal" and had always indicated the Church's self-assessment that its was the only appropriate form of worship, the only path to peace.

Long accused of being behind the times, the Catholic Church took a tremendous step forward with Vatican II, becoming perhaps the most ecumenically tolerant major worldwide religious institution. This upset a great many Catholics, at least at first. Some of them—a small but vocal number—decided the Vatican II council was invalid and established their own churches to continue the pre-Vatican II theological traditions. In fact, though many Catholics were startled by the changes, in the United States, perhaps because it lacked the Catholic heritage so key in much of Europe, Catholics were already more liberal than the Church as a whole, as demonstrated in multiple survey studies by Catholic theologian, sociologist, and author Andrew Greeley. One of the effects on American Catholics, however, was to break down the barriers and stigmas between Catholics and non-Catholics, making them more at ease with each other.

concern over illegal immigrants has been a political issue primarily in the years since this act, essentially a torch passed down the line; indeed, some of the opponents of the act were on hand in the 1980s to support stronger anti-illegal-immigrant legislation.

Despite Kennedy's assurances—which were correct insofar as discrediting what opponents considered worst-case scenarios—the act changed the demographic character and immigration patterns of the United States significantly, and it is one of the factors that transformed European Americans from an overwhelming majority to a significant, but dwindling majority (most projections show non-Hispanic whites losing majority sometime around the middle of the 21st century).

Immigration from 1965 to 1970 doubled. Much of this came from countries previously tightly constrained by the old quotas, such as Asia. But it also removed the quotas for eastern European countries, and although there was no mass immigration of Europeans as there had been in previous eras, perhaps more significantly, less tangibly, it symbolically removed the stigma of national origin. The question remains of whether the disintegration of the social boundaries between European-American ethnic groups was accelerated by the 1965 Immigration Act, or if the 1965 Immigration Act's passage boosted the in-progress disintegration of those boundaries.

WHITE ETHNICITY IN THE 1960s

A popular theory about the nature of ethnicity among non-Hispanic European Americans in the 1960s was that a family was more likely to emphasize its ethnicity—to identify strongly as German American or Italian American, for example—if it was a working-class family. The underlying assumption was that as immigrants' descendants assimilated into mainstream America, they discarded their ethnic ties and were rewarded with middle-class riches. Or, alternately, that the middle-class lifestyle constituted its own ethnicity, which drowned out what came before it. Studies that suggested that ethnicity was a lower-class preoccupation often constructed models explaining that lower-class families were more dependent on family social networks and less likely to move far away from home, which thus kept extended family closer at hand, resulting in less social and geographic mobility and therefore less likely to stray from the clan. But it is misleading to suggest that the poor cannot be mobile and to conclude that the middle and upper classes do not depend on extensive networks of family connections.

An interesting theory was aptly summed up by sociologist Marcus Hansen's maxim, "What the son wishes to forget, the grandson wishes to remember." Though Hansen's model is somewhat oversimplified, the basic idea seems to accurately describe the white American experience in the middle third of the 20th century: the first generation arrives in America and sets down roots; the second generation becomes preoccupied with the problems of adapting to

American culture, values, and institutions and in so doing sheds much of its ethnic identity, either out of necessity (when it clashes with those institutions) or vanity (when wearing traditional ethnic clothing or bringing ethnic foods in a bag lunch embarrasses one at school, for instance, when fitting in is paramount). The third generation, successfully assimilated, no longer contends with that self-consciousness and embraces the lost ethnicity—or the attractive or interesting features of it. This can include, for example, a Catholic gravitating toward the traditions specific to Ireland, Italy, or Germany; a desire to visit "the Old Country" or to do genealogical research; a desire to learn the native tongue that the second generation was so happy

The civil rights movement, which included some participants from varied backgrounds, eventually led to a growing understanding of both non-white and white ethnic identity in the United States.

to discard; an attempt to uncover old family recipes; or, more subtly, embracing or cultivating personality traits that the third generation associates with this lost ethnic identity. Ethnicity becomes a sort of explanatory text, an origin story. This embrace of ethnic heritage can often occur in adolescence or in college years, when the individual is beginning to construct a life of their own, one that transpires on their own terms, rather than just revolving around homework and lists of chores. It can be a way to move closer to family or farther from it—a way to adjust one's position.

The 1960s and beyond saw a good many "Kiss Me, I'm Irish" buttons sold, and a stronger involvement by Italian Americans with Columbus Day, which while not instituted as a celebration of Italian-American heritage was to some degree adopted as one. More and more works of world literature and ethnic literature became available in the United States as well and enrollment increased in various country- or ethnic-studies programs (not all of which can be attributed to the students' studying his or her own ethnicity). The end point of this "grandson's remembrance" model of ethnicity is the symbolic ethnicity hypothesized by sociologist Herbert Gans, which came into popularity in the 1970s. Gans contrasted—as an example—the Irish-American experience of the 1920s with the Irish-American experience of the late 1960s as the difference between "being Irish" and "feeling Irish."

CONCLUSION

Several critical and wide-spanning sociological studies were conducted and published in the 1960s on the matter of European-American ethnic groups, covering their self-identification, their treatment in the social and business spheres, and factors like intermarriage and ethnic neighborhoods. The conclusions were inescapable: the effects of ethnicity had dimmed for European Americans. They had become demonstrably more likely to marry people of other ethnic backgrounds, they faced very little job or social discrimination, and they were more and more likely to identify themselves as "American" or "a mutt" rather than "Irish" or "French and Russian." By the end of the 1960s, social distinctions between different types of European Americans had almost entirely deteriorated.

B. Keith Murphy
Fort Valley State University
Bill Kte'pi
Independent Scholar

Further Reading

Adorno, T.W., Else Frenkel-Brunswik, Daniel J. Levinson, and R. Nevitt Sanford. *The Authoritarian Personality*. New York: Norton, 1969.

Alba, Richard D. *Ethnic Identity: The Transformation of White America*. New Haven, CT: Yale University Press, 1990.

Bork, Robert H. *The Tempting of America: The Political Seduction of the Law*. New York: Touchstone, 1991.

Bukowczyk, John J., ed. *Polish Americans and their History: Community, Culture and Politics*. Pittsburgh, PA: University of Pittsburgh Press, 2006.

Charters, Ann, ed. *The Portable Beat Reader*. New York: Penguin, 1992.

Cote, James E. and Charles Levine. *Identity Formation, Agency, and Culture*. Hillsdale, NJ: Lawrence Erlbaum Associates, 2000.

DeCurtis, Anthony and James Henke, with Holly George Warren. *The Rolling Stone Illustrated History of Rock and Roll: The Definitive History of the Most Important Artists and Their Music*. New York: Random House, 1992.

Duany, Andres and Elizabeth Plater-Zyberk. *Suburban Nation: The Rise of Sprawl and the Decline of the American Dream*. New York: North Point Press, 2000.

Erie, Steven P. *Rainbow's End: Irish-Americans and the Dilemmas of Urban Machine Politics, 1840–1985*. Berkeley, CA: University of California Press, 1990.

Eysenck, Hans. *Race, Intelligence and Education*. London: Maurice Temple Smith, 1971.

Ferrante, Joan and Prince Browne, Jr. *The Social Construction of Race and Ethnicity in the United States*. New York: Prentice Hall, 2000.

Fiske, John and John Hartley. *Reading Television*. London: Routledge, 1978.

Glazer, Nathan and Daniel Moynihan. *Beyond the Melting Pot*. Boston, MA: The MIT Press, 1970.

———. *Ethnicity: Theory and Experience*. Cambridge, MA: Harvard University Press, 1975.

Gordon, Milton M. *Assimilation in American Life: The Role of Race, Religion, and National Origins*. New York: Oxford University Press, 1964.

Halberstam, David. *The Fifties*. New York: Villard, 1993.

Hefner, Hugh and Gretchen Edgren. *The Playboy Book: Fifty Years*. Koln, Germany: Taschen, 2005.

Herbold, Hilary. "Never a Level Playing Field: Blacks and the G.I. Bill," *The Journal of Blacks in Higher Education* (Winter 1994–95).

Hobsbawm, Eric. *The Age of Extremes*. New York: Pantheon Books, 1994.

Jackson, Kenneth T. *Crabgrass Frontier: The Suburbanization of the United States*. Oxford: Oxford University Press, 1985.

Jones, James H. *Alfred C. Kinsey: A Public/Private Life*. New York: Norton, 1997.

Kenny, Kevin. *The American Irish: A History*. Harlow, UK: Longman, 2000.

Kinsey, Alfred C., Wardell B. Pomeroy, Clyde E. Martin, and Paul H. Gebhard. *Sexual Behavior in the Human Female*. Bloomington, IN: Indiana University Press, 1998.

Levinson, David. *Ethnic Groups Worldwide*. Phoenix, AZ: Oryx Press, 1998.

Marling, Karal Ann. *As Seen on TV: The Visual Culture of Everyday Life in the 1950s*. Cambridge, MA: Harvard University Press, 1996.

Mettler, Suzanne. *Soldiers to Citizens: The GI Bill and the Making of the Greatest Generation*. New York: Oxford University Press, 2007.

Novak, Michael. *Unmeltable Ethnics: Politics and Culture in American Life*. Edison, NJ: Transaction Publishers, 1995.

Omi, Michael and Howard Winant. *Racial Formation in the United States from the 1960s to the 1980s*. New York: Routledge, 1986.

Sowell, Thomas. *Ethnic America: A History*. New York: Basic Books, 1981.

Steinberg, Stephen. *The Ethnic Myth*. Boston, MA: Beacon Press, 2001.

Takaki, Ronald. *A Different Mirror: A History of Multicultural America*. New York: Back Bay Books, 1994.

Trommler, Frank and Joseph McVeigh. *America and the Germans: An Assessment of a Three-Hundred Year History*. Philadelphia, PA: University of Pennsylvania Press, 1991.

Waters, Mary C. *Ethnic Options: Choosing Identities in America*. Berkeley, CA: University of California Press, 1990.

Watts, Steven. *Mr. Playboy: Hugh Hefner and the American Dream*. Hoboken, NJ: John Wiley & Sons, 2008.

CHAPTER 9

European Americans Today: 1970 to the Present

ETHNICITY WAS A hot topic during the 1960s and 1970s, but looking back on those decades, what stands out are the fight for African-American and Native-American rights and the resurgence of Chicano identity and literature. Typically overlooked is the great deal of discussion over European-American ethnicity. Although today distinctions are made between "ethnicity" and "race," predjudices persisted, and the effects race has on social treatment are acknowledged, for most of the 20th century. It was still common for an Italian-American mother to tell her children that she expected them to marry other Italian Americans, for Anglo-American children to be forbidden from playing with Hungarian-American children, for Irish Americans to be denied work on the basis of their ethnicity, and for third-generation Americans to be called "wop," "mick," or "kraut," words that may not have become as taboo as racial slurs, but that were certainly intended to be just as hateful. By the end of the century, these social distinctions between different types of European Americans had disappeared almost entirely.

One contributing factor to this—the most significant factor, in the minds of most of the sociologists and historians commenting at the time—was the slowdown of European immigration. The 1924 Immigration Act had imposed country-of-origin quotas on immigration, intended to preserve the 1910 ethnic mixture of the United States and to slow down immigration over-

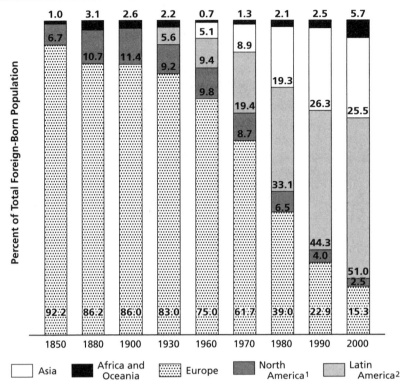

Origin of U.S. Population by Region of Birth, Selected Years, 1850–2000

Asia | Africa and Oceania | Europe | North America[1] | Latin America[2]

[1] North America includes Canada, Bermuda, Greenland, and the islands of St. Pierre and Miquelon.
[2] Latin America includes Mexico.

Note: The source from which these figures are drawn defines foreign-born as "people residing in the United States on census day or on a survey date who were not U.S citizens at birth." Slaves are not included in these figures. Figures for 1960–90 are based on the resident population. For 2000, figures are for the civilian noninstitutional population plus armed forces living off post or with their families on post. Figures include some but not all undocumented immigrants.

Source: Dianne A. Schmidley, Profile of the Foreign-Born Population in the United States: 2000. U.S. Census Bureau, Current Population Reports, Series P23-206. Washington, D.C.: U.S. Government Printing Office, 2001, p. 9. Available online. URL: http://www.census.gov/prod/2002pubs/p23-206.pdf.

© Infobase Publishing

all. But when the act was effectively revoked by the subsequent Immigration Act of 1965, the influx of immigration that followed was principally Asian, not European. Asians immigrated to the United States in great numbers in the 1960s and 1970s, contributing to the doubling of immigration between 1965 and 1970. European Americans become, in some parts of the country, a less dominant majority as new ethnic communities were established not only in the major coastal urban centers that had customarily been home to new immigrants, but, in places like Houston, Texas, where large numbers of Vietnamese refugees settled in the suburbs along Interstate 10. The numbers of European immigrants were surprisingly low: many families had already relocated to join their now-American relatives, and the Europe of the 1960s and 1970s was in a much different state than the Europe of the first half of the century.

Even after the slowing of European immigration and further assimilation, it was still possible to distinguish the diverse backgrounds of European Americans. Some of the prominent groups remained the Dutch, French, Scandinavian, and German people who had long been part of the mix in the United States, as well as the descendants of mostly later immigrants from central Europe, Italy, Russia, Poland, and southeastern Europe, including Greece. In terms of religion, most European Americans are either Christian or Jewish, and in socioeconomic terms, they cover every level of American society ranging from the wealthy and the powerful to poor migrant families.

Emigration from western European countries to the United States declined further during 1990–2007. By 2007, the United Kingdom (UK) was the only European country in the top 20 regions of birth for new U.S. legalized permanent residents. Very few refugees or asylum-seekers entered the United States from western European countries, reflecting the region's relative political stability and democratic governance. Emigrants from the UK came seeking educational and career opportunities and stayed in the United States for reasons of employment.

In terms of population makeup, a majority of the U.S. population is of European descent, comprising roughly 75 percent of the country's population as of the 2000 census. Two centuries of immigration have made it difficult for many citizens to trace their ethnic identities beyond the general category "American." In many ways, the history of European Americans during the late 20th and early 21st centuries is the history of mainstream culture within the United States. However, political events in eastern Europe spawned new waves of immigration that are worthy of note.

The Republic of Yugoslavia broke into multiple independent countries beginning in 1991, and more than 100,000 political refugees sought asylum in the United States within that decade. New waves of immigrants also arrived from Russia, Poland, the Ukraine, and former Soviet bloc countries during the 1990s. Between 1992 and 1999, the United States admitted over 250,000 political refugees from the former Soviet Union countries. Most of these immigrants settled in the northeast, with significant numbers in New York, Washington, D.C., and other major urban centers on the eastern seaboard.

EDUCATION

The history of immigration in the United States is closely tied to the history of education, as the children of immigrants seek new opportunities through

Whiteness Studies

Many, perhaps most, of our white students in the United States think that racism doesn't affect them because they are not people of color; they do not see "whiteness" as a racial identity . . . In my class and place, I did not see myself as a racist because I was taught to recognize racism only in individual acts of meanness by members of my group, never in invisible systems conferring unsought racial dominance on my group from birth.

—Peggy Mcintosh

The above quote from Peggy Mcintosh's essay "White Privilege: Unpacking the Invisible Knapsack" introduces key ideas about the subfield of ethnic studies known as "whiteness studies." This field is founded on the contention that the majority of European-American races have been grouped together as ethnically "white," and that these descendants of former immigrants have inherited specific privileges of power by virtue of their race that contrast with the rights and privileges available to people of color. In examining "white" as a race, Mcintosh examines how white culture is seen as the norm to which other subcultures are compared. Other scholars apply these critical theories to history, literature, and the humanities. For example, Noel Ignatiev's *How the Irish Became White* examines from a historical viewpoint how the Irish Americans went from being an oppressed minority to being part of the U.S. mainstream within two generations, and examines the intersection of religious and racial identities.

Critiques of whiteness studies are numerous. Scholars argue that the field commits the same error it protests against by denying the individual experiences of oppression endured by multiple nationalities of European immigrants. They point to the lack of a firm definition of "whiteness" as a problem, since it is unclear who may claim a white identity. Others make points regarding the time needed for immigrants to assimilate, and note that the groups most recently arrived in the United States often face the biggest hurdles in finding employment and learning the English language regardless of skin color. A third argument is that socioeconomic class appears to play a significant role in access to the American dream, regardless of race—that is to say, poor whites are equally as likely as poor people of color to have limited access to education and other tools of social mobility. As whiteness studies become better known as a field, scholars will need to address these arguments to justify the study of these controversial social theories.

schooling. During the late 20th century, the story of American public schools was one of attempted reforms. In 1994, Republican senators and representatives wanted to avoid increased federal involvement in public education and derailed President Bill Clinton's "Goals 2000" legislation. While the federal government was in gridlock, individual states began to take up the challenge of public education reform. One goal of this reform was to reduce "white flight," the demographic trend occurring when middle-class European Americans leave urban areas and public schools for suburban areas and private schools. Another was to close the gaps in achievement across ethnic and socioeconomic groups. Reformers believed that improved public education would increase the number of middle-class students in public schools and thus strengthen the tax base in urban areas, providing more funding for education. By 1998, 38 states had independently developed standards for education in some core subjects, regardless of federal government regulation.

In 2001, sweeping federal legislation entitled "No Child Left Behind" (NCLB) built on those states' core standards in an effort to return America to a "back-to-basics" curriculum. NCLB required states to develop their own educational standards and assessment tests in reading, math, and science. A primary criticism of NCLB is that it encouraged "teaching to the test" or developing test-taking skills over creative and critical thinking skills difficult to measure in a multiple-choice format. Because of the teaching time devoted to reading, math, and science, it became more difficult to provide adequate instruction in history, social studies, performing arts, foreign languages, fine arts, or vocational training. In 2006, the Northwest Evaluation Association Study examined results from reading and math tests administered to 500,000

Despite attempts at reform spanning decades, achievement gaps continue to exist between European-American children and minorities in the United States.

students in 24 states during the 2004–05 school year. The study found that achievement gaps persisted between European Americans and ethnic minorities in each grade and subject studied and between students from high-poverty schools and those from wealthier ones.

NCLB requirements also requested schools to submit educational achievement data on recent immigrants, allowing researchers to study some of the impacts of immigration on U.S. classrooms. Unfortunately, NCLB data did not track students who had been in the United States for more than three years, and so did not represent a full 75 percent of children with immigrant parents. Many schools and districts released information regarding foreign-born students without any geographic detail, making it difficult to determine whether recent European immigrants were succeeding academically in U.S. public schools.

In higher education, two areas of research in the social sciences drew attention to European Americans' history in the United States. The field of ethnic studies expanded during these two decades, and the subfield of whiteness studies was born in the early 1990s. These interdisciplinary areas study the intersections of ethnicity with culture, history, and socioeconomic status. Ethnic studies departments were first established in the late 1960s and early 1970s as outgrowths of the civil rights movement. Proponents of ethnic studies argued that Eurocentric bias marginalized Asian-American, African-American, and Latino contributions to the history of the United States. By the 1990s, prominent scholars including Toni Morrison and Peggy Mcintosh began to theorize around the concept of whites in America as a race of invisible privilege and people of color as "others," leading to the field of whiteness studies. This sociological subfield remains controversial because of its core concept that race has been socially constructed to maintain European-American socioeconomic privilege.

YOUNG ADULTHOOD, MARRIAGE, AND FAMILY LIFE

The generation following the Baby Boomers was born between 1965 and 1980 and takes its name from the book *Generation X* by Douglas Coupland. Sometimes called the "baby bust," the generalizations that characterize this age group are cynicism, reluctance to marry, and a deep awareness of the social problems created by the preceding generation. Generation X is the first generation likely to make less money than their parents' generation, according to studies that predict economic mobility. As children, many of them witnessed their parents' divorces; most had mothers who worked outside the home, and many were raised by single mothers. These circumstances inspired a pragmatic, self-reliant approach to life that is also distrustful of traditional social institutions such as marriage. For European Americans who were second- or third-generation immigrants, increasing geographic mobility, in combination with delayed marriage and pursuit of higher education, speeded up the assimilation process.

Perhaps because of the prevalence of divorce in their childhood homes, and also because of women's increasing academic achievements, the average age of first marriage went up by more than a year over these two decades. According to a U.S. census study, by 2003, young women's average age of marriage was 25.1 years of age, and men's was 26.7. These later marriages resulted in a corresponding delay of childbearing. The higher percentage of women having their first children in their thirties and forties resulted in a shift in parenting models. Instead of choosing between working motherhood and stay-at-home motherhood, increasing numbers of mothers tried to "sequence" parenting, working part-time or seeking flexible schedules in order to spend more time with their children than their parents had been able to. This shift was most noticeable at higher socioeconomic levels, where education and professional expertise made it possible for working women to demand such employment concessions.

By 2000, the oldest of the Baby Boomers's children, known as Generation Y or the "millennials," had entered college. Born between 1980 and 2000, this generation was the first to be raised with computers and cell phones. The millennials are tech-savvy, with a short attention span and well-developed multitasking abilities, and tend to be idealistic and politically involved. They believe in the power of networking and communications, and more will attend college than any previous U.S. generation, in spite of the rising costs of higher education. This generation is the most ethnically diverse in American history and was born after the civil rights movement, so diversity and racial tolerance have been common ideas during their youth.

WHITE ETHNIC INTERMARRIAGE

Today, marriage between two European Americans is more likely to be between two different ethnic groups than between members of the same ethnic group, and is likely to elicit little comment. The 1970s was the era in which this first occurred. Intermarriage had been becoming more common since the immediate post–World War II years; to put it another way, one generation after the Immigration Act of 1924 had slowed the replenishment of the nation's supply of first-generation immigrants.

For instance, according to the 1980 census, Polish Americans born in 1920 or before were 47 percent likely to have married another Polish American, and 5 percent were likely to have married someone of partial Polish heritage. Those born after 1950 were only 17 percent likely to have married someone with any Polish heritage. For Italian Americans, the figures dropped from 59 percent combined to 25 percent combined. English, German, Irish, and French Americans were the least affected, with their intermarriage rates already at about 50 percent. Because intermarriage among those groups had been common for so long and because in the 1970s they were the largest ethnic groups of European Americans, a significant number of potential white partners for a member of that group would include some shared heritage. In only a quarter of the marriages of people born after 1950 did partners come from the same ethnic background, a reversal of what had occurred a century earlier.

Religious intermarriages had also become more common by the 1970s. For instance, before the 1960s, only a tiny number of Jews married non-Jews, and in most cases did so without the approval of their religious community and perhaps their extended family. By the end of the 1970s, a quarter of Jews were marrying non-Jews, and most stigma had worn off, except in especially conservative religious communities. In that same period, marriage of Catholics to non-Catholics rose to a full half of Catholics' marriages, in part a result of the Second Vatican Council's liberalization of Catholic identity.

EUROPEAN-AMERICAN ETHNICITY AND RELIGION

Denominational affiliation in the United States has tended to fall along ethnic lines, for historical reasons. A nation of immigrants, the United States is younger than most of the major denominations and has drawn members from all of them. For instance, the four major divisions of Christianity are Catholic, Eastern Orthodox, Anglican, and Protestant. Anglicans, needless to say, are nearly always ethnically English, Welsh, Scottish, or Irish. This is true too of the Episcopal Church, which was formed by Anglicans after the Revolutionary War because it was no longer appropriate for their clergy to swear allegiance to the King of England. Similarly, members of the Eastern Orthodox faith are frequently of eastern European extraction—the growth of the church in the United States is strongly associated with late-19th-century and early-20th-century immigration, as Greeks, Russians, Bulgarians, Albanians, and others left their native lands. They arrived in great numbers after the Bolshevik Revolution in Russia and the formation of the Soviet Union.

One of the major changes to the Eastern Orthodox church in the United States has been the increasing number of converts from other ethnic backgrounds, a trend evident by the 1970s. Just as eastern-European Americans became less of a marked group by the 1970s and inarguably part of the American mainstream, Orthodox Christianity—the second-largest Christian affiliation in the world—became a mainstream American faith and not simply an immigrant practice. Most of the converts to Orthodox Christianity had been raised in some denomination of Christianity or in mixed-faith households.

"Protestant intermingling" is a distinctly American phenomenon. Only in the United States and Canada is there frequent use of the term *mainline Protestantism*, referring to the Protestant denominations represented in the bulk of the populace before World War I. The six largest of these are the Baptists (typically English), Episcopalians, Lutherans (typically German, Baltic, or Scandinavian), Presbyterians (typically Scottish), Congregationalists (typically English), and Methodists (typically English and Welsh); smaller mainline groups include the Moravian Church, the Reformed Church in America, and the Quakers.

Just as those denominations have traditionally correlated strongly to ethnicity, so has there been a creation of "American mainline Protestantism" analogous to that of the "European American" identity. Indeed, particularly since the 1970s (the Fourth Great Awakening, in the view of some historians and religious scholars, a period of great religious and social change in America), there have been an increasing number of Americans who identify as "Protestants" rather than as a denominational affiliation or as "nondenominational Christians."

Catholicism is not divided into denominations as Protestantism is. Worldwide, it is the largest Christian affiliation, though it lags behind Protestantism in the United States. In the 1970s, the reputation of Catholicism as an "immigrant religion" had only recently worn off. Catholicism was expected to be an obstacle to the 1960 election of President John F. Kennedy and did affect his popularity in some parts of the country, but the election showed that the perception of anti-Catholic sentiment was stronger than its actuality.

There are broadly four different ethnic strains of Catholicism in the United States: Spanish and French Catholicism, in their former colonies; British Catholicism, historically centered around Baltimore; and the Catholicism of the immigrant populations (especially the Italians, Irish, and Germans) who arrived in the 19th and 20th centuries. It is this last type that is responsible for the biggest increases in Catholic populations. To a lesser extent than in Protestantism, there was a growing American Catholicism in which Irish and Italian families might attend the same churches. Even the adoption of St. Patrick's Day as a holiday celebrated by much of the country—Irish or not, Catholic or not—represented the lessening of ethnic differences among European Americans.

THE NEW EUROPEAN AMERICANS

The net effect of all the intermarriage among ethnic groups was the self-proclaimed "mutt"—the German-Irish American, the French-Italian-Russian American, or the Hungarian-Dutch-English-Welsh-French American with a Cherokee great-grandmother. By the 1980 census, 47 percent of non-Hispanic whites born in the United States had ethnically mixed heritage. There are reasons to suspect this is a vast understatement: in-depth sociological studies have shown people are very poor at reporting their heritage. For instance, a man with a German-American father and a German-French American mother may simply report his heritage as German. A woman whose father is Italian and Irish and whose mother is Irish and French, who lives in a predominantly Italian neighborhood, and who has an Italian last name may refer to herself as Italian. A man whose parents represent an admixture of many ethnicities, but whose only significant contact with his extended family was with his Irish grandparents and cousins, may call himself Irish. Various researchers discovered that asking follow-up questions in person, which the census cannot do for reasons of practicality, revealed significantly more ethnic information. Once the subject starts thinking, he may remember that one of his grandmothers was "French-Canadian, but never talked about it much" or that his grandfather "had an eastern-European accent," after previously identifying himself only as Irish American. As white ethnicity ceased to be a factor in obtaining employment or education—as it ceased to have a social cost—it became only selectively emphasized. Why should someone whose great-grandparent was French but who has no contact with French-American culture think of themselves as part-French? What does it even mean to do so?

At the same time, Americans remained highly aware of their ethnicity, in certain ways. The modern conception of the European American, of whiteness as ethnicity, had essentially been born. Such Americans were the product of the melting pot—a little bit of this, a little bit of that, with not too

Southeastern Europeans

The 1980s saw the emergence of two Greek Americans on the political scene. Michael Dukakis, the 1988 Democratic Party presidential candidate, was born in Brookline, Massachusetts, the son of Greek immigrants partly of Vlach origin. Dukakis was not the first Greek American to be active in politics. Twenty years earlier, Spiro Agnew, also of Greek ancestry, had been elected vice president.

In 1979, Paul Tsongas, the son of a Greek father (the son of a poor migrant) and a Massachusetts mother, was elected to the U.S. Senate for Massachusetts, a position he held until 1985 when the seat was taken by John Kerry. A liberal, Paul Tsongas contested the 1992 Democratic Party primaries. A very famous Romanian American is Holocaust survivor and writer Elizer "Elie" Wiesel, who was born in Romania in 1928, survived Auschwitz, and moved to New York in 1955, where he wrote more than 40 books. In 1986, he was the recipient of the Nobel Peace Prize, being described as a "messenger to mankind" involved in the "practical work in the cause of peace."

Former Massachusetts Governor Michael Dukakis, who ran for president in 1988, is of Greek descent.

much attention to specifics. Any ethnic expression beyond that had become voluntary.

Voluntary ethnicity is sometimes called symbolic ethnicity, especially in psychological literature. Symbolic ethnicity carries little to no cost: in today's America, a person does not give up any rights or privileges to say "I am Irish" or "I am French" in the same way that identifying as a non-white ethnicity would. There is no *French Like Me* as a follow-up to *Black Like Me*, John Howard Griffin's exposé of how he was treated differently while passing as a black man. Many psychologists, following Erik Erikson's example in his theories of identity, see ethnicity—especially this symbolic white ethnicity—as part of identity formation. One perceives similarities between one's personality and one's perception of those personality traits that correlate to part of his/her ethnic heritage—or one reacts against those perceived traits. One may describe talkativeness as part of one's Irish nature, or a love of food as part of an Italian background, even if one has little or no connection to any Irish or Italian culture or relatives.

That symbolic ethnicity can extend to interaction with the world. Irish causes receive a surprising amount of support from Americans whose Irish-American ethnicity can only be described as symbolic. St. Patrick's Day, for example, has become a more popular celebration in the United States in the decades since the boundaries between white ethnic groups have eroded.

DUTCH AMERICANS

Some of the earliest settlers in the United States were the Dutch, and as a result, a number of prominent Americans whose families have been in North America since the 17th century can claim Dutch antecedents. The most famous of these during the 1980s was former president George H.W. Bush, who has the Dutch Schulyer family in his ancestry and often appears in lists of Dutch Americans, although most of his ancestors were English. Michigan Congressman Pete Hoekstra is also of Dutch descent.

The famous realist painter Andrew Wyeth—the "Painter of the People"—also had Dutch ancestry dating back to the 17th century. His ancestor, Nicholas Wyeth, a stonemason, came to Massachusetts in 1645. Wyeth also had German ancestry, and it is not uncommon for many Dutch Americans to also have other European ancestry. David Hartman, who hosted the television program *Good Morning, America* during the 1980s, was of Dutch, Swiss, English, and German ancestry.

Although many Dutch Americans came from New York or New England, there have been some who came from the Midwest. Filmmaker Paul Schrader was born in Michigan of Dutch parents. There are also Dutch Americans born in the Netherlands who have only recently settled in the United States. Soccer player Johan Cruyff—European football player of the year during the 1970s—moved to the United States in 1980–81, before returning to the

Netherlands; and Nobel Laureate for Physics in 1981, Nicolaas Blembergern, was also born in the Netherlands, then moved to the United States in 1945 to study at Harvard. After years of campaigning during the 1980s, in a bid to make the community more well known, from 1990, November 16 was designated Dutch-American Heritage Day.

FRENCH AND BASQUE AMERICANS

Given the proximity of French-speaking Canada, it is not surprising that there have been many French Americans who have risen to prominence in the United States. Jimmy Carter's Secretary of Housing and Urban Development Maurice "Moon" Landrieu was of French ancestry; political maverick Lyndon Larouche also has claimed French ancestry. Republican House minority leader from 1981 until 1995, Robert H. Michel was the son of a French migrant factory worker. Economist Gérard Debreu was born in Calais, France, just after the end of World War I; in 1948, he moved to the United States on a Rockefeller Fellowship, became a prominent economist, and was awarded the Nobel Prize for Economics in 1983.

In the realm of literature, many French Americans have distinguished themselves. The most prolific during the 1980s was Louis L'Amour, whose output of fiction, especially westerns, or "frontier fiction," as he called them, continued until his death in 1988; L'Amour published 16 books during the 1980s. There was also renewed interest during the 1980s in the work of Jack Kerouac, whose family was from Quebec; and museum administrator Philippe de Montebello was director of the Metropolitan Museum of Art in New York from 1977 until his retirement in 2009. Born in Paris, France, he moved to New York with his family when he was 14. Another famous French American was Tamara Faye Bakker, daughter of Carl and Rachel Fairchild LaValley of Minnesota and wife of the televangelist Jim Bakker. Her grandfather was the son of migrants from French Canada.

Closely linked to the French and Spanish communities, but separate from both, are the Basques. Although there were Basques in the crew of Christopher Columbus,

Sausage preparation in a Basque-American kitchen in Nevada in 1979.

Basque-American cattle ranchers talking at a community barbecue in northern Nevada in 1978. Basques have traditionally been involved in sheep herding, farming, and ranching in the west.

and Basques among many Hispanic settlers in the Americas, there was also a significant Basque community that settled in Idaho and other states in the 1890s. During the 1970s, they started to form Basque community groups that drew together French and Spanish Basques, which led to the formation of the North American Basque Organization. One of the most prominent Basque American politicians was Pete T. Cenarrusa, who served as Idaho's secretary of state from 1967 until 2003. In 1982, he arranged for three seedlings grown from acorns from the famous Gernikako Arbola ("Guernica Oak"), which has a famous role in Basque history. One of the seedlings was planted on April 18, 1982, on the grounds of the statehouse at Boise. Unfortunately, the following day it was discovered that the seedling had been dug up and stolen; for that reason the second seedling was planted in a secret location.

SCANDINAVIAN AMERICANS

The first Europeans to arrive in North America were the Vikings, and there are claims of Viking settlements in Minnesota as evidenced by various rune stones. However, most of the Scandinavian community in the United States descends from those who came in the late 19th century. The most famous Scandinavian in the U.S. news during the 1980s was Chief Justice William H. Rehnquist of the Supreme Court. Born in Wisconsin, his family was Swedish, and he joined the Supreme Court in 1972, becoming chief justice in 1986, a position he held until his death in 2005. He was the second Scandinavian American to sit on the Supreme Court, the first being Chief Justice Earl Warren, who had a Norwegian father and a Swedish mother. Other prominent Scandinavian Americans during the 1980s included Robert Bergland, U.S. secretary of agriculture from 1977 until 1981, who was from a Swedish family; anthropologist Donald Johanson, who was the son of Swedish migrants; and astronaut Buzz Aldrin, the second man to walk on the moon in 1969, a Swedish American.

Of Norwegian Americans during the 1980s, the most famous was Walter Mondale, who started the decade as U.S. vice president and unsuccessfully contested the 1984 presidential elections. Mondale was the second vice president of Norwegian ancestry, the first being Hubert Humphrey, who died in 1978. And political adviser Karl Rove, who worked on George H.W. Bush's failed presidential campaign in 1980, was also of Norwegian ancestry. A more recent migrant to the United States, organic chemist Charles J. Pedersen was born in Korea to a Norwegian father and a Japanese mother. He moved to the United States in 1922, and five years later he started working for DuPont, where he was involved in the synthesization of crown ethers, earning him the Nobel Prize for Chemistry in 1987.

GERMAN AMERICANS

The U.S. German-American population has always been significant, and a number of prominent German Americans during the 1980s descended from families that had been in the United States for generations. The largest group of European Americans during the 1980s were German Americans who made up about 23 percent of the entire country's population in 1990 and a quarter of the non-Hispanic white population of the United States—although the latter includes people of German and other heritages. German Americans are also the most-reported ancestry in nearly half of the 50 states in the Union, with most having assimilated easily into U.S. society.

Some 58 million Americans identified themselves in the 1990 census as having German ancestry. Edwin Meese, who was counselor to President Ronald Reagan from 1980 and attorney general from 1985 until 1988, was the great-grandson of German migrants who had moved to San Francisco during the California Gold Rush of 1849. Many decades later, Julius George Schwarzkopf, the grandfather of General H. Norman Schwarzkopf, also migrated from Germany. Schwarzkopf led the U.S. forces in the 1983 invasion of Grenada (Operation Urgent Fury) and later in the Gulf War (1990–91): he was one of many German Americans who served with distinction in the U.S. armed forces, the most famous being Dwight D. Eisenhower. The person under whom Schwarzkopf served, Secretary of Defense Caspar Weinberger, was also a descendant of German migrants.

Politician Dick Gephardt was born at St. Louis, Missouri; both his parents were grandchildren of German immigrants. His family were among the large wave of German migrants who moved to the United States in the late 19th and early 20th century, and whose descendants were well-represented among famous Americans in the 1980s: poet Kenneth Rexroth and chess player Bobby Fischer (of German and Polish ancestry) are probably the most famous.

The rise of Adolf Hitler in Germany in the 1930s caused many people, both Jewish and non-Jewish, to seek refuge in the United States. Biologist Ernst Mayr was born in Germany and moved to the United States in the 1930s; in the 1980s, he was hailed as one of the leading evolutionary biologists in the world. It is especially notable that a number of other children who arrived during this period also distinguished themselves throughout the 1980s. One of the most famous is Henry Kissinger, who fled Germany with his parents

President Gerald Ford (left) and then-Secretary of State Henry Kissinger on the grounds of the White House in 1974. Kissinger remained a prominent political adviser throughout the 1980s.

in 1938 when he was 15. Although he had retired from government in 1977, he was still a prominent political adviser throughout the 1980s. Madeleine Kunin was born in 1933 in Switzerland, the daughter of German Jews who fled their homeland after the rise of Hitler; in 1940, they managed to reach the United States. Madeleine Kunin became the governor of Vermont in 1985 and served in that position until 1991. Economist and financial consultant Henry Kaufman, president of Salomon Brothers in the 1980s, was born in Germany before his family fled Nazi Germany. Jack Steinberger was born in 1921 in Bavaria and migrated to the United States with his family in 1934; he was awarded the Nobel Prize for Physics in 1988. Psychologist Ruth Westheimer was born in Frankfurt, Germany, in 1928, the only child of Orthodox Jewish parents who moved to Palestine and then to New York. Pulitzer Prize–winning journalist Max Frankel was born in Germany in 1930, moved to the United Kingdom and then to the United States with his mother after World War II. Frankel worked at the *New York Times* for 50 years, and later wrote about his time as a journalist. Broadcast journalist Ted Koppel was born in England, the son of parents who had fled Nazi Germany and were heading to the United States. Migration continued after the war, and included another Nobel laureate. Hans G. Dehmelt was born in 1922 in the city of Gorlitz and served in the German army during World War II. He migrated to the United States in 1952, taking a position at Duke University; he was a corecipient of the Nobel Prize for Physics in 1989. Artist Hans Haacke was born in Germany in 1936, the son of a Social Democrat; he also remained in Germany during the war and moved to the United States in the 1960s.

CENTRAL EUROPEAN AMERICANS
The upheavals in central Europe from the 1840s had seen many central Europeans migrate to the United States. One who left Switzerland in the mid-19th century was Joseph Burger, who joined the Union Army in the American Civil War when he was only 14. His grandson, Warren Burger, was chief justice of the Supreme Court from 1969 until 1986, during which time he presided over many controversial decisions on abortion, capital punishment, and school desegregation, among other political and social issues. There were also a number of other Swiss Americans: geneticist Mathilde Krim was born in 1926 in Como, Italy, the daughter of a Swiss zoologist and a Czech mother; oboist Heinz Holliger was born in Switzerland in 1939 and came to the United States in the 1980s.

There are many Hungarian Americans who distinguished themselves during the 1980s. Actor Paul Newman was born in Cleveland, Ohio, of Hungarian, German, and Polish ancestry; George Soros, the currency speculator, was born in Budapest to a Jewish family who survived World War II and first migrated to Britain and then to New York. Christoph von Dohnanyi, music director of the Cleveland Orchestra, was from a Hungarian family; and D. Carleton Gajdusek, the son of Slovakian and Hungarian migrants, was a famous biomedical scientist who worked on virus infection. Author and journalist J. Anthony Kukas was born in New York in 1933, with Hungarian and German ancestry; and lecturer on art Rosamond Bernier was born in Germantown, Pennsylvania, circa 1920, the oldest child of a Hungarian Jewish father who was the vice president of the Philadelphia Orchestra. Tom Lantos, U.S. Representative for San Francisco from 1981 until his death in 2008, from Hungary, remains the only Holocaust survivor to have served in the U.S. Congress.

In the 1980s, Arnold Schwarzenegger was a prominent bodybuilder and actor. When he was elected governor of California in 2003, he famously said that he would never have expected that a boy who grew up in an Austrian town, and who moved to the United States in 1968, speaking little English, could become such an American success story, ending up as governor of the wealthiest state in the nation. Although he had not entered politics yet, the 1980s saw him become wealthy through films such as *Commando* (1985), *The Running Man* (1987), *Red Heat* (1988), and *Total Recall* (1990). At his marriage in 1986, his biographer Wendy Leigh noted that he had become famous "through the traditional virtues of hard work, talent, charm, intelligence, positive mental attitude, and persistence" and that he "epitomized the classic rags-to-riches hero." Also of Austrian descent is operatic tenor Alfredo Kraus, born in 1927, to a Viennese father and a Spanish mother.

From a Czechoslovakian background, Thomas Cech was born in Chicago in 1947 and went on to receive the Nobel Prize for chemistry in 1989. From a Czech Christian family, academic Jaroslav Pelikan (famous for his books on the history of Christianity) was the son of a Lutheran minister from Czechoslovakia and a schoolteacher from Serbia.

A Czech American also played a major role in the political scene during the 1990s. During the Clinton presidency, Madeleine Albright served as the United States' first female secretary of state. Albright, a Czech American born in Czechoslovakia, fled with her family to England in 1938 during the years leading up to and including World War II. By 1948, the rise of Communism led Albright's father to seek a position in the United States in the political science department of the University of Denver. Albright's first diplomatic post was as U.S. ambassador to the United Nations, to which she was appointed in 1993. She served as secretary of state from 1997 to 2001 and played a large role in the shaping of U.S. foreign policy toward Bosnia, Herzegovina, and Croatia during the wars that reshaped the former Yugoslavia.

ITALIAN AMERICANS

Italian Americans were important in many aspects of U.S. life in the 1980s. President Jimmy Carter's last attorney general, Benjamin Civiletti, was of Italian ancestry, and in 1988 the Democrat vice presidential challenger was Geraldine Ferraro, the fifth child of Italian migrants. Among the Republi-

Breakup of the Soviet Union

Near the end of the Cold War, Russia's economic system edged toward complete collapse. The expense of a never-ending war in Afghanistan and of maintaining superpower status made economic reforms essential for the survival of any kind of state. When Mikhail Gorbachev came to power in 1988, he instituted two types of reforms, *glasnost* and *perestroika*, which eventually led to the breakup of the Soviet Union in the early 1990s.

For the first time since the Bolshevik Revolution, *glasnost*, or political openness, brought improved journalistic access and reporting to the Soviet Union. Other political changes included mass releases of political prisoners and dissidents, and the opening of state archives to social science researchers.

As the media reported on organized crime, alcoholism, government corruption, and the aftermath of the Chernobyl nuclear plant disaster, the public saw the flaws inherent in the Soviet system and the government began to lose popular support. *Perestroika,* the economic restructuring of the Soviet Union, was even less successful. In attempting to gradually reform state controls of industrial and agricultural production without removing price subsidies or ceding control to private industries, the government's spending spiraled out of control.

Given the Soviet Union's power structure, Gorbachev could be removed from office at any time, which did not suit his programs of reform. To hold on to power, he created the position of president of the Soviet Union, which was independent of the old Communist councils. The Communist Party of the Soviet Union voted to give up central control of the country in February 1990. Gorbachev was elected the Soviet Union's first president in March 1990, and nationalist reformers won many seats in the government in that same election.

In the month that Gorbachev took office, Lithuania and Estonia declared independence from the Soviet Union. After a failed coup attempt in August 1991, Gorbachev's power was extremely limited. On December 8, 1991, Russia, Ukraine, and Belarus left the Soviet Union, forming the Commonwealth of Independent States (CIS). On December 21, the Alma Ata Protocol was signed by all remaining republic states except Georgia. Gorbachev resigned on December 25, and the Soviet Union officially dissolved on December 31, 1991.

The turmoil caused by these political and economic changes within such a short time period led hundreds of thousands of eastern Europeans to migrate to the United States in order to escape the poverty, lack of employment, poor public health, and civil unrest in the emerging independent states.

cans, Ronald Reagan's deputy secretary of defense and President George H.W. Bush's secretary of defense Frank Carlucci was the grandson of an Italian immigrant stonecutter.

In business, Lee Iacocca, the son of Italian migrants from San Marco dei Cavoti, south of Rome, saved the Chrysler Corporation and wrote best-selling books on management. In his memoirs, he describes how he grew up in Allentown, Pennsylvania, which was largely comprised of Dutch Americans who were, he felt, prejudiced against Italians. On the back cover of his book there is a photo of his mother visiting Ellis Island 63 years after her first arrival there. His mother was from Naples, which he notes was "the birthplace of pizza," but his parents were in Venice when he was conceived. Venice was also where Gore Vidal's ancestors hailed from. In the late 1980s, playwright and author Gore Vidal helped produce a television documentary on Renaissance Venice in which he traveled to Venice and spent time in the archives there, finding a 16th-century Vidal who had been jailed as a criminal.

A procession for the Italian-American festival of San Rocco in Paterson, New Jersey, in 1994. Growing interest in genealogy and improved access to records has led some European Americans in the 1990s and 2000s to renew ties to ethnic communities or rediscover lost roots in Europe.

Other prominent Italian Americans during the 1980s included New York choreographer Michael Bennett, born in 1943 as Michael Bennett DiFiglia to a New York Italian family; art dealer Leo Castelli was born in Trieste when it was still part of the Austro-Hungarian Empire; and film director Martin Scorsese, whose parents were migrants from Italy. Other Italian Americans involved in the film industry during the 1980s include Francis Ford Coppola, Robert DeNiro, and Al Pacino, as well as Frank Sinatra, who was still performing in his 70s.

The United States has continued to attract many talented Italian Americans, including Franco Modigliani, who won the Nobel Prize for Economics in 1985; and Rita Levi-Montalcini, also born in Italy, who received the Nobel Prize for Physiology or Medicine in 1986. Modigliani was from a Jewish family and left Italy in 1939; and Levi-Montalcini, also Jewish, left Italy for the United States in 1946.

RUSSIAN AMERICANS

During the 1890s and 1900s, many Russian-Jewish families fled the pogroms and moved to the United States, bringing much talent—literary, artistic, and musical. Broadcaster Larry King was the son of Russian-Jewish immigrants, as was Carl Sagan, an astrophysicist who popularized astronomy and science through his books and his television series *Cosmos*. Author Herman Wouk rose to fame in 1951 with *The Caine Mutiny*, and later wrote *The Winds of War* (1971) about the coming of World War II and its sequel *War and Remembrance* (1978); both were turned into television miniseries in the 1980s by ABC, *The Winds of War* in 1983, and the sequel in 1988.

Artist Jacob Kainen was born in Connecticut in 1909, the son of Russian migrants; author and winner of the Nobel Prize for Literature in 1976, Saul Bellow was born in 1915 in Montreal, Canada, his father having worked as an onion importer in St. Petersburg, Russia. Comedian Jackie Mason was born in 1936 in Wisconsin, the son of an Orthodox Jewish rabbi from Minsk, Russia (now Belarus).

Daniel J. Boorstin, historian of the Library of Congress during the 1980s, was descended from Russian-Jewish migrants; and violinist Nadja Salerno-Sonnenberg was born in Rome, her father a Russian who abandoned the family, and she took her name from her stepfather.

There were also some Russian Americans who were from families that had supported the Russian Revolution of 1917. Poet and literary figure Allen Ginsberg was the son of a Russian-born Marxist. Editor, painter, photographer, and sculptor Alexander Liberman was born in 1912 in Kiev, Russia (now Ukraine); his father was an economist who worked for Lenin, and the family left Russia in 1921. Joseph Brodsky, born Russia in 1940, only moved to the United States in 1972 after being expelled from the Soviet Union—he received the Nobel Prize for Literature in 1987.

EASTERN EUROPEAN AMERICANS

Also of Ukrainian ancestry was 1976 Nobel Laureate for Economics Milton Friedman, who played a significant role in the 1980s as a leading exponent of monetarism and a major influence on the Reagan administration. Professional football coach Mike Ditka of the Chicago Bears was the son of Ukrainian immigrants; and New York tennis player Mike Bossy was of Ukrainian and Austrian ancestry.

A large number of migrants from Lithuania settled in the United States, the most famous probably being the poet Czeslaw Milosz, who was born in 1911 near Kaunas in what was then part of the Russian Empire and later became a part of Lithuania. Milosz was living in Warsaw during the German Occupation and ended up as a diplomat for the Polish Communist government, defecting in 1951 and seeking asylum first in France, and then moving to the United States in 1960. A lecturer at the University of California, Berkeley, in 1980, he was the recipient of the Nobel Prize for Literature.

Another Lithuanian American—from a very different background and career—Paul Marcinkus was born in Cicero, near Chicago, Illinois; his father had fled Lithuania in 1914 to avoid serving in the Russian army. After his ordination as a Roman Catholic priest, he went to Rome and worked for Pope Paul VI. In 1981, Pope John Paul II appointed him a Pro-President of Vatican City, becoming the third most powerful person in the city-state after the pope and his secretary of state. He retained that position until 1990. In contrast to Marcinkus, Yonatan Netanyahu was born in 1946 in New York, all four of his grandparents having been from Lithuania, his mother's family having migrated from there to Minneapolis, and his father's family having lived in the British Mandate of Palestine (later Israel). Soon after Yonatan was born, the family moved to Israel, and then in 1963 migrated back to the United States. Yonatan Netanyahu was killed in 1976 in the rescue of hostages from a hijacked plane at Entebbe; one of his younger brothers, Benjamin, born in Israel in 1949, was elected to the Knesset in 1988 and became prime minister of Israel in 1996–99 and again from 2009.

Actor Hal Linden was born in New York in 1931, the son of

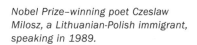

Nobel Prize–winning poet Czeslaw Milosz, a Lithuanian-Polish immigrant, speaking in 1989.

Lithuanian Jewish migrants who moved to New York in 1910. Art historian Meyer Schapiro was also born in Lithuania, moving to the United States with his family when he was 2 years old; publisher and human rights activist Robert L. Bernstein was the grandson of German and Lithuanian migrants; and famous skateboarder Natas Kaupas, one of the innovators of street skating in the late 1980s and early 1990s, was of Lithuanian heritage.

Among the Latvian Americans active during the 1980s, anthropologist Lionel Tiger was the only child of a Latvian migrant; and the 1981 Nobel Laureate for Physics, Arthur Leonard Schawlow, was the son of Jewish migrants from Latvia. Of the Estonian Americans, editorial cartoonist Edmund S. Valtman from Tallinn fled Estonia in 1944 when the Red Army took it for the second time. He and his wife escaped to Germany and then migrated to the United States; he was awarded the Pulitzer Prize for Editorial Cartooning in 1962, and his cartoons continued to be published for many years after his retirement in 1975.

The descendants of Jewish immigrants from eastern Europe also included playwright Harvey Fierstein; Nobel Laureate Robert Solow; recipient of the

The number of new immigrants from Western Europe is relatively small. This U.S. Army combat medic who is a native of Denmark obtained his U.S. citizenship at a mass naturalization ceremony for 107 foreign-born U.S. service members in Iraq on February 15, 2010.

Nobel Prize for Physiology or Medicine in 1989 Harold E Varmus; New York–based writer and literary critic Harold Bloom; Yiddish comedian Billy Crystal; and Chicago-born filmmaker William Friedkin. Other descendants of Jewish migrants from eastern Europe who became notorious during the 1980s were stockbroker Ivan Boesky—made famous by the character Gordon Gekko in the Oliver Stone film *Wall Street* (1987)—and "junk-bond king" Michael Milken.

POLISH AMERICANS

In 1980, two Polish Americans held key posts in the administration of President Jimmy Carter. Secretary of State Edmund S. Muskie, the son of a Polish immigrant who anglicized his name from Marciszewski when he arrived at Ellis Island, was born in Rumford, Maine. He served as governor of Maine, then U.S. senator from 1959 until 1980, before taking over from Cyrus Vance as secretary of state from May 1980 until January 1981. He then retired from politics and worked as an attorney. Carter's National Security Adviser Zbigniew Brzezinski was also a Polish American. Brzezinski was born in Warsaw in 1928; his father, a diplomat, was posted to Germany from 1931 until 1935, and then to the Soviet Union, and finally to Canada in 1938, where he was living when World War II broke out. Brzezinski completed his doctorate at Harvard, became a U.S. citizen, and moved to Columbia University. After his service in the Carter administration, he served President Ronald Reagan as a member of the Chemical Warfare Commission and in 1988 was appointed by George H.W. Bush as a co-chairman of the National Security Advisory Task Force.

In the literary field, Chaim Potok, the son of Polish-Jewish immigrants, grew up in the Bronx and wrote a number of important books from the late 1960s through 2001. In 1985, his novel *Davita's Harp*, the only fictional work by Potok to have a female protagonist, was published to great acclaim. Writer Robert A. Caro was also born in New York of Polish ancestry; and psychologist and educator Jerome Bruner was born in Alabama, the youngest child of Polish immigrants. Motion picture director Billy Wilder, whose films such as *Some Like it Hot* (1959) were being rediscovered by a new generation, was born in Galicia, then in the Austro-Hungarian Empire but now in Poland. He had moved to the United States in 1933, the same year that astrophysicist Arno Penzias, the son of Polish-Jewish parents, was born in Germany. The Penzias family left Germany for the United Kingdom and in 1940 moved to the United States. Educator and journalist Marvin Kalb was the son of a Polish father and Ukrainian mother; and Harvey Lichtenstein, the president of the Brooklyn Academy of Music, was born in New York in 1929 of Polish-Russian immigrants.

Post–World War II immigrants to the United States from Poland included Roald Hoffmann, born in Zloczow, Poland (now Ukraine), in 1937; his family managed to survive the Holocaust, and they moved to the United States in 1949. Hoffmann, who had been named after the Norwegian Antarctic explorer Roald Amundsen, became a prominent theoretical chemist and was the recipient of the 1981 Nobel Prize for Chemistry. In the year that the Hoffmanns crossed the Atlantic, Emanuel Ax was born in Lvov, Poland, both his parents having survived Nazi concentration camps. The family moved to New York when Ax was 12, and he went on to be one of the most famous classical pianists during the 1980s. Mathematician Benoit Mandelbrot was born in Poland in 1924, and moved to the United States in 1958.

Because of the changing national borders in Europe and intermarriage between people from different countries or backgrounds, there are a large number of Americans of Polish descent who also have German or Russian ancestors. Singer Neil Diamond was born in 1941 in New York City of Polish and Russian descent. Already famous in the 1970s, his popularity continued in the 1980s, and in January 1987 he sang the national anthem at the Super Bowl. The following year his song "America" became the theme song for Michael Dukakis in his presidential bid. Alan Greenspan, who was appointed chairman of the Federal Reserve in 1987 (holding that position until 2006), was also born in New York, his father being German Jewish and his mother Polish. And Federal Bureau of Investigation (FBI) agent Robert Hanssen was of mixed Polish, Danish, and German descent. During the 1980s, he worked in the FBI Counterintelligence Unit and was also a Russian spy; he was eventually arrested in 2001.

The Polish community, spread throughout the United States, has managed to fund its own newspapers such as *Nowy Dziennik* in New York, *Dziennik Zwiazkowy* in Chicago, and two papers in Detroit, as well as its own radio stations and even its own television station. The community still helps maintain the Polish Museum of America, which was established in Chicago in 1935, and holds regular cultural festivals and gatherings.

CONCLUSION

The loosening of immigration restrictions in 1965 did not result in a surge of European immigration, but it did implicitly remove any stigma attached to national origin. And because there was no surge sufficient to seriously impact the ethnic makeup of European Americans, whites settled into a new sort of comfort with the melting pot beginning in the 1970s. Just as more and more Protestant Christians began to identify as "Protestant" rather than "Baptist," "Methodist," and so on, or moved between those more specific designations as they changed churches for the sake of convenience or as a result of intermarriage, so too did white Americans identify less often as German, French, Italian, particularly if not specifically asked. By the last third of the 20th century, the more recent whites, the 19th- and early-20th-century immigrants, had been integrated into a casual, vague group of "white Americans." Whiteness itself had ceased to mean "pale and Anglo" and now included olive-skinned Greeks, Italians, and eastern Europeans.

Although a majority of the U.S. population is still of European descent, in 2000, the percentage of Americans who identified themselves as white fell to

75 percent, the lowest level recorded since such records began with the 1790 census. The country's white population had never before dropped below 80 percent, and had peaked at almost 90 percent (89.8 percent) in both the 1930 and 1940 censuses.

Recent census projections predict that the majority of the country will be nonwhite by 2050. Barring the arrival of an unexpected influx of new European immigrants, such as the Russians who arrived in the 1990s and 2000s, European Americans as a group are expected to decline in population numbers in the 2030s and 2040s, and to make up only 46 percent of the total population in 2050. While for many years the history of mainstream culture in the United States has been a history of European Americans, this may be about to change.

BILL KTE'PI
INDEPENDENT SCHOLAR
HEATHER BEASLEY
UNIVERSITY OF COLORADO

Further Reading

Alba, Richard D. *Ethnic Identity: The Transformation of White America*. New Haven, CT: Yale University Press, 1990.

Bukowczyk, John J. *And My Children Did Not Know Me: A History of the Polish-Americans*. Bloomington, IN: Indiana University Press, 1987.

———. ed. *A History of Polish Americans*. Somerset, NJ: Transaction, 2008.

Capps, Randy, et al. "The New Neighbors: A Users' Guide to Data on Immigrants in U.S. Communities." Washington, DC: Urban Institute, 2003.

Cote, James E. and Charles Levine. *Identity Formation, Agency, and Culture*. Hillsdale, NJ: Lawrence Erlbaum Associates, 2000.

Erie, Steven P. *Rainbow's End: Irish-Americans and the Dilemmas of Urban Machine Politics, 1840–1985*. Berkeley, CA: University of California Press, 1990.

Ferrante, Joan and Prince Browne, Jr. *The Social Construction of Race and Ethnicity in the United States*. New York: Prentice Hall, 2000.

Fitterer, C. Ann. *Russian Americans*. Chanhassen, MN: Child's World, 2003.

Glazer, Nathan and Daniel Moynihan. *Beyond the Melting Pot*. Boston, MA: The MIT Press, 1970.

Habenicht, Jan. *History of Czechs in America*. St. Paul, MN: Czechoslovak Genealogical Society International, 1996.

Hobsbawm, Eric. *The Age of Extremes*. New York: Pantheon Books, 1994.

Iacocca, Lee, with William Novak. *Iacocca: An Autobiography*. New York: Bantam Books, 1984.

Ignatiev, Noel. *How the Irish Became White*. New York: Routledge, 1996.

Jackson, Ronald L. *The Negotiation of Cultural Identity: Perceptions of European Americans and African Americans*. Westport, CT: Praeger, 1999.

Kazal, Russell A. *Becoming Old Stock: The Paradox of German-American Identity*. Princeton, NJ: Princeton University Press, 2004.

Kendall, Francis. *Understanding White Privilege: Creating Pathways to Authentic Relationships Across Race*. New York: Routledge, 2006.

Kishinevsky, Vera. *Russian Immigrants in the United States*. New York: LFB Scholarly Publishing, 2004.

Kourvetaris, George A. *Studies on Greek Americans*. Boulder, CO: East European Monographs, distributed by Columbia University Press, 1997.

Lagarde, François. *The French in Texas. History, Migration, Culture*. Austin, TX: University of Texas Press, 2003.

Louder, Dean R. and Eric Waddell. *French America. Mobility, Identity, and Minority Experience across the Continent*. Baton Rouge, LA: Louisiana State University Press, 1993.

Mcintosh, Peggy. "White Privilege: Unpacking the Invisible Knapsack." In *Re-Visioning Family Therapy: Race, Culture, and Gender in Clinical Practice*. New York: Guilford Press, 1998.

Morrison, Toni. *Playing in the Dark: Whiteness and the Literary Imagination*. Cambridge, MA: Harvard University Press, 1992.

Moskos, Charles C. *Greek Americans: Struggle and Success*. London: Transaction, 1989.

Novak, Michael. *Unmeltable Ethnics: Politics and Culture in American Life*. Edison, NJ: Transaction Publishers, 1995.

Omi, Michael and Howard Winant. *Racial Formation in the United States from the 1960s to the 1980s*. New York: Routledge, 1986.

Pula, James S. *Polish Americans: An Ethnic Community*. New York: Twayne, 1995.

Steinberg, Stephen. *The Ethnic Myth*. Boston, MA: Beacon Press, 2001.

Takaki, Ronald. *A Different Mirror: A History of Multicultural America*. New York: Back Bay Books, 1994.

Tamburri, Anthony Julian, Paolo A. Giordano, and Fred L. Gardaphé, eds. *From the Margin: Writings in Italian Americana*, Rev. ed. West Layfayette, IN: Purdue University Press, 2000.

Waters, Mary C. *Ethnic Options: Choosing Identities in America*. Berkeley, CA: University of California Press, 1990.

Acadians: Ethnic group inhabiting North America that is mostly made up of descendants of French settlers.

Adamson Act: Legislation that required an eight-hour workday for interstate railroad construction workers.

agricoltura: Italian word for "farming."

Américain: French word for an American male.

Américaine: French word for an American female.

Americanization: The process by which an ethnic individual or community assimilates into American mainstream culture and society.

Amerika: Russian term for "America."

Anarchist Exclusion Act of 1903: This act was passed largely in fear of foreign anarchist subversion following the assassination of William McKinley in 1901; the act allowed the deportation of individuals who followed or promoted anarchist philosophies.

anglophobia: Fear or distrust of the English or those of English ancestry.

assimilieren: German word for "to assimilate."

baas: Dutch word meaning "boss."

baby boom: The period following World War II that saw a great increase in the birth rate in the United States, generally thought to have lasted "from the Bomb to the Pill" (from August 1945 to the introduction of birth control pills in 1961.

banlieue: French word meaning "suburb."

buitenwijk: Dutch word for "suburb."

California Alien Land Law: This law restricted newly arrived immigrants from owning land.

chain migration: Refers to immigrants following their families and/or friends to ethnic communities in the United States.

Chicano: An American of Mexican descent.

città: Italian word for "city."

colon: French word for "settler."

colonizzatore: Italian word for "settler."

combattenti: Italian-American veterans of World War I.

coup d'état: An overthrow of a government, usually done abruptly.

dix: French word for "10" that was printed on local Louisiana currency during a short period following the American Revolution.

dollar: Spanish word that was later adopted by the Continental Congress for the new nation's currency system.

Emergency Quota Act of 1921: Stipulated that only three percent of the United States's existing ethnic population could be allowed to immigrate into the United States. For example, only three percent of the existing French-American population was allowed to immigrate from France to the United States.

etniciteit: Dutch word for "ethnicity."

etnicità: Italian term meaning "ethnicity."

Espionage Act of 1917: Legislation that required, among other provisions, that the German-American press print English translations to ensure that no subversive comments were made in German newspapers.

First Red Scare: Spurred by the communist revolution in Russia, the movement lasted from 1917 to 1920 and was dominated by anti-Communist sentiment in the United States.

frankfurter: The German name for a popular sausage, changed during the anti-German hysteria of World War I to "hot dog."

Francophobia: A fear of all things French, founded largely on the Reign of Terror that occurred during the late 18th century in France.

German Belt: Geographic phrase referring to an area between Ohio and Nebraska that boasted a high German-American population.

Gilded Age: A term, created by Mark Twain, referring to the age of political corruption following the Civil War; although not precise, the period usually refers to the 1870s and 1880s.

Immigration Act of 1965: Congressional act that granted 300,000 visas to newly arrived immigrants on a first-come, first-serve basis.

janke: Dutch word meaning "yankee."

Know Nothings: Members of an American Party of the 1850s, who, when asked about the party platform, were reputed to answer "I know nothing." The party believed that American ideals were corrupted by foreign immigrants.

Ku Klux Klan: A hate group that focused its energies on disrupting the harmony and collective goodwill of many ethnic communities.

laissez-faire: French term for an economic theory that states that government should have a "hands-off" role in a nation's economy, allowing free market capitalism to take its course.

landbouw: Dutch term for "farming."

landwirtschaft: German term for "farming."

langue: French word for "language."

l'appartenance ethnique: French phrase meaning "ethnicity."

melting pot: Metaphor used to describe the mixing together of many different ethnicities and cultures in the United States.

mercantilism: Economic theory that states that wealth is the primary indicator of a country's power.

minstrelsy: A type of performance where, typically, white actors would don blackface and lampoon the African-American community.

muckraker: One who seeks to expose the corruption of businesses or government. Muckrakers were common during the Progressive Era, and included Upton Sinclair and Lincoln Steffen.

misión: Spanish for a missionary system designed to convert inhabitants of a region to a particular religion or faith.

nativism: Philosophy that espouses the superiority of native peoples over newcomers and immigrants.

Naturalization Act of 1790: Congressional legislation requiring that all foreigners must live in the United States for 14 years before attaining residency status.

Northwest Passage: Sea route connecting the Pacific and Atlantic oceans.

osadnik: Polish word for settler.

Palmer Raids: A series of arrests conducted under the direction of Attorney General A. Mitchell Palmer in 1919 and 1920, rounding up and deporting aliens suspected of subversive activity.

patroon: Originating with Dutch settlers, the term applies to a landowner who holds significant leverage over tenants.

pauper: Term originating in England to describe someone who is poor and officially a recipient of government relief.

pogrom: A violent mob action, often sanctioned by government, against a particular minority group. In particular, pogroms against Jews in Europe often led to waves of emigration.

Proto-industrialization: Term for the early period of the Industrial Revolution.

razzismo: Italian word meaning "racism."

reisepass: German word for "passport."

Risorgimento: The unification effort in Italy that took place in the 19th century.

siedler: German word for "settler."

Smith Act of 1940: Required all non-citizen adults living in the United States to register with the government and have their fingerprints taken.

sobborgo: Italian word for "suburb."

Social Gospel: Protestant movement that emphasized social reform, such as curbing child labor and improving labor unions.

stadt: German term meaning "city."

Vereinigte Staaten: German phrase for "United States."

verfolgung: German word for "persecution."

vestiti: Italian word for "clothes."

ville: French word for town, used in America as a suffix to many town names, such as Rockville, Maryland.

War Brides Act of 1945: Legislation allowing spouses of U.S. military personnel, particularly those who served in World War II, to enter the United States.

WASP: A white, Anglo-Saxon Protestant.

White Flight: Term used to describe European Americans leaving urban areas and settling in the suburbs.

xenophobia: A severe dislike of foreigners or outsiders in general.

INDEX

Index note: Page references in *italics* indicate figures or graphs: page references in **bold** indicate main discussion.

Produced by Golson Media

President and Editor	J. Geoffrey Golson
Layout Editors	Oona Patrick, Mary Jo Scibetta
Author Manager	Susan Moskowitz
Copyeditor	Barbara Paris
Proofreader	Mary Le Rouge
Indexer	J S Editorial

DATE DUE